QUEER SOCIAL PHILOSOPHY

RANDALL HALLE

Queer

Social Philosophy

CRITICAL READINGS FROM

KANT TO ADORNO

UNIVERSITY OF ILLINOIS PRESS

URBANA AND CHICAGO

© 2004 by the Board of Trustees
of the University of Illinois
All rights reserved
Manufactured in the United States of America
C 5 4 3 2 1

∞ This book is printed on acid-free paper.

Library of Congress Cataloging-in-Publication Data
Halle, Randall.
Queer social philosophy : critical readings from
Kant to Adorno / Randall Halle.
p.   cm.
Includes bibliographical references and index.
ISBN 0-252-02907-0 (cloth : alk. paper)
1. Social sciences—Philosophy.
2. Homosexuality—Philosophy.
3. Social change.
I. Title.
H61.15.H35   2004
300'.1—dc22   2003019952

Contents

Acknowledgments

There are many people I would like to thank for their contributions, insights, and support in the writing of this book.

Jim Steakley, Jost Hermand, and Mary Layoun offered ideas, advice, and influence at an early stage. The National Endowment for the Humanities offered generous support for the German Social Philosophy Seminar at the University of Chicago; Don Levine's direction and the participants' contributions made it a lively and truly interdisciplinary experience. Likewise, the Deutscher Akademischer Austauschdienst offered its generous support for the Queer Theory Seminar at Cornell; it was a privilege to have that level of engagement with Biddy Martin and the many participants. I want to thank Dagmar Herzog in particular. The seminar offered valuable comments that propelled earlier versions of the work into a more developed form. I would especially in this regard like to thank Bruce Bethell, at the University of Illinois Press, whose engaged commentary and careful editing helped give the manuscript its final shape.

The University of Rochester has provided me an intellectual home for a number of years. In the Department of Modern Languages and Cultures I have experienced the support of not just colleagues but real friends. Our Susan B. Anthony Institute creates a community of scholars from which I and this book have benefited greatly. Additionally, the programs in visual and cultural studies and film and media studies have provided welcome forums for the exchange of ideas. Kamran Ali, Rachel Ablow, Janet Berlo, Joanne Bernardi, Lisa Cartwright, Elizabeth Cohen, Ayala Emmett, Robert Foster, Mary Fox, Hal Gladfelder, Tom Hahn, Patricia Herminghouse, Cilas Kemedjio, Rosemary Kegl, Bette London, Andrés

Nader, Kathleen Parthé, Jean Pedersen, David Rodowick, Raul Rodriguez-Hernandez, Joan Saab, Claudia Schaeffer, Timothy Scheie, Reinhild Steingröver, Donatella Stocchi-Perucchio, Jeffrey Tucker, and Janet Wolff have offered comments, critiques, and support. Moreover, all of us engaged in queer work at the university have benefited greatly from Douglas Crimp's work and simple presence on campus.

My respect and affection for John Michael are boundless. Empty are the days when I do not enjoy Sharon Willis's keen insight and limitless wit. Where would I be without Sue Gustafson, my colleague, mentor, and friend? Your engagement has made a world of difference. I am privileged to know Tom DiPiero, and I owe special thanks to him for his energy and generosity and for sharing many beers and countless ideas. My fondest thanks to my oldest friend and critic, James Scannell McCormick. Here is to old friends!

Finally, how can I even begin to thank Mohammed Bamyeh? The globe spins, the tulips grow, the ashes scatter, planes fly, ideas become words shared, and we remain at each other's side, even when apart.

QUEER SOCIAL PHILOSOPHY

Introduction:
In Which the Terms of a Critique
Are Discussed

> Rather, I aim at having an experience myself—by passing through a determinate historical content—an experience of what we are today, of what is not only our past but also our present. And I invite others to share the experience. That is, an experience of our modernity that might permit us to emerge from it transformed. Which means that at the conclusion of the book we can establish new relationships with what was at issue.
>
> —Michel Foucault

Could a historically grounded queer critique of social philosophy contribute to new forms of political life? The following pages explore this obviously complicated question. Before we explore how to weave together the elements of the answer, however, and by way of introduction, we need to specify the referent of each term of the question. Doing so will illuminate not only the question's pertinence but also its fundamentally consequential nature in its relationship to modern life, desire, and philosophy. In this introduction we will consider the term *queer* through considerations of queer critique, queer politics, and queer history. We then move on to social philosophy and its relationship to the heterocoital imperative and heteronormativity.

Queer

What does *queer* mean? This book investigates social philosophy from Kant to Adorno by virtue of queer readings or queer critique. Such activity, the methods and techniques of such an undertaking, may not appear immediately obvious. I want to pause, therefore, to contemplate what the term *queer* designates and what theoretical work can be accomplished with this terminological tool.

In this book queerness is brought into relation with instability, fracturing, disruption. Further, the book explores how the term relates to specific historical content. Both these relations prove significant in that the study seeks to avoid reducing queerness to a *technology of exclusion.* Up to this point queer theoretical explorations undertaken synchronically have tended to present queerness simply as a condition of (individual) outsider status.[1] Technologies of exclusion certainly play a part in any account of queer. In the context of this study, however, queer is understood as part of an approach to history that recognizes that within the sum of all social structures of a period—that is, its *socius*—certain moments of disruption and exclusion will appear alongside moments that constitute and bring stability.[2] In this usage, *queer* draws our attention to the interconnection of structure and instability or form and mutability. In an approach that combines synchronic and diachronic analysis, a dynamic of transformation, disruption, subjectivity, and epistemology becomes apparent as part of a queer dynamic.

It is possible to think of the operation of this dynamic through social philosophy. In this regard some of the directions in social philosophy under examination here have proven productive for queer theory. Hegel, Marx, Nietzsche, and Freud constitute a familiar set of names. Moreover, it is also possible to use social philosophy to fill the term *queer* with historical content. This requires careful attention to the history of social philosophy. It requires a historicization of these names and directions. As much as these names have proved productive in the development of queer theory, they have rarely been the object of any historically based queer critical analysis. Therefore, to open new terrain for queer theory, the exploration of queer undertaken by this study further takes place not only through and against social philosophy but within its history. The queer critique of this project sets for itself the task of writing a history of social philosophy.

It is possible to understand what is meant by *queer* in this study by thinking through a brief résumé of the various directions in social philosophy under examination. Through psychoanalysis we could turn to

Freud's notion of repression as describing a process that might hold some insight into the functioning of the queer. Psychoanalytic discourse has formulated repression as a psychic process that also represents a social dynamic. Beginning from the individual psyche, the repressed marks an exclusion from conscious representation that comes through the expenditure of a certain amount of psychic energy. At the same time, there is a social component enforcing the act of censorship or exclusion. Repression involves a drive force that is unavailable for sublimation into productive cultural energy in part because (a particular) culture is threatened by the manifestation of the drive. Unavailable for manifestation, repression initiates signifying chains, substitutions that disrupt and leave symptoms behind. The psychoanalytic concept of repression has proven useful in describing the disruptive acts of queerness, but repression carries with it certain presumptions of healthy structures, a hope for "asymptomatic" (though certainly infected) representations and substitutions. Moreover, as a discourse that relies on particular kinship structures, especially where they are elevated to a transhistorical and transcultural status, psychoanalysis has not proven able to account for the historical specificity of desire. I return to this model in chapter 4 for a lengthier discussion.

The operation of queer can be contemplated through Hegel's concept of negation as well. In a formulation central to his philosophical project, a "knowledge" confronts the "one-sidedness" of another "consciousness" (*Phenomenology*, §79). Hegel recognized that the exclusions of any one-sided structure will generate a "determinate negation" that challenges the partiality of consciousness. Consciousness might, for example, strive toward absolute or universal truth based on claims such as those that take heterosexuality as a universal of consciousness. This consciousness will be brought up short by any individual whose knowledge of self does not coincide with such a truth claim. For our understanding of the term *queer*, such a negation of heterosexual consciousness presents a queer confrontation. It is not the homosexual or the female-to-male transsexual who is queer but rather the challenge such individuals present to the socius. A queer confrontation becomes a *determinate* negation when it becomes the "truth" of the other. Homosexuality, for example, has become the truth of a whole category of people who are unassimilable to heterosexuality in the present order. In this confrontation, the challenge to the one-sidedness of consciousness can end only with a dialectical synthesis of the "truth" of the other. Thus, in a socius that relies on heterosexuality as a structuring term, only a synthesis with those whose self-knowledge is queer will allow the socius to speak the truth of all its subjects.

Hegel understood this process of confrontation as providing the motor of history and a drive toward universal truth. Such a dialectical process results in a serial progression; each new synthesis undoes the one-sidedness to a certain degree. Hegel's work is thus filled with a sense of historical progress and hope that we are always moving toward freedom. However, as I discuss at length in chapter 2, the Hegelian dialectic proved unable to take into account the power involved in the primary exclusion of a repressed knowledge. Ultimately, what had seemed to compel us toward positive liberation became an advocate of negative separation and domination because queerness presupposes that something cannot be *contained* in the synthesis.

Derrida's uncontainable excess, or *différance*, which disrupts totality and displays the partiality of all seemingly stable structures, proves useful in capturing the excessive dimension of queer. Deconstructive procedures have the advantage of operating without the assertion of serial progression that the Hegelian dialectical procedure implies. *Différance* or excess appears as part of any system, not necessarily as negative determination, but certainly as disruptive potential isolated to the margins and borders of the socius. At the same time, deconstructive strategies become more difficult to employ in a political arena, because they do not immediately evince freedom. To resolve this problem, Lyotard's formulation of the *différend* might prove more useful. Lyotard's work drew directly on Derrida but also on Kant to engage more explicitly with questions of exclusion and injustice in the socius. The *différend* marks that which disrupts social and psychic structure "ask[ing] to be put into phrases" but also "suffer[ing] from the wrong of not being able to be put into phrases right away" (Lyotard, 13). The *différend* compels the socius "to institute new addressees, new addressors, new significations, and new referents," "new rules for the formation and linking of phrases." Such analysis is significant for an understanding of queerness, yet while Lyotard's concentration on the *différend* provided insight into the function of the queer elements, it could not provide an adequate historical explanation of particular formations. We know that history happens and even to a certain extent why historical change must happen, but, like deconstructive notions of iterability, supplementarity, *revenant*, and so on, we cannot explain how it happens. To address such lack, later chapters of this study explore in more detail Marxist terms of production and desire and Nietzschean notions of genealogy and power.

Nevertheless, here we can recognize the contours of a path, the coordinates of a trajectory. We can recognize that queer has the possibility to operate both according to historical specificity and as metahistorical motor, compelling historical change. *Queerness and not freedom compels Hegel's* Geist. *Queer desiring-production and not class conflict fuels Marx's materialism.* To give the queer its due means to understand queer as a site of desire that unleashes events other than those involved in a discharge of desire. The disruption in which it is involved may be no more than the "scandal" of a kiss between two men, but it resides in the unattainable luxury good that attracts yet foils desire and in the energy behind explosive gatherings that unleash mob behavior or even all-out revolutions; such disruptions are part of queer's complicated workings on the socius. They are not aberrations to be overlooked, excised, negated, forestalled, or foreclosed.

Queer Critique, Queer Politics

The writings examined here have tended to rely on the *dread of the queer.* Marx's famous lines about the specter that haunted Europe identified within capitalism a fundamental dread: the dread of the proletariat. There is likewise a specter that haunts heterosexuality: the specter of queerness. The dread of this specter fills all the texts examined here. Where the tautology of heterosexuality comes to fashion social philosophy, it is easy to find this dread. Queer dread repeatedly establishes limits to the philosophical systems as they strive for universality. It is what transforms these systems from rational universals to coercive totalities. This dread, however, seems apparent only for those who have eyes to see. For example, long ago, when I was a student, I went to the office of a faculty member who was a specialist on the Frankfurt School and a proud member of the New Left. I had my copy of *Dialectic of Enlightenment* and a question about a particular line. The line, which seemed to say that homosexuality was the cause of fascism, had caught me up short. The professor replied that, although he had read the passage "countless times," he had never noticed the line and or its implications. It had been passed over in silence. He then shrugged his shoulders and directed me toward the door. But the matter seemed worth more than a shrug. I thus used the line as the red thread that guided my readings backward and forward in the work of the Frankfurt School. It turned into a web, and when I turned my attention beyond the boundaries of the Frankfurt School to the general tradition of critical philosophy and critical theory, I found more and more instances: similar lines that appear marginal but on closer examination begin to reveal themselves as central to the argument. This book is the result.

This queer dread results from a social philosophy that is based on a tautology. Those who follow the dictates of the heterocoital imperative seek to relieve themselves of this dread not by undoing the tautology but by "treating" or in some way responding to the queer. What happens to those who are constantly the object of response? In the modern era some seek to lull themselves through misplaced faith in their position as speaking subjects within the tolerant liberal democratic system. They hope for a communicative practice that allows them to ward off the treatment, to respond to the response. They take a sense of tolerated complacency as evidence of success, believing in the promises of liberalism, proud of their place at an exclusive table filled with postgays.

At the same time countless others experience the danger of a response that forces them into silence. They experience the very real violence of the "treatment." They experience the pain of state-enforced coercion directed at eradicating queer desire. While some are off close dancing at inaugural balls, popular politicians are gaining electoral support by attributing every form of disaster, whether natural or otherwise, to the very tolerance that allowed the balls to occur in the first place. In the United States the Christian coalition offers a "treatment" for "curing" gays that makes it appear "kinder and gentler." These efforts to "heal" homosexuals, however, bolster prohibitions against *every* expression of desire, queer or otherwise.

Queer desire seems too contested, too fraught, too much an object of response. The more it is discussed, the more it becomes a central problem that needs resolution, a knot of modernity. The more queer desire is discussed, the more heterosexuality is pulled into this problem. Dare one hope that in the midst of this contention, with its gaps and ruptures, we can recognize a state of *late heterosexuality?* Are the transformations begun in the early modern period playing themselves out? Is the web of modernity fraying and unraveling? If the answer were yes to any of those questions, I would still not suggest that this is the end of history—for certain subjects history is just beginning. I fear, however, that the problem here has a long life, and it is precisely in this problem that heteronormativity continues to find its existence. As I explore in chapter 5, Nietzsche teaches us to recognize here an inversion of cause and effect. As heterosexuality's problem, queer desire is set up as a cause of calamities great and small, from the decline of civilization to a dwindling tax base. Ultimately the problem is an effect of heteronormativity. Queer desire is only queer by virtue of the definition of heteronormativity. Remove those definitions, and you remove the queerness itself. This awareness suggests that attempts to respond to heterosexuality—for example, by seeking equal rights, marriage, and military rights—are at a political, liberatory, emancipatory, and revolutionary dead end.

This standpoint suggests that the kind of politics to which a book such as this one must orient itself should be charted through nonrepresentative forms. These involve questions of autonomy and civil society rather than rights and juridical equality as ends in themselves. It is, in other words, a book oriented toward what Nietzsche frequently refers to as life rather than ossified forms of prescribed relations. While this orientation toward life may not alter the eternal present of our lived time, it does lead us to push beyond queerness *in itself* and bring queer theory to examine the potentials of queerness *for itself.*

Queer History

The term *queer* is linked at this point to certain configurations of desire that emerged in the nineteenth century. To describe these configurations of desires as identities, social philosophers developed designations such as *homosexual, heterosexual, sadist, masochist,* and *transvestite.*[3] The historically specific emergence of these terms can certainly lead us to conclude that homosexuality, heterosexuality, sadism, masochism, and so on could not have existed as such before then. Without the specific denotations and connotations of these designations, the configurations of desire existed in radically different semantic fields. The sodomite occupied a different cultural, ideational, and material world. Such a question was hotly debated in the 1980s in regard to the designation *homosexual.* The general conclusion to that debate seems germane to all these designations. It would be a mistake to presume that the coining of any term marks a sudden break, an overnight shift. There were historical precursors and processes that led up to the emergence of the terms, a *longue durée* of developments as opposed to an epistemic explosion whose crater marks the discourse's point of origin. It would also be a mistake to assume that the terms' appearances mark the emergence of exclusive, universal, stable identities. Certainly the medical and disease models from which words such as *homosexual* sprang were neither universally accepted nor uncontested, either then or now. Certainly the liberal models of democratic representation through which the terms came to designate political subjects were likewise historically and socially specific. At the same time, regardless of the designation—whether, for example, *homosexuality, gayness, sodomy,* and *pederasty* or *transgendered, transvestite, berdache,* and *hijra*—certain configurations of desire constitute historical and cultural constants. Thus to claim that, for instance, the homosexual as such did not exist before 1870 or the transvestite did not exist before 1910 does not negate the historical processes that led to the emergence of these personages. There is some genealogy that connects the sodomite of the eighteenth century to the modern homosexual.

As a result of these debates, two sets of questions have confronted historians since the 1980s. On the one hand, we want to know how to look back and understand the specificities of configurations of desire, how to avoid clouding the understanding of this specificity by attributing it to a transhistorical type, and how to see life as it was, *wie es gewesen ist*. On the other hand, and somewhat antithetically, we want to know how we can contain the transhistorical quality of certain configurations of desire, acknowledge the genealogy that connects desire across history, and account for the *progresus* of history that has led to us.

We can rely on the term *queer* to avoid the conceptual problem of the "gay history from Plato to Quentin Crisp" or the "transgendered history from Hermaphroditus to Renee Richards." Queer offers the possibility of maintaining both a historical specificity and a transhistorical genealogy. But then queer must be understood as a temporary placeholder without essential meaning, a fluid marker of difference waiting to be replaced later when we have understood its historical specificity. The same-sex desire of Goethe or Winckelmann, for instance, or the cross-dressing of Joan of Arc and Charlotte von Mahlsdorf could be the grounds for marking them as queer, but then queer in itself will be understood not as identical with same-sex desire or cross-dressing but as something more expansive yet fundamentally rooted in desire. How does this term come to have specific content?

Until recently the accepted understanding of Johann Joachim Winckelmann (1717–68) was that he was tolerated by a heterosexual society despite his homosexuality—a "queer" insider. Such a position rests on a transhistorical understanding of hetero- and homosexuality. Simon Richter's work on Winckelmann and the larger project initiated by Alice Kuzniar on the "Age of Goethe" has challenged such a view of the eighteenth and early nineteenth centuries.[4] They have unearthed forms of relations, especially same-sex ones, that later generations effaced. Much as was the case with Marlowe and Shakespeare in the Anglo-American world, such effacement often resulted simply from an embarrassment over the avowed passions and warm embraces in which the cultural giants indulged. After Goethe wrote Egmont into Ferdinand's arms or placed Götz as the spectacular center of homoerotic attraction, a later age found itself compelled to skip quickly over those spots in the text. The fact that Winckelmann, the "father" of modern art history, developed an aesthetic on the basis of homoerotic attraction had to be more than glossed over, however; it had to be subjected to an active forgetting. Whereas once individuals felt compelled to *actively forget* certain aspects of the Age of Goethe, now we feel compelled to *actively remember* precisely those aspects.

To remember the past, however, the historian must be displaced from the present. The status of Winckelmann continues to provide a good example. When seeking to explicate the status of same-sex desire and foster the project of active remembering, Kuzniar made a significant plea to unhinge the term *homosexuality* "from a solely sexual definition: it cannot be conceptualized apart from homoeroticism, homoplatonism, homoaesthetics, and passionate friendship" (16). The latter terms filled the ideational superstructure of Winkelmann's world, providing links between persons and rationale for material production. Winkelmann's sexuality related directly to these other terms, which constituted one another. If Winckelmann is designated as homosexual, then that designation has to be understood through the social-sexual field Winckelmann inhabited.

The importance of this suggestion cannot be overemphasized, and in an examination of queerness this insight can be moved one step further. If a historian attends to the configuration of Winckelmann in his own era, his same-sex desire comes to appear not as queer at all but rather as a *stable* element in a particular arrangement of the socius. It is queer only when set against a different arrangement of the socius, that is, when viewed as a negative determination to *our* socius. Indeed, it becomes evident that queerness *in itself* is not transhistorically coincident with same-sex desire. Along with systems of patronage in the eighteenth century, other systems come to mind, such as the *paiderastēs* in ancient Greece, in which same-sex desire acted to stabilize the socius. Even in the current historical context certain configurations of same-sex desire appear as socially stabilizing, including those activist configurations that fight defensively within the terms of the socius; the struggles for marriage, market shares, and military participation, the call for a "place at the table," and so on—all are initiatives that do not set out their own logics of operation.

The story told here begins with the nineteenth century, when queerness and sexuality were joined, as they largely continue to be today.[5] To examine this joining, it became important not to remove sexuality from queerness but to unhinge it as the primary defining point. The joining of sexuality and queerness to which this study attends took place in a mutually constitutive field of larger social philosophical concerns that included democracy, capitalism, nationalism, justice, rationality, subjectivity, and so on. In general I suggest that queerness cannot be conceptualized apart from its bases in desire communicating with problematics of gender, sex, race, erotics, pleasures, needs, wants, drives, and so on. Furthermore, queer *in itself* cannot be conceptualized apart from norms, forms of governance, principles of communication, and economics.

Eve Sedgwick warns against attempts, such as the one being pursued here, to evacuate the term *queer* of a fundamental relationship to same-sex desire. She writes, "Given the historical and contemporary force of the prohibitions against *every* same-sex sexual expression, for anyone to disavow those meanings, or to displace them from the term's definitional center, would be to dematerialize any possibility of queerness itself" (*Tendencies*, 8). This warning is well taken, yet I take exception with the statement's final direction. The emphasis on same-sex sexual expression risks setting homosexuality as the permanent victim of heterosexuality. I caution against understandings of queerness that reduce it to victim status. Homosexuality might be abjected, but homosexuals are not abject in themselves. Queer theory must search for the historical mechanisms of abjection. In queerness we find not that which is always prohibited but that which is always disruptive to the homogeneity of any system. Such disruptions often must be prohibited, but they can nevertheless serve a significant social role.[6] This leads me to a point equally significant, if not more so. Sedgwick's cautionary statement effaces from queerness desires outside same-sex desire, outside sex altogether, and even beyond erotics: for example, the cross-dressed heterosexual or the narcissist whose object of desire is the self or the desires elicited by the image of Huey Newton on the steps of the capitol building in Sacramento.

Sedgwick is correct in warning against a disavowal of the prohibitions, but the problem is the prohibitions, not same-sex sexual expression. Contrary to Sedgwick, I suggest, relying on Hegel's terminology, that within current configurations same-sex desire falls away from being *the* queer determinate negation. Because of its own history, "homosexuality" is fraught with tensions brought on by a certain one-sidedness within configurations of homosexuality itself. It breaks apart out of certain claims for normalcy and inclusion that cannot contain the *queer knowledge* of the homosexual. The final chapter explores this question of queer knowledge, or queer epistemology, but at the moment I want simply to suggest that queer knowledge was never a property of the homosexual. Queer knowledge adhered to and often accrued to the homosexual, but it never belonged to the homosexual.

Ruptures with queer epistemology occur in the contemporary political and economic configuration of homosexuality: gay versus queer; normal versus deviant; inclusive versus partisan; post–disease model, essentialist, "I was born this way" lobbyists versus in your face with my sassy Don't Panic® T-shirt, street-savvy queens. Moreover, where it appears as queer, homosexuality appears as only one form of a host of nonnormative queer desires. Other queer forms of desire seem to be emerging as political agents. Transgendered and S&M activists are throwing off the fetters of pathologizing discourse. The Internet presents Web pages of individuals with all sorts of nonheterosexual objects and directions of desire, from fetishists and necrophiles to voyeurs and exhibitionists. Well beyond sexual desire, moreover, there seems to be something queer to our entire historical context with its nervous attention to disruptive tensions and gaps well beyond those wrought by sexuality. These contemporary tensions and gaps become especially productive when we look back and struggle with the comprehension of history *wie es gewesen ist*. Undertaken from a queer perspective, a project of historicism easily undermines a stabilized essential hetero- versus homosexual paradigm, informing us that at one point in time the structure of the socius was different and assuring us that at another point in time it will be different again, but not promising us what shape it will take.

The current historical perspective almost makes the entire eighteenth-century socius appear queer. For certain forms of sexual desire, the absolutist era may actually have been more open and inciting. I present the possibility that the end of the eighteenth century did not introduce tolerant society, as claimed by liberalism. Indeed, this study's considerations of the eighteenth and nineteenth centuries make clear that in considerations of queer the past and present are fundamentally related. The history of then tells us the story of now. The eighteenth century relates queerly to the present, revealing how the order of things arrived at the present configuration.

The descriptions of the homosocial cultural arrangement of the eighteenth century, the Age of Goethe, the Age of Winckelmann, or the Age of absolutism, can now describe only small pockets of ghettoed culture. Somehow we got from there to here, so that transformations begun at the end of the eighteenth century must have come to frame our current cultural and political thought. If we compare then to now, we are confronted with two seemingly contradictory and paradoxical commonplaces of the present. On the one hand, homosocial arrangements have come to preclude the representation and expression of queer desire, bringing forward, as Foucault observed, certain "silences." On the other hand, such a foreclosure of queer desire paradoxically facilitated the emergence of certain speaking subject positions, individuals who express queer desire, what Foucault called "personages." Silence and speech become knotted together in our modern era. In the first chapter I look more closely at the way some of the threads of this knot were drawn together at the end of the eighteenth century to give strength to the web of modernity.

Social Philosophy

In his essay "A Child Is Being Beaten," Freud noted that "perverts who can obtain satisfaction do not often have occasion to come for analysis" (197). This interesting observation leads to a reconsideration of all the unanalyzed people of the world—perhaps not what Freud intended. Taken to its extreme, then, this remark suggests that the unanalyzed are not the opposite of the perverts. Indeed, the analyzed and the unanalyzed are both perverts, with the real difference being a question of the ability to find social satisfaction in perversion. Freud did chart out the complete route that an individual would have to traverse on the way to a healthy psychosexual configuration. This route proves to be long, passing through early partial drives into the Oedipal conflict through the latency period and out.[7] The travelers ride wild horses on this journey, all the while being battered by the winds of the death drive. A superego rides with them, constantly engaging in exacting criticism and never refraining from unsympathetic commentary. Repressive mechanisms force blinders on them. They are confronted with countless detours and rest stops along the way, and the journey becomes so tiresome that no individual could ever hope to complete the passage. With some bit of baggage lost here or too many souvenirs acquired there, we travelers on this journey are perverts, one and all. Only some of us come in for analysis, however; in only some cases does our perversion find no social satisfaction.

The writings of Kant, Fichte, Herder, Hegel, Marx, Freud, Adorno, and Habermas can fall under the rubric of social philosophy. This group comprises central theorists of modernity, men who defined the parameters of what is socially satisfiable. These figures have been analyzed extensively—but rarely as perverts. This assessment would change a bit if the group was expanded to include Nietzsche, a figure whose philosophy has been extensively analyzed as madness and degeneration. Nevertheless, for the most part these figures belong to the class of satisfied perverts. In their work, lives, and psyches they found outlets and satisfaction in their social settings.

The writings of this group of satisfied perverts present a desiring individual as central subject. In their social philosophy, an understanding of the appropriate manner and object of this individual's desire marks the difference in their divergent conceptions of society. This study explores how their work defined the parameters of desire—and not just for themselves. It examines in addition how they identified the permissible, the normal, the satisfiable. The various social philosophical limits to the desiring individual provide the central subject of each chapter. Further, this book describes how they established these limits through a construction of heterosexuality. Heterosexuality is understood here, as it is in the works I critique, not simply as object choice but as the route through which desire may be associated with something other than desire: universal rationality, morality, national community, bourgeois subjectivity, freedom, and equality. Heterosexuality became the positive direction of desire. Of course, heterosexuality as limitation foreclosed satisfaction for large groups of perverts. Blocked from satisfaction, their desires frozen, their social and psychic beings immobilized, they were sent in one way or another to the "analyst's couch"—frequently a site of horror and torture.

The term *social philosophy* as I use it here has three levels of meaning that become apparent through the preceding description. The first is the immediate level of the *texts* produced by the figures mentioned. This level will be my primary object of critique.[8] It is also the level that distinguishes social philosophy from epistemology, ontology, aesthetics, logic, and so on. This level is most closely implicated in setting social philosophy close to what we call "science."

Living in an age and a place where science is equivalent to objective, verifiable truth, where the *natural* sciences have gained almost full disposition over the truth claims of science, and where the humanities have been relegated to some purely subjective undertaking, it is important to take a moment to reflect on the use of the term. In German the word for science is *Wissenschaft,* a term perhaps better translated as something like "knowledgeship," or systematic knowing. *Science/Wissenschaft,* then, is a term open to humanists as well as "naturists." In German the humanities, the *Geisteswissenschaften,* share with the sciences, the *Naturwissenschaften,* this term that designates the English "science." Likewise in French we can speak of *science humaine* and *science naturelle.* *Science/Wissenschaft* is a form of structured thought whose truth claims, whether drawn from observations of nature or "spirit," are subject to testing and critique.[9]

A second level of social philosophy emerges on recognizing the greater context in which these texts emerged. In particular, there was an oppositional relationship between text and context, between the social philosophy of the theorists and their cultural milieus. That these texts needed to be generated and produced, that they emerged at a particular point in time, indicates that their authors sought to shift material, political, or social structures. If they had been fully of the "common sense" of their period, they would have found no incitement to write. These texts were somehow out of joint with their times. Common sense, time, and material political social structures all refer to another greater field of social philosophy through, against, and within which social philosophy was produced. The texts went on to achieve a transhistorical quality through such oppositional aspects.

In this study, then, social philosophy also marks the constantly changing field on which struggles for historical direction are fought. This field, where heterogeneous interests and identities intersect, cannot be represented by one individual contained within one book. The field of social philosophy is a space of negotiated power relations, and in negotiating the relations of power, Kant, Hegel, Marx, and the others both determined and were determined by this greater field. It is possible within historical analysis to note broad conceptual and philosophical developments and to note that, in those transformations, the writings of Kant and Hegel have influenced the field of social philosophy more than have, say, context-bound social commentators or quantitative sociologists. Why? Certainly Kant and Hegel adopted a more panoramic vision in responding to the debates of their era. Their contributions were ultimately more comprehensive, more synthetic. Hegel himself might suggest that their works gave voice to the *Zeitgeist,* the spirit of the time. Both Marx and Nietzsche, however, would warn against attributing consciousness to these changes ex post facto. Nevertheless, historical awareness lets us acknowledge that out of the immediate possibilities present in any field of social philosophy these individuals negotiated the relations of power that would propel historical transformations.

There is then a third and final level of social philosophy at work here, one discernible in the negotiation of power relations in the socius. Power relations shift as a result of something's being "out of joint" or not working, experienced as a rupture, a crisis, a question. Social philosophy responds to that question. It provides an answer, a new way of knowing that ends the crisis. In this regard Michel Foucault used the term *epistemic shift* to describe such a process. I will use a more metaphoric and less philosophical term: *knot.* At a moment of crisis in social philosophy various figures pull together threads of discourse that threaten to break apart into incoherence or sociopathology and knot them together again. These knots form the social discursive fabric. They are always unstable and in danger of fraying. These knots provide structure. They also block change and further transformation. Sometimes it becomes necessary to unravel them; sometimes, to cut them.

I do not confront the figures under examination through questions of biography; that is, I do not approach them as biographical perverts. Nietzsche's madness and Kant's neurotic compulsive behaviors certainly present enough material to explore biographically, but here I am interested in textual perversion (as, for instance, when Kant defined marriage as a contract for the spouses' mutual use of each other's sex organs). What is unique about these figures is how their social philosophy might be understood in relation to their lives. Their participation in the transformation of social philosophy meant that they actively created the social conditions for obtaining their own satisfaction; Kant and Hegel were more successful in this regard, and Marx and Nietzsche were less so. Heterosexuality came to occupy a significant role in this endeavor.

The Heterocoital Imperative and Heteronormativity

To begin with, the earlier quotation from Freud already presents a problem, for even as it suggests that we are all perverts, it also sets up a paradigm of health. This paradigm invokes a healthy psychosexual configuration toward which we all journey: heterosexuality. The deployment of the term *perversion* rests on the presumption that distance from health can be measured. The paradigm relies on a goal of healthy development. If the measure and goal are accepted as synonymous, then deviations from the goal must be approached with a certain sense of anxiety or dread, especially when the deviation is willful. Willful deviations call for an explanation, a treatment, some form of response. Freud, Hegel, Kant, Marx, and Adorno relied on heterosexuality as an a priori goal. Heterosexuality, however, is an outcome. Freud and the rest established as a priori telos an outcome that can be described only a posteriori. In this regard, this book will explore what it means that the social philosophy under examination is based on a tautology.

I should take a moment to define heterosexuality, even though it is so pervasive as to be almost self-evident. Given the anxious volumes devoted to defining nonheterosexualities, however, a few words here will hardly matter. And I do not intend to provide a better entry for the *Oxford English Dictionary*. Heterosexuality is both an outcome of desire and a historical sign system.[10] In order for heterosexuality to be an outcome, desire must adhere to a particular sign system. As in any other semiotic system, culture and history anchor or fix the terms of heterosexuality into a signifying system. The heterosexual sign system, however, has taken on a unique quality. The semiotics of heterosexuality strive for the specific appearance of language where signifiers and signifieds are bound together as signs. In a heterosexual outcome, desire passes through a certain form of comportment (a gender morpheme) that appears as a signifier. It moves onto a particular physical configuration (a body-sex morpheme) that appears as a signified. It then connects that configuration to a behavior, a syntax of activity.

Figure 1 attempts to represent this dynamic in terms familiar from Saussurian linguistics. Saussure helped explore the arbitrary relationship of the signifier and signified that nevertheless appears to a language's speaking subjects as a stable, necessary relationship. Figure 1 draws out a similarity between the relationship of signifier to signified and that of gender to sex made natural by the language of heterosexuality.

Sexological literature, one of the main grammars of heterosexuality, often identifies gender as a "secondary" sex characteristic.[11] This secondary quality of gender presents it as existing in relationship to some more essential, more real base or signified. We will see that the determinants of gender vary greatly, from dress and behavior to body characteristics such as hair patterns. Further, these characteristics shift and change wildly over time and across cultures, so that what appears as masculine in one culture may signify femininity in another. Such variation does not disrupt the coherence of the gender morpheme, because whatever configuration defines secondary characteristics, they are understood as deriving from a more primary sex characteristic. As with gender in sexological literature, the exact definition of this primary sex characteristic varies but is generally understood as genital configuration, although there is a contemporary tendency to rely on chromosomes. Further, it is im-

Figure 1. The Linguistics of Heterosexuality

Signifier			Masculinity			Femininity	Gender
————	=	Sign	————	=	♂ ↔ ♀ =	————	
Signified			Male			Female	Sex

$$\text{Sexual Desire}$$

Gender: masculinity/femininity

Sex: male/female

Sexual desire: a "natural" force of attraction between these two gender/sex morphemes

portant to note that whereas the secondary characteristics are multiple, the primary is a singular characteristic that is signified. Both sex and gender are aligned into dimorphic configurations; that is, humans are positioned in polar configurations, with the poles often understood as opposing each other. This becomes significant for the explanation of the flow of desire. With the gender and sex morphemes culturally bound together into two poles, desire then moves between these two poles, drawing them together into a particular form of genital contact. The particular requirement placed on the form of this contact is something explored throughout this study. Heterosexuality does not result in simply any contact between the two poles but must culminate in the specific form of coitus. Thus a flow of desire between masculine male and feminine female poles that does not result in this particular form of contact becomes defined as something other than heterosexuality: anal, oral, or fetishistic sexuality or even asexuality. To underscore this aspect of heterosexuality, therefore, I use the phrase *heterocoital imperative* to denote the mechanism that brings this sign-system into coherence, structuring it as sexuality by providing it with a specific outcome.

For those whose sexual desire is communicated through this "language," it can appear as a natural signifying system outside history—a language spoken by God himself. But just as in language, where closer examination shows the relationship of signifier to signified to be arbitrary yet structurally important and constantly shifting, so too are the terms of heterosexuality. In its contemporary form heterosexuality masks the arbitrary nature of its sign system. In doing so it appears as necessary and natural. Of course, there is no necessary connection between behavior culturally defined as feminine or masculine and bodies of a particular sex configuration. "Tomboys" and "sissies" from childhood made us aware of other possibilities from our earliest days onward. Further, regardless of various behavioral possibilities, the epithets *tomboy* and *sissy* taught us what we ought to do and what we may not do vis-à-vis sex and gender. But some wind up being bad pupils in this lesson. While the connection is deeply psychically entrenched, some remain aware that this relationship is arbitrary.[12] In others the awareness is an anxiety. A few remain blissfully ignorant.

In language a rupture between signifier and signified ends the possibility of communication. An examination of heterosexuality's "linguistic" structure, however, shows that the components of this semiotic system, unlike those of language, are complete morphemes. A break between the components of the signs of heterosexuality, the split of sex and gender, does not lead to a collapse of communication. Indeed, it leads to an increase of language and new rules for the formation and linking of cultural phrases. Even if we retain a strict dimorphic basis, we can recognize that breaking the ostensibly natural relationship between signifier and signified here expands the possibilities of configurations.

Figure 2 represents some of the possibilities of an expanded language of sexuality. Configuration 1 might describe "butch-femme" same-sex relationships, where two women are attracted to each other's different gender traits. The gender traits differ while the sex characteristics remain the same, and it is this configuration that allows for the desiring relationship. Configuration 2 changes the sex characteristics and therefore might describe a similar dynamic in a gay male relationship. Configuration 3 retains the typical configuration of sex characteristics in a heterosexual relationship but incorporates a cross-gender or perhaps butch-femme situation that allows for a flow of desire. Configuration 4 again retains a typical configuration of heterosexual sex characteristics, but the gender dynamic might represent a couple in which one partner cross-dresses, for instance. Configurations 5 and 6 might mark various forms of transgendered/transsexed relationships. Configurations 7, 8, and 9 might mark auto-oriented patterns of desire directed toward gender or sex. They also hint at possibilities for nondimorphic descriptions. Of course, such configurations do exist, despite any imperatives of a restrictive model of sexual language. Ultimately the point of figure 2 is not to provide a new system of cataloging or categorization; if the table appears confusing or bewildering, it has done its job. I hope that, in offering a sort of combinatorial matrix of alternatives and possibilities, it reveals some of the complexity that is lost as a result of the heterocoital imperative.

The configurations of sexual desire available could be further described by placing sexual dimorphism into question. The polarity of gen-

Figure 2. Elaborated Semiotics for Dimorphic Configurations of Sexual Desire

1. $\dfrac{\text{Masculinity}}{\text{Female}}$	$\leftrightarrow$	$\dfrac{\text{Femininity}}{\text{Female}}$	2. $\dfrac{\text{Masculinity}}{\text{Male}}$	$\leftrightarrow$	$\dfrac{\text{Femininity}}{\text{Male}}$
3. $\dfrac{\text{Femininity}}{\text{Male}}$	$\leftrightarrow$	$\dfrac{\text{Masculinity}}{\text{Female}}$	4. $\dfrac{\text{Femininity}}{\text{Male}}$	$\leftrightarrow$	$\dfrac{\text{Femininity}}{\text{Female}}$
5. Male	$\leftrightarrow$	Masculinity	6. Female	$\leftrightarrow$	Masculinity
7. Female		8. Male	9. Masculine		

der and sex that attends the heterocoital imperative has obtained a truth position in popular consciousness, a taken-for-granted, commonsense quality at the heart of social philosophy. The body exists as the material and stable term in relationship to gender and sexuality, yet within the sexological writings of the late nineteenth and early twentieth centuries—the backdrop to the works of Continental social psychology—a fundamental and stable dimorphism of the body was hardly taken for granted. In Germany Magnus Hirschfeld documented diversity in primary sex characteristics that challenged such a simplistic division. Much excellent recent work on the history of the construction of dimorphic sex, especially that by Thomas Laqueur and Anne Fausto-Sterling, restores the critique of the two-sex model.[13] This book seeks to add to that discussion. The distinction that it makes between the heterocoital imperative and heterosexuality as such lets us identify how the latter became implicated in connecting desire to themes in social philosophy, while the former connected desire to specific objects.

Furthermore, this study explores how, during the nineteenth and early twentieth centuries and within the rising system of sexuality defined by the heterocoital imperative, the heterogeneity of sexual morphemes was bound to signifiers of perversion. The emergence of terms such as *homosexuality, heterosexuality, transsexuality, sadism,* and *masochism* does not mean that the forms of interaction that these terms designate did not exist before. It does mean, however, that certain behaviors were reformulated and reclassified as a result of a new context. This new context was the rise of heterosexuality as imperative. Recall that the term *heterosexuality* appeared after the descriptor *homosexuality,* and it is possible to recognize that the establishment of a semiotic primacy for the heterosexual system of signification made heterosexuality appear natural and transparent, not requiring any descriptors at first. Nevertheless, the heterocoital imperative forces the myriad possibilities of desiring relationships alluded to in figure 2 out of transparency and into a condition in which they must be explained. The presence of these "perversions" did not (nor will it ever) result in a dreaded collapse of culture or the decline of civilization promised by authoritarian (sexual) reformers of that period or this one. The very fact that heterosexuality had to be regulated and protected indicates that it was always a tenuous and unstable undertaking and that it was always aware that it shared the field of (sexual) desire with other, more attractive forms.

At this point it should be abundantly clear that heterosexuality and the heterocoital imperative have a history. What might not yet be clear is that the awareness of this history leads us to understand that heterosexuality can exist separate from any imperative. Structurally heterosexuality can occupy the same syntactical position as other determinations of sexuality. *Eros* and *paiderastēs* were once imperatives in the language of desire among the ancient Greeks. These terms have given way to a term, *homosexuality*, that exists without being an imperative.[14] Heterosexuality can also cohere as a pattern of desire without the state and economic regulations that make it an imperative. Therefore we can identify a component of heterosexuality that exceeds its relationship to sexuality as such, so that I have had to use the term *heteronormativity* along with the term *heterocoital imperative*.

Michael Warner and Lauren Berlant have provided the following useful definition for heteronormativity:

> By heteronormativity we mean the institutions, structures of understanding, and practical orientations that make heterosexuality seem not only coherent—that is, organized as sexuality—but also privileged. Its coherence is always provisional, and its privilege can take several (sometimes contradictory) forms: unmarked, as the basic idiom of the personal and the social; or marked as a natural state; or projected as an ideal or moral accomplishment. It consists less of norms that could be summarized as a body of doctrine than of a sense of rightness produced in contradictory manifestations—often unconscious, immanent to practice or institutions. Contexts that have little visible relation to sex practice, such as life narrative and generational identity, can be heteronormative in this sense, while in other contexts forms of sex between men and women might *not* be heteronormative. Heteronormativity is thus a concept distinct from heterosexuality. One of the most conspicuous differences is that it has no parallel, unlike heterosexuality, which organizes homosexuality as its opposite. Because homosexuality can never have the invisible, tacit, society-founding rightness that heterosexuality has, it would not be possible to speak of "homonormativity" in the same sense. (547)

Historical or cross-cultural studies such as mine will of necessity take exception with this passage's final statement. Indeed, the normative and doctrinaire institutionalization of heterosexuality through social philosophy will be my focus, especially in the first two chapters.

To recognize or experience historical shifts requires a turning back, a dislocation from our culture's social philosophy. This move is never complete and certainly not to be completed without a certain amount of madness—a bit of communicative psychosis. This madness can appear even without the move of historical recognition. It can force the limits of culture defended by ossifying common sense. Cultural displacement, persecution, diaspora, exile, travel of a sort, and education can burden an individual with cultural skepticism or cultural relativism. Historical awareness, knowledge of the broad stretches of time, can bring this madness too. The safety from even a touch of this madness is the luxury of the sedentary and complacent, the "discriminating" traveler who prefers the package deal with its protective resort and enclave exoticism, the student whose education only reinforces what he already knows. Nevertheless, those touched by this madness bring new phrases into existence, new linkages, new formulations.

This study takes as its point of departure a moment of historical and cultural displacement, so that new phrases, new linkages, and new formulations may be brought into existence. The story it tells moves us beyond our culture and outside our social philosophy, beginning in the late eighteenth century, the Enlightenment, in Kant's Königsberg, moving to Hegel's Jena, winding its way with Marx to London and with the exiled to New York and Los Angeles, and then turning back to Nieztsche's Basel. Nevertheless, the story told here is about you. The story told here is for you.

Notes

1. Whether knowingly or as a result of participating in a similar problematic of liberal structures, the authors of these studies return to a model presented by Hans Mayer.

2. Leo Bersani wrote critically of *queer* as a politico-cultural organizing term. He rejected especially the form of voluntarist liberal protest that motivated the deployment of queer in Queer Nation, a queerness of dress-up and play, of liberal shock. Ultimately he rejected the term and pleaded instead for a more structural understanding of disruption that adheres to "homoness." He wrote "there is a more radical possibility: *homo-ness itself necessitates a massive redefining of relationality.* More fundamental than a resistance to normalizing methodologies is a potentially revolutionary inaptitude—perhaps inherent in gay desire—for sociality as it is known" (76). Bersani called for an analysis embedded in specificity, a gay specificity that does not "commit us to the notion of homosexual essence" (76). We can call this specificity history and its determinations. We can recognize that homosexuality, male-male sexual desire, has been for a great deal of the modern period a particular site of anxiety and disruption. I attend to this specificity in this book, yet the matter must not be confused. I also recognize that homosexuality, once a bearer of the spirit of freedom, is not inherently so. Bersani wrote further: "There are some glorious precedents for thinking of homosexuality as truly disruptive—as a *force* not limited to the modest goals of tolerance for diverse lifestyles, but in fact mandating the politically unacceptable and politically indispensable choice of an outlaw existence" (76). There is now, however, urgent evidence that homosexuality can also act as the opposite. In a period when gays and lesbians are lining up at the altar simply to gain the same rights as heterosexuals, they relinquish their ability to demand greater freedom for *all.* It seems that we are living through a flight from freedom, from the outlaw existence Bersani hopes to find among homos. We must attend to that specificity as well. Yet Bersani's *homoness* as inapt sociality, as that which forces a failure of sociality, is precisely what the term *queer* can contain.

3. Magnus Hirschfeld coined the term *transvestite* in his 1910 publication *Die Trans-vestiten* (a slightly later study has been translated into English [*Transvestites*]). Nevertheless, there were a number of earlier discussions of this "type." Charles Geneviève d'Eon de Beaumont (1728–1810), who spent the better part of his life as a woman, became the object of great interest in the nineteenth century. Havelock Ellis borrowed his name for the "sexo-aesthetic inversion" "Eonism." In the years following the publication of Hirschfeld's book, the literature was filled with discussions of the transvestite and other "clothing fetishists."

4. See Richter; see also Gustafson; Tobin.

5. Of course Foucault's *History of Sexuality* made great contributions to this discussion, along with the now classic work of Weeks (*Coming Out*) and Halperin.

6. We can recall Bataille's articulation of the heterogeneous and recognize it also as a site of queerness. The heterogeneous is outside the order of the homogeneous system. Bataille described not only the "freak" but also the leader as heterogeneous. Bataille actually condenses the two, making them possibilities of each other. Such a condensation is unique to Bataille and bears further analysis (see *Visions of Excess*).

7. In his further theoretical elaborations Freud went on to identify the Oedipal conflict, the primary mechanism of the formation of heterosexual object choice, as a neurosis-producing mechanism; see "On Narcissism" and "Three Essays on Sexuality."

8. For this level of social philosophy, Axel Honneth has noted a divide in the semantic fields of the German and Anglo worlds. He writes: "In this confused terrain, social philosophy in the German-speaking world has increasingly taken on the role of a residual discipline. Indeterminant in its relation to the neighboring fields of study, by default it functions as an overarching organization for all practically oriented subdisciplines, a normative supplement for empirically oriented sociology, and in an interpretive undertaking that is time diagnostic. In Anglo-Saxon lands, on the other hand, since the early days of utilitarianism an understanding of social philosophy has emerged that is roughly what in Germany has been conceived as 'political philosophy': a study which emphasizes normative questions that are revealed in the places where the reproduction of civil society requires the intervention of the state (the maintenance of property, the apportioning of punishment, healthcare, etc.)" (367). In the one realm the breadth of social philosophy threatens it with dissolution; in the other its focus threatens to subordinate it to political philosophy. Having noted this problem in the semantic and discursive field, I chart a different path that in effect appeals to neither German nor Anglo-American social philosophers. Rather, I follow a path similar to the one charted by Hegel and explore the discourse in its historical (diachronic) development.

9. I turn to the term *critique* rather than *criticize* out of appreciation for its deployment within German philosophy. Rather than express some form of positive or negative evaluation (as in "to criticize"), *Kritik* involves a systematic analysis of the components of an argument with the goal of testing their truth claims.

10. For an original discussion of the history of heterosexuality, see Katz.

11. This distinction is made especially in German sexological or sexual-scientific literature. In German the word *Geschlecht* denotes both sex and gender. Hence *primär Geschlechtscharakteristik* (primary sex/gender characteristic) denotes a similar semantic field covered by the English *sex*.

12. For an excellent discussion of the possibilities of gender insubordination, see Butler, "Imitation."

13. For a direct discussion of dimorphism in Freud, see Laqueur; see also Fausto-Sterling, *Myths of Gender*.

14. We can add to this observation the absence of trans imperatives, object imperatives, or whatever other directions in which desire does flow. Such nonexistent imperatives are perhaps potentials structurally inherent to all the sexual morphemes. There have been many literary descriptions of parallel universes defined by such imperatives, often undertaken as a means to confront heterosexual homophobia. Such descriptions invite fictional imaginings along the lines of "what if the world were different and straights were oppressed instead of gays" (see Piercy; LeGuin).

1   *Kant and the Desiring Individual*

> The super-ego—the conscience at work in the ego—may
> then become harsh, cruel and inexorable against the ego
> which is in its charge. Kant's Categorical Imperative is
> thus the direct heir of the Oedipus complex.
>
> —Sigmund Freud

The Queer Turn to Kant

Indispensable to the history of sexuality and the project of
queer theory is the work of Michel Foucault.[1] Just as the cliché about the
three influences on Marx, it is possible to suggest that Foucault's inspiration was drawn primarily from three similar sources: German philosophy, French history, and American sexual economy. Certainly French
history's influence is obvious, and the biographies have made clear the
impact of the American sexual economy. In terms of German philosophical influence, the Frankfurt School is underexamined, but Foucault himself made explicit the influence of Nietzsche and Kant.

In the work of Immanuel Kant (1724–1804) Foucault recognized "the
outline of what one might call the attitude of modernity" ("Enlightenment," 38). Kant signified a certain shift in the order of things, the emergence of "a historical ethos that could be described as a permanent critique of our historical era" (42). Foucault located his own project in this
critical ethos. "The critical ontology of ourselves has to be . . . conceived
as an attitude, an ethos, a philosophical life in which the critique of what
we are is at one and the same time the historical analysis of the limits
that are imposed on us and an experiment with the possibility of going
beyond them" (50). The revised project that Foucault began in the sec-

ond volume of *The History of Sexuality* belongs to such a critical ontology. In undertaking a history of sexuality, Foucault understood himself
as charting out a genealogy of the modern subject. Foucault sought to
describe not our essence but the way "Western man had been brought to
recognize himself as a subject of desire" (*History,* 2:6). "In short, with this
genealogy the idea was to investigate how individuals were led to practice on themselves and on others, a hermeneutics of desire, a hermeneutics of which their sexual behavior was doubtless the occasion, but certainly not the exclusive domain" (2:5). These remarks also offer a glimpse
of what will be the starting point of our approach to Kant. Kantian philosophy certainly represents the outset of the critical project Foucault
described, but it also marks one of the primary points of emergence of
this modern subject of desire. Through a close examination of Kant we
can further recognize how this subject of desire became bound to heterosexuality as the bearer of norms.

A queer turn to Kant affords both a contribution to and critical assessment of the history of sexuality, but the turn is not to Kant as person. Kant's bachelorhood, his daily walks, his self-constructed adjust-
able sock suspenders, or even his belief in extraterrestrials could
certainly serve as sufficient material for a quirky review. It might prove
useful to keep in mind that modernity's great philosopher of rationality
exhibited a panoply of neurotic symptoms. For queer theory, however,
Kant serves as a locus on a discursive trajectory that continues to the
present. Through Kant we can identify both the attitude and the genealogy of modernity; we can mark the emergence of a modern discourse
of social organization, the logic of which intersected with the emergence
of modern social institutions.

Kant's discourse of politics, economics, and subjectivity relied on a
conception of the universal human and thereby supported a political
institutional system that was ready for export—the republic.[2] Such universality relied on an essential homogeneity that came to collide with
historically, socially, economically, and psychically determined heterogeneity. If we recognize how the individual subject of this philosophical
discourse, the citizen of this republic, is constructed in an intersection
whose focus is a heteronormative containment of desire, we will extend
the project of the history of sexuality formulated by Foucault. We can then
examine the genealogy of "the manifold relations, the open strategies, and
the rational techniques that articulate the exercise of powers" (*History*
2:6) and finally come to understand how heterosexual attachments submitted homoeroticism in particular to active forgetting and suppressed
representation.

Entering Kant's Corpus

How do we enter Kant's corpus? When we turn to the ethical Kant, it is probably most often a turn to his "categorical imperative." The categorical imperative seems to be the most admired and pursued aspect of his ethics. It is a fascinating piece of critical philosophy easily contained within a simple principle: "Act so that the maxim of your will could always hold at the same time as a principle establishing universal law" (*Practical Reason*, 30).[3] It is a little sinew that holds his body of thought together, a muscle that keeps it in motion. If we poke around at it, try to follow what it anchors and what it leverages, we can find in it almost everything at stake in Kant's philosophy.

The categorical imperative emerges in the *Critique of Practical Reason* as the conclusion of a story designed to illustrate the a priori status of moral law. This illustration, a thought experiment, gets lost in the attention paid to the renowned maxim that immediately follows it. Let us then take a step back from the categorical imperative and listen attentively to the story Kant tells, the story of a voluptuary, a libertine who is bound to his desires. His story is the prototypical queer story in modernity. "Suppose that someone says his lust is irresistible when the desired object and opportunity are present" (30). Note that the story of the voluptuary begins with a confession. The libertine reveals the truth of himself: he is controlled by his passions. He is unable to resist the object of his desires. The account begins with the lowest of the low: this someone, a *man*, is governed by his desires. In the logic of the story, being led by his emotions sets this character as far from reason and the reasonable control of his will as Kant could imagine. It also introduces a certain tension. This is hardly the sort of character from which one would expect the moral law to emerge. It is all the better as a trope, then, when the rake turns out to be moral.

But before I get ahead of myself, note how Kant adds a twist to the story. Having gotten the hero to confess to his desires, Kant poses a question designed to draw him up short. "Ask him whether he would not control his passion if, in front of the house where he has this opportunity, a gallows were erected on which he would be hanged immediately after gratifying his lust" (30). Confronting the sensualist with the gallows instead of postorgasmic bliss is certainly a rupture, an interruption in his desires that should make him think twice. This is a gallows that seems to be set up only for him and for his transgressions, much as, in Kafka's famous parable, the door to the law was set up there only for the man from the country. The gallows of the law waits for our lecher to sneak into this house and satisfy his lusts. He is free to enter, much as Kafka's man from the country is free to leave. Kafka's man wants to enter the law. Kant's man, however, does not yet know the law; he discovers it through trying to enter the door to his desire. It is unclear exactly whose house this is. Perhaps the police are waiting for him to commit the transgression and are ready to break through the door and catch him in the act. This would have been well within the purview of Reformation-era discipline masters, *Zuchtherren,* and certainly within the powers of the Prussian *Polizey.* If we object that this was an abrogation of the right to privacy, a still hotly contested right, we would be evincing our temporal and legislative distance from Kant's period.

That Kant turned to the gallows is significant. He went well beyond the usual punishments meted out to libertines, fornicators, and adulterers in his era, suggesting not just jail, or the stockade, or a scarlet letter, or a hat with bells on it (a *Springer*).[4] Kant confronts our voluptuary with the punishment reserved for sodomites and rapists: death. According to common law, however, the sodomite confronted death by fire, while the rapist got the sword. Nevertheless, his deployment of death here indicates the libertine to have been an extreme criminal. Moreover, it is not surprising that Kant invoked his era's most extreme "sex criminals" for his example. He wrote his critiques at a time when legal reform was in the air and sexual behaviors received a great deal of attention. The 1780s and 1790s saw intense juridical debate throughout the German territories, the most notable result of which was the Prussian *Allgemeines Landrecht,* adopted in 1794 after years of debate. This legal code eventually evolved into that of the Second Reich. In the last two decades of the eighteenth century, moreover, Austria, Baden, and Bavaria were undergoing similar legal reform, and just across the border, in France, 1789 set off the biggest legal reform of the modern era. Sex crimes and especially sodomy came under reexamination in all these reform efforts. Holland in the 1730s and then Austria in 1787 had lessened the penalty for sodomy from death to imprisonment. Prussia did likewise in 1794. Baden and Bavaria went as far as *almost* decriminalizing consensual sexual acts entirely, retaining language that marked those acts as criminal but with no legal means of prosecution.[5]

In Kant's story, however, contrary to the reforms of the early modern period, the libertine (imagine him to be like the Marquis de Sade, a rather polymorphous perverse type given to all sorts of acts and committed only to the heightening of his own desire) confronts the gallows. Here Kant strategically turned to the premodern formulation of the law. The gallows represents the actualization of the rule of the sovereign, or as

Foucault would have identified it, the right of death over life. Up through absolutist monarchy, the law's relation to life—the source of its control and ultimate threat—was in its ability to end life. Confronted with such a law, the roué is brought up short. Given these conditions, "We do not have to guess very long what the answer would be" (30). Apparently the hero would obey the law, repress or sublimate his desire, and avoid the death penalty. This whole story would be about external restrictions placed on his freedom to desire. But since the answer is not given explicitly, we may have to guess.

There is a slight problem, however. Kant requires that our eudaemonist do more than simply submit to the law. Recall that Kant is searching for the a priori basis of morality. Obeying the law simply because it is the law is hardly a transcendental a priori, making it an insufficient ground for morality as Kant understood it. Now with the legal reform in the air, acts once deemed eternally immoral and evil were being treated according to a different rationale. In Baden and Bavaria jurists promoted the decriminalization of consensual sexual acts; sodomy was about to become, as Nietzsche might say, extramoral, beyond good and evil.[6] As Enlightenment jurists sought to base legal systems in rational processes of legislation, the law revealed itself as historical and cultural, not transcendent. Kant, an Enlightenment philosopher with his own commitment to rationality, nevertheless searched for some other basis; indeed, the search here is for a transcendental ground for morality. Therefore the story would and does continue. "But ask him whether he thinks it would be possible for him to overcome his love of life, however great it may be, if his sovereign threatened him with the same sudden death unless he made a false deposition against an honorable man whom the ruler wished to destroy under a plausible pretext" (30). There are three possible ways to read this turn in the story. First, if our hero has obeyed the law and avoided the death penalty, then in the continuation of the story a shift occurs away from his desire. This move to something other than the sodomite's desire is significant. Desire seems to be contained to the first half of Kant's thought experiment. Personal wishes, needs, longings, pleasures, drives and so on seem to disappear entirely from the second half. The libertine appears to be confronted with an entirely new form of coercion, that of the evil monarch.

In a different reading, however, it is possible that our libertine may *not* have submitted to the law and is actually on his way up the scaffold to the gallows. If this is the case, we must read the plot very differently. It is the early modern period, recall, and the story has two new characters, the honorable man whose existence is endangered and the corrupt monarch. The corrupt sovereign seems to have no power over the honorable man but apparently has a certain power over our hero, for the death penalty is in effect. If the death penalty is still in effect because our hero has acted on his nature, it is possible to read the story as continuous. Sovereign law has failed to deter him, and his desire compelled him to revolt against determinations on his freedom. Now he is facing the same not yet executed sentence, walking the steps to the gallows, and the monarch is coercing him in his weakness. The monarch has the goods on him, the libertine is a weak pederast, and if he wants to save his life, he will have to do something that he does not desire.

There may be yet a third reading: the death penalty and gallows are established only to coerce the libertine into bearing false witness. Knowing the hero's desires, the sovereign established the gallows, a repressive mechanism designed to keep the libertine in check, and indeed he never entered the house. In this reading, too, the nature of the libertine plays an important role in both parts of the story. The corrupt monarch is offering him, for the price of false witness, a complete freedom to act on his desires. If he bears false witness, the monarch removes the gallows in front of the house, and our libertine has free passage to enter.

Kant apparently intended the first reading and simply experienced a lapse in his narrative technique. Nevertheless, the other two readings underscore (sexual) desire's significance to all the readings, which replace a gallows that differentiates good and evil as absolutes at the cost of life with a ruler who is corrupt in his disposition over his subjects. This ruler is willing to deploy the law to achieve his own ends. In such a case the individual needs the moral law more than ever, and here the tension builds in the story. From which corner will morality appear? By what means? Will our libertine, our Lothario, our rip, our prototypical queer, wishing to serve only his own desires, be able to rise to the occasion, go beyond selfish interest and become a true hero, protect the honorable man and save the day?

Suddenly the tension drops. Kant's story takes another unexpected turn. A form of indifference or disappointment arises. "Whether he would or not he perhaps will not venture to say" (30). Our voluptuary, it seems, will no longer follow the thought experiment. He does not present himself as a revolutionary hero, willing to take on the existing powers. He is a nervous character, unwilling to linger any longer. Perhaps his desires are getting the better of him. Perhaps he is suffering from attention deficit disorder. The man is low, corruptible, base, indifferent—but not entirely. Before he could run after some pretty young molly, Kant managed to get in one last question, asking him if he at least might say no to the

corrupt monarch: "but that it would be possible for him he would certainly admit without hesitation" (30). And from this point Kant was able
to draw the story to a close.

In the acknowledgment of the possibility that the libertine might say
no lies the key to Kant's conception of morality and the key to modernity. Kant recognized in this behavior a higher principle that precedes temporal law and the individual. Removed from the law of the sovereign, out
from under the shadow of the gallows set up to condemn his actions, the
sodomite acknowledges that there is some other a priori law. Interestingly
for Kant, it is only in the absence of state coercion and punishment that
such a law can become visible; only in these conditions can one behave
morally. This becomes apparent when our voluptuary acknowledges the
possibility that he could behave differently and save the honorable man
at the cost of his own life: "He judges, therefore, that he can do something because he knows that he ought, and he recognizes that he is free—
a fact which, without the moral law, would have remained unknown to
him" (30). The moral law appears here, separate from the corrupt monarch, inherent and a priori in the libertine. It is also interestingly separate from juridical law. Moral law is what gives the libertine an inkling
of his own freedom and makes it possible that he might not endanger the
freedom of others, to the point of giving up all his pleasures and becoming a martyr. The libertine could become indifferent to the corrupt monarch because there is a law before him by which even the monarch can
be judged. From here Kant leaped directly to the first definition of the
"law of pure practical reason": "Act so that the maxim of your will could
always hold at the same time as a principle establishing universal law"
(30). According to this a priori principle of freedom, our voluptuary does
not bear false witness, because a world that permitted false witness would
constrain his own freedom more than prohibitions against false witness
would. Hence he is willing to restrain himself from constraining the freedom of others in order to maximize his own freedom. He forgoes coercion to increase the possibilities for pursuing "his own" enjoyment. The
more coercion there is in the world, the fewer are the possibilities available for the individual to pursue. Kant's story is thus supposed to show
that the basis of this moral law lies in the libertine's identification with
the honorable man. The libertine must recognize himself in the honorable man's predicament of being endangered by the corrupt machinations
of the sovereign—"that could be me." He must join with the honorable
man to circumscribe the desires of the monarch. The moral law is thus
also the source and mechanism of (bourgeois) sociability. The libertine
nobly climbs the scaffold to the gallows because he would rather die than

live in a world in which he coerced the honorable man. The moral a priori and the rationale of choice coincide to provide a happy end to the story.

Kant made quite a leap to reach his conclusion, however, a leap that may appear to require seven-mile boots, and not everyone will want to follow. I myself want to linger a bit longer, but not because I am an enervated voluptuary unable or unwilling to follow Kant. There is something about the libertine's sudden departure; recall that he did not ascend the gallows but rather mumbled an answer and ran off. That leaves me puzzled, so I would like to look around just a bit longer. I wonder where he went. Is it possible that he could return? What happened to all that desire contained in the first half of the story? Kant concluded that the libertine was motivated by an a priori "moral" law, but the lukewarm acknowledgment of the possibility suggests that he was much more motivated by desire. So it is important to recognize that the ending to Kant's story is not the only one available to us, nor was it the only one available to Kant. A different conclusion is perhaps possible.

Kant suggested that the libertine is motivated to recognize a moral a priori by a form of *identification with* the honorable man. Consider the cast of characters and ask who has the most power, tradition, and strong feelings to draw the libertine's desire and his identification. Is it the innocuous honorable man? Or is it the corrupt monarch? Instead of concluding that the refusal to bear false witness would be done out of the libertine's identification with the honorable man—"that could be me"—we could rather conclude that the refusal would be undertaken out of identification with the monarch—"*that* could be me!"

Note that the corrupt monarch has disappeared as well; perhaps he has slunk off having realized the bind he is now in vis-à-vis his own legitimacy. We might even conclude that this is a tale not about the moral law but about a rerouting of desire. Certainly the libertine has avoided the gallows—that is, the law of the sovereign—by acquiring internal control over his own desire. (Here Freud might toss in a new character, the agency of the superego, but we do not need a cast of thousands.) So if the voluptuary is motivated to wield morality as a weapon in a struggle with the sovereign, it might be possible to understand the tale as one of a sublimation of desire where desire now expresses itself not sexually but rather in a will to power. Morality can be the name for a struggle for autonomy between sovereign and subject. What appears as morality could simply be the attainment of control over one's own (sexual) desire in order to attain the power of self-governance. As a result of this sublimation, not only has he learned to avoid the gallows by containing his own desires, but in the second half of the story a new world of power has opened up to him through the assertion of his own will and his willingness to go to the gallows. In the second half of the tale the monarch does not abide by the sovereign law but rather exposes the libertine to schemes and tactics that undo the monarch's own sovereignty. When the monarch banks on his subject's newly learned containment of desire, the voluptuary's refusal of the pardon and his willingness to go to the gallows create a crisis of legitimacy for the monarch himself. If the monarch kills the voluptuary for not carrying out the monarch's corrupt desires, he kills an innocent man. If the monarch moves to wield the law as a tactic, to rob it of its sovereignty, it becomes possible to open up a will to power on the part of the subject, because the sovereign no longer appears constant in his application of the law.

With this conclusion to the tale of the libertine, the prototypical queer, we move from the lowest of the base to the highest of the transcendent. Kant would never offer this conclusion, however, although Nietzsche might, and with it I make my own leap from the early modern to the postmodern. I do so only to illustrate briefly what is at stake here. Here we confront what I will identify as knots of modernity. In the early modern period certain aspects of the social fabric based on divine order and revelation began to fray, and new threads were introduced: transcendence, nature, law, desire, sexuality, rationality, morality, and freedom. Kant tied together the problems that bind and support the web of modernity: individual and society, "freedom from" and "freedom to," morality and coercion, power and desire, repression and incitement. And these knots have proven to provide both structure and stricture. Those strictures have been most painfully felt by queer subjects who have sought to undo them, who have compelled other social philosophies to emerge. Nevertheless, as I suggested earlier, Kant marks the emergence of a modern discourse of social organization, the logic of which intersected with the emergence of modern social institutions. In the following sections, then, I concentrate more precisely on the problem of desire and subjectivity in Kantian social philosophy as the site of the central queer dynamic of early modernity.

The Universal Human Confronts the Modern Individual

As early as the seventeenth century burgeoning bourgeois liberal theory introduced certain key terms for understanding the individual and society, thus shaping modern social debates. The source of these terms has been traced back variously to a decline of tradition as justification for political action, a similar decline of religion's ability to confer political principle, and the rise of the bourgeoisie within the new economic system of capitalism. Certainly by the eighteenth century the institutions of estate, confessional, and guild were often experienced as shackles binding productive forces. In addition, terms such as *freedom* and *equality*, constitutive to the modern ideological framework, presented contentious attacks on the existent system.

The emergence of the radical political critique propelling the developments of modernity brought with it a split between equality and freedom. Most discussions of political and social philosophy, however, paired equality with law and morality with freedom. Of course, these discussions were interrelated. The inalienable legal rights of all men were affronted by the inequality that resulted from privileges limited to some men. Meanwhile, the universal human, constituted through those properties of reason and morality common to all, came under examination, supporting the claim to freedom for all. Although these discussions were interrelated, they were also distinct, giving rise to two directions in social philosophy.

These two directions both appear in the development of the German term *der Mensch*, the human being. *Mensch* became inflected by a denotation that looked beyond differences of class, religion, and culture to a moral, rational, civilized core of fraternal humanity. The emphasis on this expansive and inclusive notion of the human paralleled an interrelated emphasis on the free development of the individual personality and the individual pursuit of happiness. The promise of freedom, once accorded to all, could result in the full unfolding of an individual. The promise of this unfolding confronted social systems that emphasized the significance of the whole over the one. The individual was distinct and at odds with everything that sought to emphasize the significance of a superindividual absolute. Thus the same revolutionary spirit spawned the mutually antagonistic conceptions of the universal human and the contingent individual, a queer conflict in social philosophy.

Kant's philosophy strove to synthesize various seemingly antinomic philosophical and social movements and to resolve the tension between the universal human and the contingent individual. The resolution of this tension provided the source of a new understanding of subjectivity.[7] Certainly Kant understood himself as accomplishing the synthesis of rationalism and empiricism. These movements, representing seemingly irreconcilable conceptions of subjectivity, reflected the broader social political developments. Rationalism distrusted the senses and emphasized the role of reason in the perception of eternal truths. Reason thus had the quality of a universal human phenomenon. Empiricism recognized sense perception—that is, material experience and experimentation—as the source of knowledge. It thereby emphasized the individual's relationship to the world.

Drawing on both movements, Kant put forth a new conception of ego that remained the dominant model until Freud's reformulation over a century later. Drawing on the rationalists, Kant recognized the presence of an a priori framework distinct from sense perceptions—hence the significance of the a priori basis to morality in the *Critique of Practical Reason* (1787) discussed previously. This a priori framework, a *transcendental ego*, gave shape to the empirical world by providing certain categories of perception. In the *Critique of Pure Reason* (1781) he wrote:

> We have therefore wanted to say that all our intuition is nothing but the representation of appearance; that the things that we intuit are not in themselves what we intuit them to be, nor are their relations so constituted in themselves as they appear to us; and that if we remove our own subject or even only the subjective constitution of the senses in general, then all constitution, all relations of objects in space and time, indeed space and time themselves would disappear, and as appearances they cannot exist in themselves, but only in us. What may be the case with objects in themselves and abstracted from all this receptivity of our sensibility remains entirely unknown to us. (185)

And yet paradoxically, like Freud's unconscious, the direct experience of transcendent ego and of objects in themselves remained inaccessible to the subject formed by the a priori categories. Direct experience of self became foreclosed to the individual. Drawing from empiricists, however, Kant also acknowledged the significance of material sense perceptions. Kant thereby added a further twist to this conception of the subject that distinguishes his work from earlier forms of metaphysics.

> We are acquainted with nothing except our way of perceiving them, which is peculiar to us, and which therefore does not necessarily pertain to every being, though to be sure it pertains to every human being. We are concerned solely with this. Space and time are its pure forms, sensation in general its matter. We can cognize only the former *a priori*, i.e., prior to all actual perception, and they are therefore called pure intuition; the later, however, is that in our cognition that is responsible for it being called *a posteriori* cognition, i.e., empirical intuition. The former adheres to our sensibility absolutely necessarily, whatever sort of sensations we may have; the latter can be very different. (185)

The a priori activity of pure reason brings structure to the material sense impressions through the forms of space and time. Even though we can recognize a priori principles of reason shaping empirical experience, these principles are still tied to the phenomenal world. To leave the level of abstract pure thought and lead to knowledge, pure reason must have the possibility of being realized through empirical objects.

It is an ingenious answer that Kant offers to a world questioning the role of divine revelation and legitimacy. Kant affirms the existence of the metaphysical but focuses his metaphysics on the construction of the physical subject, the individual human psyche. In joining the realization of the subjective world with the objective world, Kant made way for the absolute individuality of the subject. The individual is the product of specific sense perceptions. Each empirical subject, however, stands in relation to others as a result of the structure of the ego. This structure of the ego is universal. Georg Simmel described the reconciliation of the universal and the contingent in Kant by pointing out that the Kantian ego is not an individuality; rather, it has individuality (*Kant,* 277). Having individuality means that universal ego, subjectivity, *Geist,* or psyche becomes apparent in phenomenal, contingent individuals. *Being* is set off as universal. It might seem like a slight distinction, but it is significant that subjects are not ontologically individual—not, that is, monads; rather, it is universal being that is individuated.

This distinction—between truly being an individual and having individuality—shows that the Kantian subject postulated in the critical works relies on a *homogeneity of individuality* that will conflict with the *heterogeneity of individuals* examined in his social-philosophical and anthropological works. The confrontation with heterogeneity figured directly in Kant's own oeuvre and marks a central conflict of modern individualism. This conflict is where the queer conflict in early modern social philosophy becomes visible in Kant. Kant's social philosophy shows that a fundamental universal quality of the human does not guarantee a fundamental equality between humans. A glimpse of this conflict has already manifested itself in the conflict between the corrupt sovereign and the prototypical queer, the voluptuary. Their universal humanity certainly does not undo the coercive potential of the power difference between them. But that story was only a brief thought experiment. Thus, I will now examine those more explicit impediments to equality found in Kant's work, which will reveal fundamental limits to the universality of the Kantian subject.

Sexuality and Gender in Kant's System

Discussions of Kantian philosophy have generally ignored the connection between gender and sexuality, one of the principal objects of queer theoretical examination. Gender and sexuality, however, present a fundamental and immediate stumbling block to a Kantian realization of equality and freedom. Such "stumbling" forms this section's central concern. Ultimately, however, the goal of my reading is not to carve out a "space" for sexual others (e.g., to show that transgendered or gay people can or should acquire status as Kantian rational citizen-subjects). Achieving the status of rational citizen-subject would certainly be a great achievement within the present order, but my goal is to examine the price one must pay to achieve such a status. To this end, I attend to both sexuality and gender in Kant's work.

Isolated discussions of sexuality in Kant seldom do more than mention his "sex negativity."[8] Kant's sex negativity should not be overlooked for its general significance. We need only think of such lines as the following in the context of two centuries of gay suicides to find sufficient grounds to be repulsed. "That a man who defiantly casts off life as a burden is at least not making a feeble surrender to animal impulse in throwing himself away; murdering oneself requires courage, and in this disposition there is still always room for respect for the humanity in one's own person. But unnatural lust, makes man not only an object of enjoyment but, still further, a thing that is contrary to nature, that is, a *loathsome* object, and so deprives him of all respect for himself" (*Metaphysics*, 425). Stripping the quotation of its moral tones reveals the problem to be not the lust per se but rather the fact that one loses respect for oneself. The subject is brought to reject as unnatural any acts that lead away from subjectivity. To remove the morality from Kantian philosophy, however, and arrive at such an understanding of subjectivity will ultimately require a philosopher with a hammer, who will not appear until the discussion of chapter 5.[9] For Kant it would be better to commit suicide than to make oneself an unrespectable thing "contrary to nature." In reading this remark, I can only think of those signs and graffiti from the contemporary period that read, "better dead than queer." Only when the highest goal of morality is set as a flight from the "loathsome" state of queerness can suicide be considered honorable. We should remain conscious of the trauma and violence of such a position in further readings of Kant, setting it against all the teen suicides, all the victims of queer bashings, and all those lives lived in isolation and despondency out of a dread of becoming "loathsome."

Kant is not isolated in this position. Within his own age he can certainly be easily positioned within a tradition of sex reformers including Tissot, Rousseau, Campe, Pestalozzi, and Salzman. These reformers sought to reconfigure the role of marriage in defining the autonomous subject.[10] To articulate this reconfiguration they relied on a line of reasoning that instituted a heterocoital imperative, often with a further emphasis on reproduction, proving thereby restrictive to most forms of sexuality. These precursors to Kant can be remembered especially for their significant role in unleashing the antimasturbation campaign of the eighteenth century and providing the foundation for all subsequent campaigns into the twentieth century.[11]

If we were to approach Kant through gender alone, we might note an interesting point verging on contradiction in his work.[12] In terms of gender difference, Kant did not relegate women to a subordinate position based on notions of their rational inferiority. Quite the contrary, in his article "What Is Enlightenment?" (1784) Kant included the entire "fairer sex" in his general list of those needing to improve their rational capabilities through enlightenment. In doing so he indicated that he viewed women as a subpopulation in a general world that, although not essentially or inherently irrational, was definitely in need of rationality.

With such an assertion Kant positioned himself with respect to the discussions of his predecessors and the debates of his contemporaries on the nature of women and their rational potential. Among the most influential precursors to Kant's social philosophy, Samuel Pufendorf (1632–94), Christian Thomasius (1655–1728), and Christian Wolff (1679–1754) all had assigned women to a position subordinated to men, but they had relied only ambiguously on a separate feminine nature. They were ultimately more interested in tradition and self-interest as determining factors on the (male) subject. The paradigm of women's inherent irrationality, which would dominate the nineteenth century, had not yet emerged fully, although it began to take shape within Kant's lifetime. Moreover, the debates over the status of women as rational beings, with all its impact on their psychic lives, did not take place in an abstract setting. The notion had material determinations. Women's rationality, "for or against," served as a central issue in proposed reforms of marriage, family, and education, with all the economic and political consequences such reforms might effect. Hippel attempted to contribute to Prussian legal reform by arguing at length both for marriage reform and for women's *ability* to be educated.[13] By including women as "rationalizable" beings, Kant seems to have offered them a role in universal subjectivity and political participation. By 1797, however, when *The Metaphysics of Morals* was published, the "fairer sex" had assumed a different position. Women were positioned outside the autonomy afforded to the universal subject precisely because that subject was grounded in its rationality. This book, an extension and application of the principles established in the

Groundwork of a Metaphysics of Morals (1785), placed gendered limits on the universal.

The following section explores how one central ordering principle knots together the threads of gender, sexuality, economics, politics, individuality, and morality into the web of modernity. That ordering principle is *the family*. For Kant the question of marriage, the rights of married couples, and suffrage give structure to the state.[14] An exploration of the family will help make clear the unique intertwining of sexuality and gender in Kantian social philosophy. It also makes clear what stands outside the family, on its margins, the contours of what I described earlier as the prototypical queer.

Kant's Family

Kant wrote about kinship in terms that mark the emergence of the modern bourgeois nuclear family. Kant only sparingly employed the term *family*, which entered into theoretical usage first in the latter part of the eighteenth century, when Kant was writing. He rather employed the now archaic term *Haus* ("household"), designating a family structure other than our bourgeois nuclear form, one more suited for primarily agrarian production. Kant's use of the term reflects a long history starting in the fifteenth century. The outset of the early modern period saw the birth of the *Hausvater* (father—or head—of the household) literary genre, which advised households how to prosper. In law the early modern state had instituted the household as the object of its direct address, an extension of its control. Isabel Hull noted that the terms *Haus, Hausvater,* and so on were actually terms reserved for official usage and not everyday designations. The more contemporary *Familie* did not serve as an official term and entered into common usage first in the eighteenth century.[15] In Kant's discussion of *Haus, Hausvater,* and *Hausmutter,* as well as of servants (*Gesinde*), he added this "modern" twist, designating these as aspects of the *Familie,* a move indicating that Kant understood this family household as a *center of production* with a nuclear family kinship structure at its core.

This family came about through the marriage process. He defined this process as a form of acquisition, thus clearly more of an economic than an affective transaction. Based in contractual law, Kant's grounding of the family was nonetheless distinct from a simple contract. He conceived of the marriage process as belonging to the realm of personal rights guaranteed by law, but personal rights that were experienced and evinced through acquisition. In this regard Kant wrote, "a *man* acquires a *wife;* a *couple* acquires *children;* and a *family* acquires *servants.* Whatever is acquired in this way is also inalienable and the rights of possessors of these objects is the *most personal* of all rights" (*Metaphysics,* 277). He positioned women as subordinated and passive objects in this system of acquisition, therefore shut out from the experience of "the *most personal* of all rights." Marriage, the man's acquisition of a wife, was only the initial step. This system reached all the way through into the establishment of the household—an institution from which the majority of men would have been foreclosed in various ways, so that women were not alone in their excluded position; whole categories and classes of individuals become subject to the power of the *Hausvater.* The woman as wife becomes subsumed into ever-greater conceptual categories of acquisition in a process initiated by the man/husband. As a form of acquisition, marriage became the principal institution of private property. Kant set family rights synonymous with property rights and thus equated entitlement to property with the autonomy deriving from such rights. In this definition Kant, like his contemporaries, promoted the family as an autonomous sphere.

Kant's family concept seems responsive to the changing kinship patterns that gave rise to the nuclear family. Kant's descriptions evince the intensification of the marriage relationship that Heidi Rosenbaum described as characteristic of the new bourgeois family form. Rosenbaum isolated three central aspects that identify the new family form: an intensification and increase of intimacy in the marriage relation, where "love" becomes grounds for marriage; the central significance of children and their education, with childhood emerging as a specific age span; and seclusion of the family as private sphere from all other lifeworlds, especially those of profession and earning (251). As form follows function, the physical structures of homes changed to match the demands of bourgeois heteronormativity. Most significant of the changes was the appearance of the private bedroom in the late eighteenth century. Previously communal beds or beds in communal places had been the norm. If beds had been somehow enclosed, they nevertheless allowed the head of the house to check on the nighttime activities of children and servants. The material changes in eighteenth- and nineteenth-century living structures show that under bourgeois influence, marital sexuality became privatized as an example of privilege, while other forms of sexuality continued as public acts open to public scrutiny.[16] Such sexual acts can be considered nascent queer sexualities precisely because they are subjected to the voyeuristic gaze, the controlling scrutiny of a heteronormative apparatus.

The increasing historical significance of intimacy and affective relationships is born out clearly in Kant's work, yet contrary to the plethora of intimate relationships that populated the lives and letters of the sentimentalists, the "Storm and Stressers," or the romantics, Kant set aside these affective relationships as proper to heterosexuality. In his *Anthropology* (1798), under the dictum "the woman should reign and the man should rule, because inclination reigns and reason rules," Kant made room for emotional interaction (309, 303.17). In its opposition of inclination and reason, this distinction introduces *types* of rationality based on gender. Kant understood the union of the partners as being based on more than issues of production and reproduction. He elevated nonreproductive sexual relations to central reasons for marriage: "For the natural use that one sex makes of the other's sexual organs is *enjoyment*, for which one gives itself up to the other" (*Metaphysics*, 278). Later, when I discuss the role of desire in Kant, it will be important to recall the role of pleasure and enjoyment he allocated to sex and the sexual organs. It is significant at this point to note that Kant established sexuality as a giving up or a loss of control of one's own body—that is, it included a hint of irrationality.

In the context of the family Kant expanded what was proper to heterosexuality and therefore what was improper to other types of (desiring) relationships. For this discussion of heterosexual normativity, it is significant that Kant carefully refused to base marriage on reproduction, "for otherwise marriage would be dissolved when procreation ceases" (*Metaphysics*, 277). This move distinguished Kant from Wolff (and to a lesser extent from Thomasius), who had set procreation as the goal and outcome of marriage. It is perhaps reductive to suggest that Kant viewed marriage as *contractual sexuality* that went beyond simple procreation, but such a formulation certainly brings out a significant aspect of his understanding of marriage. From his *Lectures on Ethics* (1775–80) to *The Metaphysics of Morals*, the acquisition of marriage appeared throughout as contractual sexual acquisition. "*Acquisition* of a wife or of a husband therefore takes place neither *facto* (by intercourse) without a contract preceding it nor *pacto* (by a mere marriage contract without intercourse following it) but only *lege*, that is, as the rightful consequence of the obligation not to engage in sexual union except through *possession* of each other's person, which is realized only through the use of their sexual attributes by each other" (*Metaphysics*, 280). The way Kant defined the sexuality contracted is significant, for the contract clearly entails a monopoly of use, resulting in monogamy. Kant denied the possibility of polygamy, a long-standing object of fascination for Western social philosophy, precisely on the grounds that two wives would not have exclusive use of the husband's sex organs. For similar reasons he elsewhere dismissed "the concubine." As contractual sexuality not defined by procreation, however, Kantian marriage should in theory be open to a heterogeneity of sexual desire, including, for example, same-sex couples of the type who today seek marriage rights.

Questioning why such heterogeneity of form was excluded in the "Age of Winckelmann" should not appear as idle speculation from a contemporary perspective. Indeed, Kant's contemporary Johann Heinrich Gottlob von Justi (1720–71) had found it important to emphasize reproduction as the foundation of marriage precisely to foreclose such a possibility.[17] Likewise, Kant sought in marriage the institutionalization of a particular form of sexuality. In a paragraph preceding the definition of marriage, Kant defined the limits of the sexually permissible. His preemptive strike against same-sex desire had to resort to notions of nature and reproduction, yet it was configured differently than Justi's.

> *Sexual union (commercium sexuale)* is the reciprocal use that one human being makes of the sexual organs and capacities of another (*usus membrorum et facultatum sexualium alterius*). This is either a *natural* use (by which procreation of being of the same kind is possible) or an *unnatural* use, and unnatural use takes place either with a person of the same sex or with an animal of a nonhuman species. Since such transgressions of principle, called unnatural (*crimina carnis contra naturam*) or also unmentionable vices, do wrong to humanity in our own person, there are no limitations or exceptions whatsoever that can save them from being repudiated completely. (*Metaphysics*, 277)

In this definition Kant acknowledged the possibility of various forms of sexual desire. The designation *unnatural* and the ensuing repudiation provide no assurance of the lack of such desire; in fact, they testify to its presence. Moreover, such desire does not designate a class of people with a distinct ontology. Later I will focus more closely on the quality of desire in this work. As far as marriage was concerned, it provided for Kant the social mechanism that enforces heterosexuality, foreclosing other forms of desire. Marriage and heterosexuality are set up as an accomplishment bound into contractual and rational relations. This hints at the significance of heteronormativity, because such argumentation takes heterosexuality not as a given outcome of desire but rather as an outcome that must be enforced.

Indeed, as with the voluptuary of the categorical imperative, Kant seems to have recognized that individual desire is polymorphously perverse and that desire must be directed toward a heterosexual form, because heterosexuality is the form of rationality since rationality requires as precondition the kind of self-respect that "unnatural acts" destroy. All manner of desire therefore had to be rechanneled into heterosexuality. An imperative is imposed on all individuals to regulate their sexual relations, or else they risk the designations *immoral* and *irrational*. This regulation affects not only those whose desires are not heterosexual but also those whose desires might indeed be described as heterosexual, limiting the form of sexual expression to a particular configuration of cross-sex coital penetration and consummation. Exposed to this heterocoital imperative, all other forms of desire, all other configurations of pleasure, become a failure of self-regulation, immoral, irrational drives exposing individuals to the possibility of external regulation.

The heteronormativity and heterocoital imperative of the relations among marriage, gender, and sexuality are not isolated phenomena in the Kantian system. Rather, they are connected with the greater philosophical system, drawn as conclusions from the critical works. Kant himself asserted a connection between marriage and pure reason. "Even if it is supposed that their end is the pleasure of using each other's sexual attributes, the marriage contract is not up to their discretion but is a contract that is necessary by the principle of humanity, that is, if a man and a woman want to enjoy each other's sexual attributes, they *must* necessarily marry, and this is necessary in accordance with pure reason's principles of Right" (*Metaphysics*, 278). Furthermore, note how Kant continued to develop heterosexuality as an accomplishment. He moved from the discussion of reproductive sexuality into marriage by setting up an opposition between "nature" and "principle." "Natural sexual union takes place either in accordance with mere animal *nature* (*vaga libido, venus volgivaga fornicatio*) or in accordance with *principle*. Sexual union in accordance with principle is *marriage* (*matrimonium*), that is, the union of two persons of different sexes for lifelong possession of each other's sexual attributes" (277). Given that nature appeared in this discussion as unreliable, that individuals were not understood to be naturally heterosexual or at least certainly not naturally engaged in sexual expression solely for the sake of reproduction, and that Kant based his definition of marriage on the enjoyment of nonreproductive sex, distinguishing "principle" becomes all the more necessary to reinforce the accomplishment of heterosexuality.

It is perhaps interesting to note that Kant considered object choice less fully than one might have anticipated. Kant's imagination in the realm of the unnatural was limited to same-sex and human-nonhuman sex acts, leaving undiscussed a whole range of "unmentionable" acts that could involve inanimate objects and acts between opposite-sex partners that preclude reproduction. Nevertheless, even if he did not directly mention other sexual acts that can occur in a heterosexual desiring relationship, the definition of natural sex leaves open only one form of sexual behavior. While he based marriage on nonreproductive sexuality and acknowledged sex as enjoyment or pleasure, "natural" sex must include the *possibility* of reproduction. Ultimately Kant's definition arrived at the same point as Justi, institutionalizing a particular form of gender relationships but further institutionalizing a particular subset of sexual behavior within those relationships. Thus in the last instance Kant was more concerned with sexual aim or outcome, that is, what is accomplished through sexuality. The liberal reformers ended up hanging an imperative of coital heterosexuality over the Age of Winckelmann, with all its erotic possibilities, an imperative that began to draw the age to a close.

It might be beneficial to recall the contemporaneous critique that the Marquis de Sade leveled simultaneously against the Enlightenment and this form of heteronormativity as heterocoital imperative, a fundamental queer delimitation of desire. De Sade's works created what Kant would have viewed as a terrifying phantasmagoria. Presenting images of a social order based on a heterogeneity of desire, de Sade's works attacked the homogeneity of the Enlightenment socius promoted by Kantian universalism. His characters engage in a plethora of sexual acts, recognizing no limitations of sex or gender. And his characters do not constrain themselves in partner choice, indicating a sexuality without (homosexual, bisexual, etc.) identity, a freedom of object choice and outcome. At the same time de Sade's characters do present an ontological individuality, which becomes the central problem of his novels. The monadism of such ontology is broken through individual subject-object relations. Moreover, as is well known, the Marquis de Sade was not concerned with an equality or liberty of individuals, as Kant was. The hierarchical expression of power in de Sade's works results from his conception of subject-object relations. No one is equal to another, and only a few are fully free to express their desires. This is not to say that Kant's conception of subjectivity or sociability is without an expression of power or its own inequities, but de Sade—this fundamentally queer antipode to Kant—made these the basis of his social philosophy.[18] Perhaps we can now undertake a queer delimitation of desire that finds its own solution to the conflict of freedom and equality.

Heteronomy and Heteronormativity

The preceding discussion focused primarily on sexuality and the family. This section focuses more closely on gender, particularly the position of women in the family. In Kant's work marriage institutionalizes bourgeois gender inequality.[19] It also establishes a state of heteronomy, a state of social being that prevents the exercise of rationality, even if the faculty is there. Women clearly experience this state, and it resonates further throughout Kantian social philosophy; for instance, Kant's libertine exists in a heteronomous position. I suggest that the individual in a heteronomous state is a queer subject.

Undermining his assertion of the rationality of the "fairer sex," Kant more fully developed his assertion of a natural gender character, already indicated in his alignment of women with inclination or desire (*Neigung*) and men with reason (*Verstand*). He established a loose set of autonomous feminine characteristics involving passivity and weakness.[20] Such ontological difference conflicts with universal subjectivity. Kant seems to have offered women "compensation" in the form of marriage. "Civilized" women have the "privilege" of maintaining the species and civilizing ill-mannered men (*Anthropology*, 306). This offer evokes that of Wolff, who held up subordination in marriage as part of women's self-interest. In a seemingly egalitarian statement, moreover, Kant defined possession in marriage as being equal between the spouses (*Metaphysics*, 278): the household belongs as much to the wife as to the husband. Yet Kant did not recognize this equality of possession as an equality of disposition. The passive position into which he relegated women carried through into questions of authority over property. Kant justified this affront to the notion of equality, which he had established through a simple anthropological assertion. The dominance of the husband is based "only on the natural superiority of the husband to the wife in his capacity to promote the common interest of the household, and the right to direct that is based on this can be derived from the very duty of unity and equality with respect to the *end*" (279).

The lack of disposition would have far-reaching effects in Kant's conception of the state. Because Kant posited an ontological inequality of gender that foreclosed the possibility of women's disposition over property, the rationale for male dominance reveals itself to be based in tautological reasoning. Disposition of the household falls to the man because he is in a position to dispose over the household. Wherever and whenever the inconsistencies and contingencies that adhere to a power differential are accepted as logic, the tautological marks the sites of ideology at work. The ability of such circular reasoning to pass as logically adequate marks the point where power masks its expression in the taken for granted of everyday life, or in this case, where the economic familial structure of the bourgeoisie is ideologically ascendant (and thus expanding its normative appearance; Kant is caught here less as a victim of bourgeois "narrow-mindedness" and more as a subject of ideological unconscious).

Marriage served to establish a further role for women: motherhood. Kant did not discuss motherhood outside marriage, because, as has been discussed, he held that legal recognition and obligation exist only within marriage. Thus for a foil to the wife and mother, Kant was forced to turn his attention to "the concubine" (*Metaphysics*, 279), whom he compared to the wife as "a body for the use of an other" (95). In this comparison Kant established the wife's body as a presence that limits the head of the household. The wife's body is not solely for the use of the husband. This body forces the male to direct the flow of property back into the family. Kant recognized a threat of dissolution resulting from the male's privilege of disposition over the household. With no check imposed on him, the male could disburse household property according to his own desires. Presumably Kant viewed concubines as the ultimate example of that for which an unbridled male would spend household wealth. Although Kant could not assure the family that there would be no concubines, he also did not advocate a double standard. Kant placed the concubine, as an object of enjoyment, outside the "right of lasting contract." Unlike the wife, the concubine can make no claims on the male and shares no equality with him. Unlike that of the concubine, the wife's body is not solely for enjoyment, a use-body; it is a body of responsibilities. The presence of this body can assure the family that there will be no legitimate claims on the household from outside of the family. The wife holds the family intact, establishing all acts and practices outside the household as illegitimate and dissolute, however "practical" they may be.

Within the Kantian framework, moreover, the wife performs the more fundamental function of defining that family; her body is also the body of the mother. The wife's body, legally ordained as a mother's body through the act of marriage, gives birth to the family. A parental duty of care and sustenance exists only toward her offspring (*Metaphysics*, 283). The concubine, as an object of "momentary pleasure," cannot generate the family (279). In fact, Kant was little concerned with questions of generation and inheritance. He was more concerned with establishing limits on sexual expression, and it was such limits that defined the accomplishment of heteronormativity. The genetic family plays a role in his discussion of morality and rights only as a centerpiece to the greater household. The body of the wife limits the sexual expression of the husband, while marriage as a continued state of dependence limits hers.

The impact of this passive position extends beyond the household, affecting the position of women in the state. Distinguishing active citizens, who enjoy representational rights, from passive citizens, who are governed by the state, makes wives (and the rest of the household) subject to the power of both husband *and* state (*Metaphysics*, 314–15). Representational rights, Kant argued, can be granted only to truly autonomous citizens, whose decisions can represent their own wills. Kant's meticulous position contains what some might argue is a powerful critique of our contemporary democracies, where representation tacitly assumes but does not actively guarantee autonomous will. But Kant did not strive for a radical liberation of autonomy for all individuals. He accepted that certain classes of people are automatically foreclosed from autonomy. Women as wives, the best example perhaps, existed under heteronomous circumstances. Dependent on their husbands, their will was not their own, so that they had no access to the legislative process. The designation of passive citizen was not restricted to women as wives, however; it came to designate the entire category of women. Women's existence was designated a universal state of *dependence.* The possibility of this assertion rested on a rejection of woman as an autonomous social category. Actually, in the Kantian framework women do not exist simply as women—that is, outside the web of social relations. They exist only as wives and daughters, in relations of dependency on husbands and fathers. Although Kant invoked the model of the agricultural household, his scheme of kinship and economic relations within it conformed only to bourgeois experience.

Jean Bethke Elshtain argued that Kant made no room for women's bodily experiences (26–28). It would be more accurate to say, however, that despite his early acknowledgment of women's rationality, Kant defined women solely by their bodies. Options for liberation were afforded to particular subjects and not to others solely on the basis of bodily difference. The female body signified a permanent state of dependence. Kant restricted women to their bodies, understanding those bodies as the objects of first the family (i.e., their fathers and husbands) and second the state. Women cannot enter into the position of active citizenship because the female body is a priori restricted to heteronomous positions.

As central to the notion of private property, the household came to define a whole series of dependencies: wives, children, and all the people who work for the household in whatever capacity. Kant characterized this class as follows: "all women and, in general, anyone whose preservation in existence (his being fed and protected) depends not on his management of his own business but on arrangements made by another (except the state). All these people lack civil personality and their existence is, as it were, only inherence" (*Metaphysics*, §46).

Because the father-husband controls the household, those individuals who depend on the household for their livelihood are therefore in a heteronomous state. As the wife is marked by gender, these others are marked by class standing. Both are equivalent in their dependency, which makes them objects of the will of the father-husband. Drawing an important distinction, however, Kant granted, say, the woodchopper the right to change professions and become an independent carpenter, free of the dependency. He also recognized that the male child would grow up and become independent. These acts of liberation move such individuals into the category of active citizen. This option, however, remains closed to women.

Nevertheless, even though women's exclusion from the state is based on their bodies, this does not mean that the male body acts as a free-floating signifier with varied and unlimited definitions. Gender and sexuality form a complex system of restrictions and directions limiting the heterogeneity of all individuals. I have so far concentrated on the effects of such restrictions on women and feminine desire, but note that the restriction and containment of *masculine desire* was to a certain extent the more significant problem for the social philosophers of this period. Women were legally circumscribed, shut out of the new spheres of activity opened up by civil society and the bourgeois public arena. Men, who were to be the agent of the new spheres, were the real problem. All the advocates of a bourgeois private sphere, or of a civil society set off from the state, or of any such sphere of separate bourgeois activity (e.g., Wolff, Justi, Sonnenfels, and Kant), demonstrated a certain fear that men would avoid marriage, seek their enjoyment elsewhere, and let their passions run free. Social philosophy positioned women to contain men's passions, but somehow men had to be brought to marry.

Interestingly, there appeared alongside the promotions of marriage a recognition that marriage is an undesirable institution. A rather poignant example for the problems of marriage came from the pen of Johann Joachim Becher, a contemporary of Pufendorf. "And one lives together like cats and dogs, but for reasons of external honor one must stay together and be forced into a single yoke; in the marital estate to see the object of one's unhappiness, hatred, and death constantly before one's eyes, and to have it at table and in bed, what a martyrdom and hellish pain that is!" (qtd. in Hull, 183). It is of further interest to note that these anxieties were not limited to Germany. Such an image could easily have been authored in French, English, Spanish, or Dutch. By midcentury anxieties about the undesirability of marriage gave rise to general discussions of marital happiness, precursors to the contemporary advice books and sex manuals. Such advice proved necessary given that this "sex-gender system," which Kant employed, limited sexual expression to marriage, making marriage the site of both sexual function and dysfunction. Kant, himself a lifelong bachelor, disparaged any overestimation of harmony (*Harmonie* but also *Seeleneintracht*, or "accord between souls"), especially those made in connection to marriage. Without such harmony, the enjoyment that Kant promised could be had in the marital bed becomes one of almost mechanical pulsation and release. Many saw that this arrangement offers little to be desired.

If this containment of desire is so undesirable, why was it promoted, upheld, propped up, and continually reasserted? Recall that this was a period in which various jurists were decriminalizing consensual sexual acts. There were forces actually seeking a state based on a radically different delimitation of desire. Why was heteronormativity such a successful mechanism for the reformation of both socius and psyche during this period? To answer such a question, we must examine how this sex-gender system established the definition of both autonomy and individuality. In Kant's paradigmatic conception of the state it is the autonomous (male) individual, established through a containment of desires (by women, marriage, the family, etc.), who is granted the equality and freedom of the citizen. The individual's sociability is based on the proper containment of desires.

Desires, Selfish Interests, Rationality, and Sociability

To suggest that Kant was sex negative provides at best an only superficial explanation for why he found it necessary to limit desire to a particular heterosexual form. One of Kant's most significant contributions was to end the philosophical discussion of self-interest (e.g., self-love and narcissism) as a mode of operation for sociability. With Kant irrationality, desire, and contingent want were excised from rational social organization, whereas hedonists, Epicureans, Stoics, and so on had discussed the relationship of desire (particularly willed desire) to happiness and social organization. More contemporary with Kant, the cameralists and Adam Smith in particular had offered notions of passions and self-interests as a basis of organizing society. Not only was the *desiring individual,* with his or her sexual drives, accepted as model of subjectivity, but those drives and desires were understood positively. Positivity and status accorded sex and enjoyment were part of a general shift in the techniques of power then taking place. (I return to this point in the next chapter in a discussion of Foucault's concept of bio-power.) Opposing those discussions of pure desire or even desire deferred by reason, Kant put forward the strategy that would come to define a basis of sociability fundamentally unchallenged until Nietzsche.

By defining sex as enjoyment Kant seems to have begun "positively," at least allocating a certain status to hedonism, as did his contemporaries. Recall that Kant supported a shift away from the law of the sovereign or the law of the gallows to the law as tactic in the new forms of "bio-power." It was no coincidence that Kant turned to the voluptuary as an illustration, because sex, as a fostering of positive energy, became the main vector by which the new forms of power were exercised on and through the subject. If Kant began with a certain positivity, it was because his contemporaries had come to understand sexual desire and sexual passions as the basis for new organizations of socius and psyche. Kant picked up on this organizing potential. Nevertheless, he immediately undermined whatever positivity he accorded hedonism, pleasure, enjoyment, or desire. Kant defined sexual pleasure as a form of objectification. "For the natural use that one sex makes of the other's sexual organs is *enjoyment,* for which one gives itself up to the other. In this act a human being makes himself into a thing, which conflicts with the Right of humanity in his own person. There is only one condition under which this is possible: that while one person is acquired by the other *as if it were a thing,* the one who is acquired acquires the other in turn; for in this way each reclaims itself and restores its personality" (*Metaphysics,* 278). Only the condition of marriage allows for this kind of mutual acquisition, so that any value to sex for its own sake is negated. Enjoyment is ultimately not undertaken for its own sake, leaving one to wonder why it is done at all—especially given that for Kant sexual enjoyment need only have the natural form. Mutual possession in the sex act does not introduce a different level or experience of individuality per se. The act itself is defined through marriage in terms of mutual possession. This definition could be understood as providing a means to fend off loss of selfhood. Such a loss was a typical point of anxiety in bourgeois experience, a disruption to the continuity of individuality. "Possession" was presented here as the only alternative to a "loss" (of autonomy), which is an inherent danger of *enjoyment.*

Therefore, the immediate given purpose of marriage is to bring the natural sex drive, the *"vaga libido,"* under the control of the law, to contain it and impart it with a moral character (*Metaphysics*, 277). Without the moral character imparted by the law, "carnal enjoyment is *cannibalistic* in principle" (359). Why would Kant understand sexual acts as objectification? The images of mouth, teeth, and consumption that follow in this passage recall Freud's discussion of castration anxiety and the *vagina dentate* and might suggest that Kant indeed suffered from a neurotic fear of sexual expression. His discussion of masturbation, moreover, might betray an obsession with male potency (424–26). But here I drift away from the text into speculations that pertain more to Kant's own psyche. Psychological explanations might be informative about the person Kant, but they do not analyze the overall role that the discussion of sex and gender played in the formation of the human subject. This discussion displays the groundwork for the conception of the psyche that came to dominate the modern period.

In his critical philosophy Kant identified certain common principles of reason in the interaction between the subjective and objective world; these principles laid the groundwork for an understanding of a universal human mind. Such a mind is open to the sense impressions of the phenomenal world yet contains a priori organizing categories that connect it to the noumenal world. This mind, with its transcendent portion unknowable to its conscious portion, found its first elaboration in the *Critique of Pure Reason*. It was then refined and elaborated in the subsequent critical *and* moral works. In *The Critique of Practical Reason* Kant first addressed the means whereby the subject expresses itself and affects the objective world: *the will* as determining force exercised on the objective world. The discussion of the will provided Kant a bridge between pure and practical reason. As Kant wrote, "For here reason can at least attain so far as to determine the will, and, in so far as it is a question of volition only, reason does always have objective reality. This is, then, the first question: Is pure reason sufficient of itself to determine the will, or is it only as empirically conditioned that it can do so?" (*Practical Reason*, 15). Kant answered that pure reason can indeed determine the will, but only if a form of causality is inserted, namely *freedom*. Kant established freedom as an a priori category of reason that compels the will to take on a certain form. As was already discussed, the a priority of freedom made the voluptuary willing to set his will against his own desires.

The moral works are often overlooked in favor of the critical, but it is in the moral philosophy that Kant extended the practical examination of the will as the force or active component of reason. "The will is nothing other than practical reason. If reason infallibly determines the will, the actions of such a being that are cognized as objectively necessary are also subjectively necessary, that is, the will is a capacity to choose *only that* which reason independently of inclination cognizes as practically necessary, that is, as good" (*Groundwork*, 412). The moral works circle back to the critical, showing how this force of willed reason transforms subject into agent.

In his *Groundwork of the Metaphysic of Morals* Kant carefully distinguished between desire, drive, or instinct (*Trieb*) and will (395). In this definition Kant promoted a bipartite notion of the ego, constructing it on the basis of desire's separation from reason. Desire as instinct alone would suffice to ensure the survival and happiness of any being.[21] A being blessed with reason need not "submit its faculty of desire [*Begehrungsvermögen*] to that weak and deceptive guidance and meddle with nature's purpose" (395). To go beyond pleasure and attain a moral existence, however, Kant understood that reason, operating through the force of will, could allow the individual to act according to objective interests.

In this relationship to desire Kant's moral philosophy breaks with all previous conceptions of morality and ethics and provides the basis for subsequent work. In previous conceptions morality provided the way to happiness, or at least the way out of pain. Religions such as Christianity and Islam offered heaven as the reward for a moral life. Buddhism's moral conception offered a solution to discontentment in this life. Kant, however, secularized morality and separated it from happiness. Moreover, and in a unique move, Kant argued against a long tradition of the liberal reformers and natural law theorists who sought to use desire, passion, and selfish interest as a means to sociability and happiness. Montesquieu, Adam Smith, Pufendorf, Justi, and Thomasius all pursued this goal in various forms. Of course, they all accepted limits to desire, but such limits were imposed gently, most often by the presence of certain institutions or (heterosexual) love objects. In this regard Justi wrote, "There are only two main sources, or two great mainsprings [*Triebfedern*] from which all the genius, invention and industriousness of a people arise. These are the desires [*Begierden*], to make life comfortable and pleasant for oneself, and the desire [*Verlangen*] for advantage. Both are natural to people, and alike innate. They need not be planted in people. One need only guide them correctly and remove the hinderances that block their path. . . . This urge [*Trieb*] [to make life comfortable] is founded in love of self" (qtd. in Hull, 162).[22] As has already been discussed, in relationship to sex Kant did not estimate the "natural state" very highly. In addition, Kant thought little of desire or happiness as a "natural state" and viewed instinct itself, a natural attribute, as insufficient to achieve happiness. As was discussed earlier, to be moral the voluptuary had to take into account not selfish interests but the needs of others. For Kant reason through will confronts and directs what he saw to be the random subjective desires and needs of pure instinct.

In *The Groundwork of the Metaphysics of Morals* (1785), written shortly before *The Critique of Practical Reason* (1788), Kant set forth the basis of the terms through which a rejection of the position supported by Justi and the others could take place.

> The dependence of the faculty of desire upon feelings is called inclination, and this accordingly always indicates a *need*. The dependence of a contingently determinable will on principles of reason, however, is called an *interest*. This, accordingly, is present only in the case of a dependent will, which is not of itself always in conformity with reason; in the case of the divine will we cannot think of any interest. But even the human will can *take an interest* in something without therefore *acting from interest*. The first signifies *practical* interest in the action, the second, *pathological* interest in the object of the action. The former indicates only dependence of the will upon principles of reason *in themselves*; the second, dependence upon principles of reason for the sake of inclination, namely where reason supplies only the practical rule as to how to remedy the need of inclination. (414)

The passage's language of pathology is important and suggestive, a precursor to the medicalizing discourse that would come to dominate the nineteenth century. The distinction Kant made between forms of interest depends on a certain relationship of reason and will that in effect collapses the two into a formulation of *willed reason.* The significance of this move becomes clearer if we recognize what role it played in the definition of moral behavior, but it is immediately apparent that to accept the notion of willed reason is to reject the free flow of desire that Justi described as the basis for sociability.

Kant was cognizant of such discussions and actively sought to respond to them, as is apparent from the move he made in the first half of *The Metaphysics of Morals,* "The Doctrine of Right." Here Kant shifted away from his original discussion of needs (*Bedürfnisse*) to a discussion of desire (*Begierde/Verlangen*), directly in line with the language of Justi and the others. His introduction begins: "The *capacity for desire* is the capacity to be by means of one's representations the cause of the objects of those representations" (*Metaphysics*, 212). If we can generalize enough to say that the analysis in *The Critique of Pure Reason* began from asking how the transcendental subject shapes the objective world, then here the analysis began from the other direction: how does the objective world affect the subject? A series of confusing distinctions followed from this shift to desire. Kant immediately stepped back to examine desire's relation to pleasure: Pleasures provoke desires, but not the converse. There are pleasures without desire. Feeling is concerned with desire. Pleasure in representation is set off from desire for an object. This bewildering barrage of terms and distinctions is part of Kant's style and becomes more significant and more elaborate as the discussion develops. Many of these distinctions draw connections to his other works, keeping his system intact.[23] What is most important here, however, is how Kant shifted the relationship of will and reason. He wrote that "the will is therefore the capacity for desire considered not so much in relation to action (as the capacity for choice is) but rather in relation to the ground determining choice to action. The will itself . . . is instead practical reason itself" (*Metaphysics*, 213). And here we can identify a new formulation that knots together all the strands of Kant's work: the *will is reasoned desire*.

In *The Metaphysics of Morals* Kant distinguished one more significant concept, that of "concupiscence." Kant separated sexual *lust* from *desire* in its various forms (habitual desire, inclination, interest) as "a stimulus to determining desire" or "a sensible modification of the mind" (*Metaphysics*, 213). As such, sexual lust exists somewhere between desire and pleasure. The differentiation may seem to be a minor if not dubious point until its position in the larger project is recognized. Isolating sexual lust in this way leaves behind a vague realm of desires that occupy a different space in the Kantian discourse. These desires are supposed to be directly determinable by reason. They drive the individual to pursue practical and contemplative pleasures, needs, and tastes. Kant did not expound more fully on the varying nature and potentiality of such desires. They remained an indeterminate field, a homogenized entity whose only real distinction is their opposition to sexual lust. Only in marriage did Kant maintain some social space for "instinctual" sexuality. Such space did not exist for any other type of desire.

By contrast, his contemporaries viewed civil society precisely as the space of such desire. For Kant, nonsexual desires, caught up in a discussion of rights and duties, became the basis for an opposition of the individual and the social. In his famous description of individuals as evincing a characteristic "unsocial sociability,"[24] Kant bore witness to this belief in a split between the social and the individual. In this psyche the individual desires both society and isolation.[25] Individual desires oppose conceptions of the social good, the social welfare, the greater good, or the common sense of a universal socius whose desires outweigh the desires of the individual. Concretely Kant established the opposition through negating the necessity of individual desires, redefining them as personal interest, acts of arbitrary will, or the simple capacity for choice. Arbitrary will (*Willkür*), unlike will (*Wille*), is not subject to reason (*Metaphysics*, 213). This means that for Kant, to act according to arbitrary will is to assert an individuality of being at odds with the universal subject.

The Kantian framework places individuals in conflict with themselves. Reason and will oppose natural instincts of survival and pleasure—provided the individuals are indeed rational. For Kant, an ego based on conflict is not an inherent aspect of the individual psyche. But it is necessary, because this state of conflict is the price the individual pays for entry into morality and sociability. In unison with applied practical reason, will as reasoned desire elevates the individual from a state as subject *to* desire (i.e., heteronomy) to a state as subject *of* desire (i.e., autonomy). (We need only recall the voluptuary to illustrate this point.)

In his exposition of the categorical imperative Kant recognized the means whereby will as a generalizing act of reason moves individuals from acts based on their particular dispositions to acts of communal interest. This is the level of sociability in which the subject moves from an individuality of being to a universal subject having individuality. "The categorical imperative . . . is: Act upon a maxim that can also hold as a universal law. You must therefore first consider your actions in terms of their subjective principles; but you can know whether this principle also holds objectively only in this way: That when your reason subjects it to the test of conceiving yourself as also giving universal law through it, it qualifies for such a giving of universal law" (*Metaphysics*, 225). In his work on Kant Rawls distinguished between the moral law that results from application of the categorical imperative, the rational process of applying the categorical imperative, and the categorical imperative itself. Rawls identified the process of application as the "Categorical Imperative *procedure*" (CI-p) and based the universalism of his revision on this activity, not on the universality of its outcome.[26] The CI-p is an activity of will and not an a priori first principle, so that the will remains free and autonomous. If it were applying principles fixed by human nature or by an order of universals, such a will would be not free but rather in a state of heteronomy. If we follow Rawls in this distinction, we can see that Kant's separation of will (i.e., reasoned desire) from arbitrary will (i.e., unreasoned desire or desire in itself) rests on an understanding of reason as the universalizing act. Reason here is the taking into account of the other, the awareness of self as social being. Neither Kant nor Rawls acknowledges that reason, as a universalizing act, also works against the contingent desires of the individual.

Dividing the Social from the Individual

Throughout this discussion I have been seeking to address how Kant represented a summation and transformation of liberalism and modernity. Subsequently, as the division between the social and the individual was integrated into the discourse of liberalism, the ramifications of this principle unfolded in numerous ways. First, where collective needs or social desires and individual desires did not operate as a single element, this simple distinction allowed the institutions of state and social legitimacy to place individuals into an antisocial category.[27] The prosecution of "selfish" pursuits of individual interest—that is, acts not in accord with hegemonic interests—becomes a justified activity of social institutions. Such accusations were frequently leveled against emancipation movements throughout the nineteenth and twentieth centuries. Homosexuals and emancipated women were variously accused, for instance, of wasting society's valuable reproductive resources. Second, the homogenized field of desire, as separate from the universalizing act of reason, became irrational in itself. The various aspects of Kant's arbitrary will (desires, instincts, particular interests, natural drives, emotions, affectations, and hungers) were placed outside rationality. They subsequently constituted the domain of Freud's id. The rational was only that which leads from heteronomy to autonomy.

Third, the hegemonic force of this system had to be masked or denied. The definition of autonomy presented here presumed an ideal realm of the social in which the process of defining objective interests is free from any particular ideological interest, what Habermas would revisit in his discussion of the "ideal speech situation." Kant did not recognize himself as promoting the interests of a specific class, sex, or gender, even though we have seen that his system is marked by class, gender, sexuality, ethnicity, and so on; these were absolute moral interests of which the bourgeoisie might be considered the bearer. These interests resulted in individual autonomy, that is, *freedom from individual interests.* Autonomy in the socius was seen as a system of interdependence based on *objective* interests. Freedom for the psyche was the choice to enter into that interdependence. Autonomy and freedom were removed from choice, contingent determination, hedonistic desire, and so on. This resulted in a psychic dilemma perhaps best described in the Schillerian paradox of "freedom in necessity," where the individual is left free to choose what is universally required of him. To choose otherwise, to pursue individual instead of objective interest is, as Kant defined it in his *Groundwork,* to exist in the heteronomous category, where one is subject to irrational desire. (We can again recall the voluptuary.)

Finally, the state rises in significance as the political sphere in itself. This increase of state power can be understood as an opposition to feudal power, given that for Kant, the state discussed was not the existing Prussian state but the liberal constitutional republic. In "The Doctrine of Right" the significance of the state as organizing principle of the socius increased. A state of law must "leave the state of nature, in which each follows its own judgment, unite itself with all others . . . , subject itself to a public lawful external coercion, and so enter into a condition in which what is to be recognized as belonging to it is determined *by law*" (*Metaphysics*, 312). In such a state the possibility first arises that the (bourgeois male) citizen-individual, applying reasoned desire, will achieve autonomy *and* sociability not by acting according to nature and desire (as Justi and others advocated) but by acting according to rational principles.

In Kant's formulation this increase of the status of the state harmonizes with the interests of the emerging bourgeoisie. Intimately intertwined, barely differentiated from the civil or bourgeois (*bürgerlich*), the state discussed in "The Doctrine of Right" represents the body that governs civil society. The Kantian definition presumes the ideal state to be free from particular ideological interest while placing control of the state into the hands of a specific group. In this scheme all aspects of the household outside of its "head" are defined as heteronomous. Such a definition constitutes the household as outside the state, a private sphere subject to its head, while reserving the state as a public sphere of activity for a homogenized group of men.

In his essay "Perpetual Peace" (1795) Kant made clear his support for a republican government in which a constitution establishes a system of checks and balances, dividing government between three powers. The constitution here is tantamount to the act of reason invoked by the categorical imperative, "an act of general will whereby the crowd becomes a people" (13). It establishes the very basis for the social in the state. Kant clearly expressed his distrust of the despotism of democracy, preferring that the executive branch be in the hands of a single monarch. In "The Doctrine of Right" he expounded on the details of such a state. The active citizens of this system—limited, as I have discussed, to propertied males—were to be bound together on the basis of the sole innate law: "Independence from being constrained by another's arbitrary will" (*Metaphysics*, 237). Beyond this point all other forms of judicial regulation would result from a positive law decided on by the legislature.

The freedom (i.e., independence from the arbitrary will of another) that Kant admitted as the sole innate law was to be the basis for the ideal state. This freedom is possible only within the state. Yet it is a freedom only in the sense of "freedom from." The entire impetus thereby established in the state is not to liberate individual will. If there is a "freedom to" that can be identified in Kant's philosophy, it is a freedom to control individual desire: "The positive concept of freedom is that of the capacity of pure reason to be of itself practical. But this is not possible except by the subjection of the maxim of every action to the condition of its qualifying as universal law" (*Metaphysics*, 214). In the earlier *Groundwork*, Kant interwove the citizen into a web of duty designed to circumscribe the expression of individual desire. Kant defined duty as "the necessity of an action out of respect for the law" (*Groundwork*, 400). He never departed from this basic premise of the relation of duty and law, but in "The Doctrine of Right" he concentrated on the law as various duties and obligations, divining the basis for particular positive laws in metaphysical origins. The entire system of the law (*Recht*) then results solely in an *apparatus* for determining which personal desires are permissible within the social sphere—the modern technique of power.

The Desiring Individual and the Pursuit of Happiness

The homogenization of heterogeneous desires and the separation of sexuality from nonsexual desires received a weak compensation within the Kantian system. I have discussed how Kant admitted sexuality, containing it within the system of marriage. It is important to recognize, however, that this form of containment, while offering individuals access to satisfaction, happiness, contentment, gratification, and fulfillment, howsoever transitory, itself reduced and homogenized the sexual needs it admitted into the social sphere. Although Kant acknowledged nonreproductive sex, with all its pleasurable promises, as the basis for marriage, only the reproductive sexual morpheme, coital heterosexuality, was legitimated as basis for sociability. He foreclosed all other morphemes from the socius, constituting them therefore as immoral and illegal, not open for recognition as rational. This constitution of the desiring individual marks the point of emergence of the modern queer, a subjective state that can be associated with particular bodies. At the same time, it is important to note that the desiring individual does not designate a category of people in Kant's work. Indeed, in all fairness, we must recall that this system as ideal stood in opposition to the state of irrationality of the "far greater portion of humanity" ("Enlightenment," 35).

Within this scheme, a vague and elusive pursuit of happiness was left to humankind as means to fulfill nonsexual desires. Not happiness itself but only its pursuit—as regulated by the moral law—was admitted as a human right. "If eudaemonism (the principle of happiness) is set up as the basic principle instead of *eleutheronomy* (the principle of the freedom of internal lawgiving), the result is the *euthanasia* (easy death) of all morals" (*Metaphysics,* 378). If the Protestant work ethic answered an anxious need for signs of election by a silent god, the pursuit of happiness, not its attainment, propelled liberal capitalism with more force. Morality, distinct from happiness, elicited a consistent instrumental reason ensuring that the merchant has "a fixed price for everyone, so that a child may buy of him as cheaply as any other" (*Groundwork,* 397).

If in the earlier discussion it seemed that men function as free-floating signifiers in this system, it should now be clear that they are limited to specific idioms within this homogeneity. Of course, the violence of this homogenization on the heterogeneity of individuals must be qualified by the observation that Kant conceived this homogenized social sphere so that social power and privilege accrue to the males who participate *willingly.* This participation introduced a new form of heteronormative organization into the bourgeois economy. In return for a limitation placed on individual identity or modes of behavior, men benefit from a system of power differentials established along gender lines. Yet it should be noted that men may not govern as *men,* by which I mean that it is possible to modify the Kantian system and bring into it women, homosexuals, African Americans, Turkish Germans, and so on, but only to the extent that the autonomous rationality of such groups can be established on the basis of their mastery of their own fortunes. This possibility indicates that the exercise of power within this system does not take place through the control of gender. Gender serves only as a placeholder of differences in rational capacities, which could theoretically be overcome when autonomy is established. The only stable center of the system consists of a containment of desire, which has the tendency to display itself at the site of gender and sexuality. Kant's lasting legacy, one with great effect on all excluded groups, may well be that public power *requires* containing desire and acting like "men." To gain access to the power that autonomy offers, all excluded groups must become "men."

Tolerance is easy under such conditions. There are of course various conceptions of tolerance, and the Enlightenment German liberalism in which Kant participated voiced many of the configurations with which we labor today. Tolerance can have a *conservative* quality to it, as in, "We tolerate you because God or some higher instance will punish you." We can further recognize a tolerance based in *ignorance,* as in the adage "live and let live," or tolerance based on notions of *essential difference,* as in Dutch models of "pillarization" or apartheid, where one group tolerates another because the latter occupies a separate sphere with which the former need have no contact. There are models of tolerance based on inclusive universality, as in the antixenophobic campaign undertaken in Germany in the early 1990s through the slogan "Everyone is a foreigner somewhere." We might also toss in a tolerance based on a sheer lack of strong convictions. All forms of tolerance are oriented toward promoting homogeneity—making everybody into "men." They all are brought up short by heterogeneous elements—the queer.

Notes

1. Of course, Foucault had precursors in the history of the history of sexuality. See, for instance, the work of McIntosh. Nor did Foucault work in isolation; see, for instance, the works of Jeffery Weeks, Jonathan Katz, Carroll Smith-Rosenberg, and David Halperin, among others.

2. Globalization of this discourse is the explicit goal of Kant's republicanism; see his essay "On Perpetual Peace."

3. Page numbers for Kant's texts are those of the standard Prussian Academy edition.

4. For a discussion of the various forms of punishments and shaming techniques (e.g., the stone of shame or the violin) and the "appropriateness" of each of them (i.e., crimes for which they would have been used), see Hull.

5. The surveillance of sodomy offered modernizing states an important and primary means of social control. As modern institutions of governance were established throughout Europe, criminal codes against sodomy were reformed to include more lenient sentences. Along with this development came a transformation of the sodomite's social significance. Sodomy was still a vice in which any lusty sinner could possibly engage, yet conceptions of homosexuality began to make a transition from act to type. In Kant's example, it is not anyone who is engaging in sodomy but a person of a particular type, ruled by his desires, a libertine. For excellent discussions of this period throughout Europe, see Gerard and Hekma. For further background see Bray; Foucault, *History;* Greenberg; Perrot; and Weeks.

6. With the loss of a cosmological grounding of the law, sin could no longer cry out to the worldly courts with any certainty. Secularization through legal reform undermined all sorts of routes for punishment and retribution that had previously been available. In Catholic territories the confessional became voluntaristic, and ecclesiastical courts were severely curtailed. In Protestant territories pious self-regulation was supported by a new system of community policing. Community structures such as town meetings and *Zuchtherren* became increasingly secular, drawn into larger structures of governance and policing. For a discussion of these transformations in Germany see Hull; Koselleck. For transformations in the United States see Middleton; Formisano and Burns.

7. For a productive discussion of the concept of the individual in Kant's philosophy, see Simmel, *Kant.*

8. See, for instance, Lautmann. For a more nuanced discussion, see Hull.

9. This resembles what Nietzsche might have identified as nihilism: on the one hand, an affirmation of the negation of the life of the body; on the other hand, a mode for the affirmation of individual subjectivity.

10. For an overview see Hoof. For a general discussion see Geyer-Kordesch and Kuhn.

11. Note that the quotation on desires "contrary to nature," which seems to be directed at same-sex desire, actually takes as its starting point the question of masturbation and "unpurposive" sex. For discussions of the antimasturbation campaigns from the eighteenth through the twentieth centuries, see Hull; Fout; Geyer-Kordesch and Kuhn. See also Marcus; although that text is a bit dated and roundly critiqued by Foucault, it remains rich in information on England.

12. Susan Mendus was one of the first feminist critics to address directly the issue of gender in Kant. The initiative to analyze Kant's patriarchalism is certainly a welcome contribution to Kant scholarship, and Mendus's work is valuable in this regard. For further discussions on Kant from a feminist perspective, see David-Menard; Hermann; Elshtain; Okin; Jauch.

13. Hippel (1741–96), mayor of Königsberg and Kant's friend, adopted a similar position in his lengthy tract, *On the Bourgeois Amelioration of Women.* Hippel is often described as the first German to advocate women's emancipation. Of course the emancipation Hippel advocated was an emancipation into bourgeois society, an emancipation that sought to further bourgeois cultural hegemony by making universal claims in regard to the *type* "woman." The work is patterned somewhat after similar tracts regarding the Jews, for example Wilhelm von Dohm's *On the Bourgeois Amelioration of the Jews.* In his discussion of women, however, Hippel gave a distinct turn to the discussion of bourgeois amelioration. The tracts that advocated Jewish emancipation discussed *how* to educate the Jewish community in bourgeois sensibilities. Hippel found it necessary to argue that is was *possible* to educate women at all. Having proved rationality and educability in women, he then pointed to the type "woman" as having inherent sensibilities that work toward civilizing society.

14. Later on I explore more of the complexities of Kant's state conception through gender and sexuality. For further discussions see Beiner and Booth; Williams.

15. For an excellent discussion of family form during this period, see Rosenbaum.

16. Further changes in floor plans show that while private space was appearing in the bourgeois house, common workspace was disappearing, replaced by gendered spaces.

17. See the discussion of Justi in Hull (155–97).

18. For a discussion of de Sade and the Enlightenment, see Horkheimer and Adorno; Lacan, "Kant with Sade"; Deleuze, *Masochism;* DiPiero, *Dangerous Truths;* Gallop.

19. Eric Clarke provided a related and valuable discussion of Kant's "practices of value" but with a greater emphasis on the regulation of the public sphere.

20. See "The Character of Gender," a chapter in his *Anthropology.*

21. It might be interesting to note that Kant's use of the term *Wesen* (being) was meant to include *all* rational beings. Kant shared the eighteenth-century belief in extraterrestrials. He made it clear that his reflections in "Inhabitants of the Stars" were not for amusement but the product of rational deduction and must be taken seriously. For a detailed exposition of this period's discussions of life on other planets, see Crowe; Dick.

22. For a brief discussion of this development in Germany, see Hull. In addition, Hirschman has written a short but excellent and insightful study on this particular development.

23. The latter distinction of pleasure in representation and desire for object, significant for his argument, was drawn from his work on aesthetics, especially the sublime.

24. See Kant's discussion in "Idea for a Universal History with Cosmopolitan Purpose" (1784), esp. p. 20.

25. This type of distinction and analysis was highly influential for the work of Georg Simmel, for whom sociability (*Vergesellschaftung*) became a key concept. Simmel's own readings of Kant, while not directly invoked in this chapter, provided me significant insight, framing my own readings of Kant. For an English-language introduction to his works, see Simmel, *On Individuality*.

26. See Rawls, *Kant's Transcendental Deduction*.

27. I invoke legitimacy here in the Weberian sense.

2 *Hegel and Governmentality*

> What tolerates nothing particular is thus revealing itself
> as particularly dominant. The general reason that comes
> to prevail is already a restricted reason. It is not just uni-
> ty within diversity, but as an attitude to reality it is im-
> posed, a unity over something—and thus, as a matter of
> pure form, it is antagonistic in itself. Unity is divi-
> sion. . . . Measured by complete reason, the prevailing
> one unveils itself as being polarized and thus irrational
> even in itself, according to its principle.
>
> —Theodor Adorno

Emancipation and the State

One longer sequence of the 1998 film *Gay Courage* (*Schwu-
ler Mut—100 Jahre Schwulenbewegung*), by Rosa von Praunheim, documents a moment of emergence into political emancipation: German gays
pouring onto the streets in 1994 to celebrate the repeal of §175 of the legal
code. The repeal of this paragraph, the antihomosexual paragraph, was
rightly celebrated, for it marked a new decriminalized existence for gay
men.[1] The paragraph itself was rarely enforced since the 1970s; nevertheless, its presence in the penal code justified other forms of discrimination. Its repeal constituted the realization of a dream shared by political
activists for over one hundred years. Indeed, it marked a transformation
in the state and its techniques of governance. The repeal thus also marked
the transformation of the conditions of gays as citizens, therefore changing the conditions for the gay rights movement and hence radically transforming the basis of gay politics.

Von Praunheim's documentary camera panned over thousands of celebrating people, many decked out in their most splendid drag or most festive attire. In its concentration on the gathered celebrants, the camera could reveal little about the function of governance, but it could interrogate the homosexual as political subject. The film moves into documentary-style interviews with some of the celebrants, who were asked for their visions of future directions. One might object that it was unfair to expect well-articulated responses from randomly selected people at that time and place. After all, few if any were social philosophers. What the film does show, however, is the way "emancipation" dulled queerness, leaving a fundamental lack of prospects for future gay politics. Asked whether the gay movement had reached all its goals and was over, more than one interviewee answered yes. Asked what the next step would be, several passers-by simply shrugged their shoulders.

There was certainly urgency to the interviewer's question. Germany at that time faced record unemployment. Unification had transformed the German state and society. The new socialist government set out to dismantle the protections of the welfare state. A civil war raged in the Balkans, and the German government's policies were implicated. In the midst of all this social upheaval, an especially violent xenophobic hatred of all that was foreign or perceived as different had emerged, resulting in horrific racist and homophobic assaults, murders, and other types of hate crimes throughout the country.

The film seems to present a critical challenge: did anyone have an articulated vision of a future direction for the gay movement? One of its principal goals having been recognized by the state, the gay rights movement could disentangle itself from larger questions of economic justice, multiculturalism, or transnational peace—questions of other lifeworlds. Gays were freed to be just as apathetic, ill informed, and content with an inherently distant state as were any other citizens.

Having emerged as an oppositional minority, an object of the negating force of the state's heteronormativity, the homosexual emancipation movement has struggled ceaselessly to change the parameters of governmentality. From the beginning of the movement, however, the state has been the primary object of address.[2] The movement has sought to end what modern philosophers of the state such as Fichte and Hegel have described as the tyranny of the majority over a minority. In 1898, when Magnus Hirschfeld, the German sexologist and a great advocate of homosexual emancipation, filed the first petition to the German parliament for the repeal of paragraph 175, he reckoned the number of homosexuals in Germany as 1 percent of the general population. Given these numbers and the government's heteronormative moral apprehension of homosexuals, Hirschfeld thought it more prudent to seek as signatories not homosexuals but Germany's scientific, cultural, and political elite.

The homosexual emancipation movement primarily sought to help gays acquire equal political rights within the existing state; that is, it sought not to overthrow the state but to accomplish within its established contours a minor reform. We must therefore understand the state's steadfast and wearisome resistance to these requests as marking a site of crisis. Given that this resistance has not truly abated, that the repeal of paragraph 175 has not ended the struggle with the state, and given that the very mention of gay marriage legislation in the United States elicits vociferous diatribes about the deterioration of the state and the decline of Western values, it appears that this crisis of modern governmentality continues. Why should so modest a request as equal citizenship for a small minority, addressed respectfully to the state, have resulted in a crisis? What knot of modernity seems to be tied in the social philosophy of the state?

The Techniques of Governmentality

On the margins of Foucault's work on sexuality floats a discussion of *governmentality*—the term Foucault used to identify a certain problematic of modern governance. It has not appeared as central to the concerns of queer theory. The few deployments have remained marginal.[3] The work in question was Foucault's last project (see *The Foucault Effect*), left unfinished by his untimely death, and therefore we find only a direction for further research, but one that has the potential to open new and productive lines of inquiry for queer theory. Indeed, his observations can prove compelling to my analysis of the modern state.

Foucault set governmentality against older forms of governance, which he associated with *sovereignty*. For Foucault, the technique of power in sovereignty, the means whereby the sovereign accomplished the goal of submission, was primarily a deployment of law and death. "The sovereign exercised his right of life only by exercising his right to kill, or by refraining from killing; he evidenced his power over life only through the death he was capable of requiring" (136). This technique of power appeared in Kant's story of the voluptuary, who was subject to the law in the form of the gallows outside his house—undeniably this technique continues to exist.[4] Clearly thinking of his works on sexuality and on madness, Foucault suggested that in the modern era the tendency of governmentality developed a whole complex of *savoirs* ("knowledges") more ubiquitous but also less violent. Governance became increasingly an art or economy not simply interested in the maintenance of order and obedience.[5] The ensemble of governance became interested in the "things" of men and women, in their lives.

Foucault provided a provisional definition for the term *governmentality:*

1. The ensemble formed by the institutions, procedures, analyses and reflections, the calculations and tactics that allow the exercise of this very specific albeit complex form of power, which has as its target population, as its principal form of knowledge political economy, and as its essential technical means apparatuses of security.
2. The tendency which, over a long period and throughout the West, has steadily led towards the pre-eminence over all other forms (sovereignty, discipline, etc.) of this type of power which may be termed government, resulting, on the one hand, in the formation of a whole series of specific governmental apparatuses, and on the other, in the development of a whole complex of *savoirs.*
3. The process, or rather the result of the process, through which the state of justice of the Middle Ages, transformed into the administrative state during the fifteenth and sixteenth centuries, gradually becomes "governmentalized." (*Foucault Effect,* 102–3)

Foucault's discussion of governmentality, which focuses on the early modern period, includes descriptions of four regulatory domains of governmentality: the self, the family, the economy, and the state.[6] Foucault might have wanted to give equal weight to these domains, but by the nineteenth century a distinct line of force lent them a certain order. The state gradually gained significance—and not just any state but a particular form, the nation-state. In the tendency and process of governmentality described here, of course, governmentality does not promote just any life; it cultivates certain "useful" forms.[7] It is through this tendency that the nation-state comes to dominate the other domains.

For an illustration, consider population policy, which shifted significantly in the transition to modernity. Despite a population decline during the Thirty Years War, the various states had not sought to increase their populations. Rather than become involved in the reproductive lives of their subjects, states at most allowed migrations into their territory. By the end of the seventeenth century, however, shifts in governance meant that "population equaled state power" (Hull, 145). New European population policies "cultivated" citizens like other natural resources. The Prussian Legal Code of 1794 turned the family into a public function, viewing it as a resource for the ambitions of the Prussian state.[8] In Foucauldian terms, life, once simply an opposition to death, now became a route of bio-power, but this was a form of cultivation linked to territory by the state.

Of course, subjects who participate in reproduction need not experience the state's cultivation of life as a matter of force. They can act as relays of power, aligning themselves all the way through to their genealogy and generation, taking pride in their pedigree and their offspring. Those who do not reproduce, however, find themselves in a different and even conflictual relationship to the state. The link between territory and population, between life to be cultivated and life to be excluded, between genealogy and state, is the essence of national discourse. It is also why the nation-state relies on the heterocoital imperative and why it becomes a queering social apparatus.

Of course, the state's tendency to dominance took place via routes beyond just population control. For example, by the eighteenth century Foucault's four regulatory domains were discursively separated into four lifeworlds distinguished by a notion of public versus private interests.

I previously noted this distinction in Kant's analyses. Control of the self and regulation of the family became relegated to a private sphere, while government of economics and the state constituted a public sphere. These lifeworlds are not autonomous. In this mode of governance, a commonality of all citizen-individuals was accomplished through coercion—that is, coercion *within* particular lifeworlds accomplished the commonality *across* them.

Furthermore, even if these four representational areas constituted equal lifeworlds of governmentality at the outset of modernity, that equality obviously dissipated. The relegation of the state and economy to the public sphere defines the public sphere by a level of abstraction above and outside concrete individual concerns. The various forms of social philosophy in the modern period all defined the state and economy as supraindividual structures. For instance, the national economists who emerged in the nineteenth century understood the state as an enclosed social organism.[9] Liberal political theory concerned itself with large blocs (e.g., majorities and minorities) or the "greatest happiness for the greatest

Figure 3. Representational Lifeworlds

Public	Private
State	Family
Economy	Self

number." Unlike the legitimacy of the sovereign, which was grounded in God, the legitimacy of the state became in effect tautological, being grounded in self-referential terms such as "the people" or "the rule of law"; that is, the legitimacy of the state derives from its legitimate exercise of power. In the twentieth century Max Weber recognized this aspect of the modern state when he famously defined it as the human community that within a certain territory "successfully upholds the claim to the *monopoly* of the *legitimate* use of physical force in the enforcement of its order" (*Economy and Society*, 1:54).

The goal of governmentality was not to accommodate individual differences but to bring the individual into communal agreement, whether as national awareness, solidarity, or patriotic duty. The common good became a matter of uniform expectations, standard measures, proper educative accumulation, and a "scientific" disposition over territory, wealth, resources, foodstuffs, population, and so on that brought them to flourish. The administration and regulation of such concerns gave appearance and meaning to a new *total* system.

Hegel and the Spirit of Governance

I want to make the preceding discussion of governmentality concrete by focusing on a key contribution to modern social philosophy. Whereas Foucault identified in Kant the emergence of an attitude of modernity, "a historical ethos that could be described as a permanent critique of our historical era" ("Enlightenment," 42), Georg Wilhelm Friedrich Hegel was the first to consciously understand himself as a philosopher of modernity. His was "a birth-time and a period of transition to a new era" (*Phenomenology*, §11), and it was also the dusk in which the owl of Minerva flies (*Elements*, 23). From this pivotal position Hegel advocated, as a philosophical project of modernity, both the critique of the historical limits that are imposed on us and an experiment with the possibility of going beyond them.

Hegel's ponderous opus gave inspiration to the entire political spectrum, from Marxism to fascism. As social philosophy it is situated squarely in the problems of modern governmentality. His work propelled and defined the process of modernization itself. Historically Hegel was closely associated with the circle of liberal Prussian reformers who sought to modernize the old system, to foster the move into a modern form of governance.[10] This milieu, which included figures such as von Stein, von Hardenberg, and von Humboldt, helped to abolish serfdom and emancipate the Jews, promoted educational change, supported representative government, and re-created the basis of philosophy as a critical project. Against the backdrop of Napoléon ending the Holy Roman Empire, there seemed to be ample opportunity and ample need for reform, the chance to bring forth the most modern form of the state. I will not attempt an exhaustive discussion of Hegelian social philosophy here; rather, I will focus on six characteristics through which it advances governmentality, six characteristics that prove significant for a queer critique of the modern state. These characteristics act as six knots of modernity binding all individuals to a particular political form.

1. Autonomy reveals itself not as an exclusive property of separate private spheres or distinct lifeworlds but rather as an element in a hierarchical relationship, with autonomy of the subgroup *dependent* on consonance with the demands of the superior organization.

2. In this hierarchy the autonomy of the public becomes superior to the autonomy of the private, resulting in a state based in impersonal bureaucratic institutions that are "impartial" in the face of individual interests and a vision of an economy that sees no conflict between the interests of the individual and the good of the whole.

3. The state, as superior institution, then relies on an increasing deployment of more gentle yet pervasive forms of coercion, such as panopticism, norms, or performatives, to determine freedom in all the other lifeworlds.

4. The state assumes an expected pattern of relation to economy, over which it supposedly presides. The rationalization of law and administration allowed for a certainty of calculation that in turn facilitated rational enterprise. The state defines its relation to economy through a conscious policy, whether free trade, laissez-faire, partial regulation, or central planning.

5. Private autonomy becomes signified chiefly by the family as an institution of heteronormativity.

6. And finally, individual autonomy becomes signified chiefly by a pursuit of happiness based in a limited freedom of choice. This autonomy is not based in unfettered desire in the sense of hedonistic freedom but rather is subordinate to the economy and increasingly finds its expression in consumerism. Kant's division of morality and happiness shifted happiness away from attainability as social virtue to a pursuit of lack, a pursuit with no culmination. As a result of this distinction asceticism, a Schopenhauerian concentration on the repression of desire, develops logically out of Kantian morality. Repression becomes the morally "allowed" response, while hedonism and Epicureanism present a certain threat to the stability of this organization of lifeworlds.

Hegel among Some Hot Numbers

1. Autonomy reveals itself not as an exclusive property of separate private spheres or distinct lifeworlds but rather as an element in a hierarchical relationship, with autonomy of the subgroup dependent on consonance with the demands of the superior organization.

Hegel's works describe an integrated and fully elaborated system of social philosophy. They contain, furthermore, a discussion of what we have identified as the four areas of governmentality. Hegel undertook his discussion as an examination of the operations of Spirit in various forms, from individual psyche (*Geist*) to the supraindividual socius (*Volksgeist, Weltgeist*). This discussion is most fully articulated in his two great works: *The Phenomenology of Spirit* (1807) and *Elements of the Philosophy of Right* (1820),[11] which, although written years apart, are structurally integrated. His elaboration of government in the *Philosophy of Right* parallels the *Phenomenology*, progressing stage by stage between the different forms of *Geist*. Nevertheless, the two works move between what Hegel identified as the moral and ethical stages in opposite directions. In the *Philosophy of Right* he sustained a primarily synchronic analysis, charting the path an individual follows. In the *Phenomenology* he took a primarily diachronic approach, charting the progress of the social order with its incumbent determination of individual consciousness.

The difference rests on the perception that the individual confronts morality as a level of abstraction beyond the experiential level of ethics. The individual consciousness experiences ethics in the family structure and then moves on to moral behavior in civil society, while for the socius the abstract level of morality provides a foundation for concrete experiential ethical interaction. And while the *Phenomenology* culminates in religion as the penultimate stage before the absolute, this is revised in the *Philosophy of Right*, where religion is acknowledged as "only a foundation" of the state, and the state is viewed as absolute and as the substance of Spirit.[12] The state as the culmination of individual and social consciousness provides the *self-conscious* ethical substance, the unification of the family principle with civil society.

Figure 4 charts these different trajectories. Readers less familiar with Hegel's texts need simply recognize the extent of Hegel's system. For thirteen years he elaborated and refined the project begun in the *Phenomenology*, so that all his works constitute a unified whole. The chart does indicate how the two trajectories are interconnected, with the later conception, which benefited from years of further reflection, being a more elaborate and organized schema.

Figure 4. The Stages of Consciousness in Hegel

The Stages of Individual Consciousness in *The Phenomenology of Spirit*

Stages of Consciousness	Consciousness	Self-consciousness	Reason	Spirit	Religion
Shorthand	"I" = "I"	"I"/not "I"	"I" = "not you"	"I" = "we"[1]	
Social form	Slavery	Individuality	Family	(Nation-)state	
Means of relating to object	Sense perception	Mastery	Law	Mores (*Sitte*)/ morality	

The Stages to National Consciousness in *The Philosophy of Right*

Stages of spirit	Abstract spirit	Moral	Ethical	Absolute spirit
Social forms		Individual	Family/ civil society	
Ideational	Substance	Knowledge	Abstract universality	Resolution
Historical epochs	Oriental	Greek	Roman	Germanic
Political economic	Theocracy	Slave state	Civil society	Nation-state

1. Hegel uses a shorthand formula of "I" = "I" to define the first stage of consciousness where being is *in itself*. The other designations are my own shorthand to describe the further states of consciousness. Self-consciousness, or consciousness *for itself* appears in a relationship of difference or alterity in which the "I" is aware of itself through the not "I". The "I" that is confronted with and comprehends the specific properties of the other (especially gender) stands on the cusp of the ethical order. The move into communion of spirit, "I" = "we," comes with the recognition of moral duty to a community. This final stage is the sublation of alterity and the restoration of the absolute of consciousness.

In Hegel's work, then, the terms that concern modern governmentality appear. Hegel used the term *civil society* (*bürgerliche Gesellschaft*) to mark the sphere of economy, expanding the notion beyond any narrowly defined concern with finance, production, consumption, and supply and demand. Civil society acts as an all-encompassing term in which forms of financial and social exchange are interconnected.

Hegel's dialectical stages display the four concerns of governmentality as aspects of an absolute whole: the nation-state. Through his model of dialectical progression, Hegel was able to describe the four areas as distinct stages, yet—and this is specific to Hegel and part of the far-reaching and enduring impact of his model—this distinction does not describe a false autonomy. Indeed, Hegel's model makes explicit the relationship of coercion and domination in each stage. Each stage is based on and sublated (*aufgehoben*) into a successive moment.[13] The sublation draws the preceding term into commonality with it and contains it, but not the other way around. The family, for example, contains the individual, drawing the individual into a specific community, coercing the individual through its specificity. Civil society, likewise, sublates the family, thus drawing both individual and family stages into a further specificity.[14]

The individual, family, economy, and state continue as representationally distinct stages. Through sublation, however, each is integrated into and ultimately regulated by the succeeding stage. Hegel's analysis of autonomy, therefore, places the fact of regulation in each term, but ultimately the final term bears the full weight of legitimacy over the preceding terms. Conversely, the preceding stages cannot govern themselves. The private sphere is revealed here as incapable of maintaining itself as a truly autonomous moment or term. As Hegel described it, the movement toward totality contains the distinct terms as stages but grants only "autonomy in necessity" to each preceding stage.

2. *In this hierarchy the autonomy of the public becomes superior to the autonomy of the private, resulting in a state based in impersonal bureaucratic institutions that are "impartial" in the face of individual interests and a vision of an economy that sees no conflict between the interests of the individual and the good of the whole.*

Hegel designated the state as the point at which individual interests unite. As he described it: "The relationship of the state to the individual is of quite a different kind. Since the state is objective spirit, it is only through being a member of the state that the individual himself has objectivity, truth and ethical life" (*Elements*, §258). In civil society the individual had been sublated into the term *Bürger* in its sense as one who is bourgeois. In the state the second aspect of *Bürger*, citizen, sublates the individual. The stage of citizen means that the lifeworlds of individual and family, erstwhile defined as private, come to be contained by the public lifeworlds. Universal rights disappear, leaving behind only those of the citizen.[15] Such a citizen is subject to the dictates of the state and the vicissitudes of the economy—not vice versa.

Hegel did not distinguish between active and passive citizens, as did Kant, although he did recognize only certain members of civil society as having the right to elect deputies (*Elements*, §301, 311). This distinction resulted in an exclusion from representation, similar to Kant's, along gender and class lines. Nonetheless, there is a positive quality of Hegel's social philosophy where it goes beyond description into active reformism. For Hegel's fundamental conception of the nation-state, representation, and certainly the representation of minorities, is a minor question. The complete and effective sublation into the totality of the nation-state is portrayed as creating the perfect society. Minorities as antagonistic dissent do not exist in such a state conception.

Akin to Kant, Hegel recognized the citizen as bound by duties. Duties, or the necessities of sociation, guarantee the privileges of citizenship, and therefore such duties are also their rights. Here the double sense of Hegel's *Recht* in the *Philosophy of Right* makes itself evident. *Recht* as both right and law carries a sense of simultaneous proscription and permission, limitation and privilege, ability and obligation. *Recht* draws our attention to the rights resulting from citizenship and the rights incumbent on citizenship, for example, the right to vote and the right to pay taxes. *Recht* makes explicit how nineteenth-century concepts of the citizen left little room for freedom and autonomy. The individual retains only the bathetic pursuit of happiness. Individual citizens are not the free center of the state; rather, all that is left to them is the freedom to navigate their ships of happiness on the confined seas of the state. This state does not facilitate the individual's realization of happiness. It should outfit the individual for his or her expedition, but it provides no map to follow. This state circumscribes individual desire with duty and obligation. As rational and self-conscious totality, it is "desire in itself."

In Hegel's express critique of Kant's conception of right, freedom and autonomy dominate only when coupled by necessity. Hegel denied the categorical imperative's ability to generate right. In a critique of Kant similar to my own in chapter 1, Hegel recognized this procedure as establishing only a negative freedom. "Once this principle [the categorical imperative] is accepted, the rational can of course appear only as a limitation on the freedom in question, and not as an immanent rationality, but only as an external and formal universal" (*Elements*, §29). Yet Hegel does not follow this critique with a general rejection of negative determinations on freedom. Such a rejection might have carried the potential to liberate the desiring individual. Rather, Hegel used his dialectics to chart the process through which the state comes to contain both negative determination and positive determination; thus right *must* contain not only a negative but also a positive determination, freedom from *as well as* freedom to: "The association of duty and right has a dual aspect, in that what the state requires as a duty should also in an immediate sense be the right of individuals, for it is nothing more than the organization of the concept of freedom" (§261).

The dialectic that establishes the course of all Hegel's work precisely and clearly describes the union of freedom and necessity or the freedom in circumscription offered by modern governmentality. Ultimately, with more terrifying urgency than the categorical imperative procedure entails, Hegel's dialectics made clear the process whereby the freedom of the state acts only as a limitation, or rather a negative determination.

The ideal ethical citizen-individual here approaches his or her freedom to enjoy through an imagination that does not exceed the circumscribed limits of legality. A desiring imagination that does not even recognize the limits placed on it transforms the individual into the ideal citizen. Through panopticon, norms, performatives, or whatever mechanism of achieving what Simmel would identify as sociation, the ideal citizen must remain oblivious to its function. But it is difficult to keep the citizen subject unaware of this subjugation. To be unavailable to conscious reflection, such subjugation would have to be, like the Kantian forms of apperception, constitutive of the psyche. The limits on the citizen-subject's desiring imagination are tenuous; indeed, the nation-state is filled with individuals beset with less-than-ideal consciousness.

We might consider mind-altering substances as a test of and temptation for a citizen-individual. As when Kant exposed his voluptuary to the gallows to test the metaphysical a priori of morals, we can expose the citizen to cheap drugs to test the a priori of the state. Drugs or anything else the state rules illegal must be approached as not only illegal but also as unenjoyable, actually outside desire, not an object in the citizen's pursuit of happiness (see figure 5 for the possibilities). A citizen who wants drugs and abstains only because they are illegal might remain a citizen, but she experiences her own "arbitrariness," her "*own particularity*" (*Elements*, §139). She realizes, in Hegel's words, that she is "capable of being *evil*" (§139). In such a realization this citizen-individual consciously confronts the coercion of the state, experiencing the domi-

Figure 5. The Outcomes of Desire on the Citizen-Subject

Individual	Citizen	Status
1. Drugs not desirable	Accepts as illegal	Ethical citizen
2. Drugs desirable	Accepts as illegal	Immoral individual Conscious of state coercion
3. Drugs desirable	Does not accept	Unethical noncitizen
4. Drugs not desirable	Does not accept	Ethical noncitizen

nation inherent in modern governmentality. Until she acts on her desires, however, she remains comfortably closeted in the totality of the state.

If the citizen-individual refuses legality and acts on her desire (type 3 in the figure), "the *will* of others," that is, the totality of the state, ceases to be "the external subjectivity which is thus identical with me" (*Elements*, §111). She loses the status of citizen altogether and indeed becomes evil, presenting a crisis for the state. A fourth position can exist, however, the moral individual who strives for the liberation of other citizens' pleasures. This position, typified by Antigone confronting Creon, can present the state a profound crisis. Such an individual remains moral and ethical but drops from the status of citizen. She actualizes a higher ethical instance than that embodied by the state. She actually negates the totality of the state. Given the disinterest of the individual in this position, however, such a challenge is highly unusual. It is certainly appropriate that Antigone comes to us in a play, in that such an ideal would have to present itself as performative. My example contains little to prompt an individual to recognize the unfettering of the pleasure of others as a higher ethical instance. Only someone operating according to an ethics of masochism might rise to the occasion.[16]

Short of achieving the telos of totality—a perfect society—an ethical struggle for a positive freedom to fulfill desires has little possibility. The individual who is conscious of a coercion on his or her desires is exposed to the force of the modern state as criminal or alien. The modern state proves capable of offering only a negative "freedom from" to its citizens, freedom from the desires of the other citizens. Adorno would later identify positive freedom as the fiction of the modern state: "no single thing [*nichts Einzelnes*] is at peace in the unpacified whole" (*Negative Dialectic*, 156).

The state would be able to provide positive freedoms only as attained totality, the achievement of the telos of totality. Without such an achievement, the trajectory of the state becomes the total negation of all other lifeworlds, a violence masked as legitimacy. "The determinations of the will of the individual acquire an objective existence through the state, and it is only through the state that they attain their truth and actualization. The state is the sole precondition of the attainment of particular ends and welfare" (Hegel, *Elements*, §261). With historical knowledge Hegel could not possess, we can recognize with horror the ends of this negation in the step he defined beyond the state. Here the nation-state, bearer of the World Spirit, is revealed as the negation not only of the lifeworlds of its own citizens but also of lifeworlds beyond its own borders. "The same determination entitles civilized nations to regard and treat as barbarians other nations which are less advanced than they are in the substantial moments of the state . . . , in the consciousness that the rights of these other nations are not equal to theirs and that their independence is merely formal" (§351).

3. *The state, as superior institution, then relies on an increasing deployment of more gentle yet pervasive forms of coercion, such as panopticism, norms, or performatives, to determine freedom in all the other lifeworlds.*

Adorno recognized the descriptive accuracy of Hegel's work. He also recognized its formative force. "The tit for tat of history as well as the totality-bound principle of equivalence in the social relation between individual subjects, both proceed according to the logicity which Hegel is said merely to interpret into them—except that this logicity, the primacy of the universal in the dialectic of universal and particular, is an *index falsi*. That identity exists no more than do freedom, individuality, and whatever Hegel identifies with the universal. The totality of the universal expresses its own failure" (*Negative Dialectic*, 317). Perhaps it proved a failure, but for the better part of modernity somebody or something certainly hid that failure. Somebody or something made the totality of the universal succeed, and that somebody was certainly not Hegel. In appearing as logic the logicity here cannot simply have relied on the "scrabbling together [of] senseless and maddening webs of words."[17] The *index falsi* required an organizing principle to act as if true. The totality of the universal required much grander agents of coercion to succeed. Here the nation-state rose to predominance drawing "a general line of force that traverses the local oppositions and links them together" (Foucault, *History*, 1:94). Moreover, the nation-state's organizing structure continues to function as the chief agency of surveillance and coercion.

I do not want to belabor the point of coercion and surveillance. Without trying to draw a direct historical relationship between the Hegelian concept of the state and the Third Reich, we can recognize how the modern nation-state in itself, based on a conception of governance through the universal, marks an increasing capacity to obliterate or marginalize the particular:

> The atomic situation is now at the end point of this process: the power to expose a whole population to death is the underside of the power to guarantee an individual's continued existence. The principle underlying the tactics of battle—that one has to be capable of killing in order to go on living—has become the principle that defines the strategy of states. But the existence in question is no longer the juridical existence of sovereignty; at stake is the biological existence of a population. If genocide is indeed the dream of modern powers, . . . this is because power is situated and exercised at the level of life, the species, the race, and large-scale phenomena of population. (Foucault, *History*, 1:137)

In this exercise of bio-power, economy, family, and the self as instances of particularity within the state all become subject to the state's totalizing force, domination, and appeal. Eugenics as an outgrowth of population control is one of the most obvious nexuses of state coercion and all the other lifeworlds. Here we can see how bio-power was deployed to "help." We may reject it now, but for a century eugenics—especially its positive form—was understood as offering a progressive, positive "revitalization" of the nation. And positive eugenics came to fruition in Nazism, along with negative eugenics: the racial state whose citizens enjoyed a liberating commonality through total coercion. We need not go so far as to tread the political waters polluted by the totalitarian state. We can remain in the relatively clear waters of the welfare state even as this form experiences a global dismantling. The welfare state might benefit the particular individual, but it does so not because its massive bureaucratic institutions ever cared for citizen 918–27–364. The modern state has always been fundamentally concerned only with the universal.

Whereas Hegel, the partial reformer, marked out the primacy of universality in the modern state, Max Weber, the "impartial" observer, recognized its results. In *Economy and Society* Weber charted out the emergence of certain qualities drawn together by the modern state, which made it the chief agency of coercion: the reliance on monocratic bureaucracy as the most rational means of exercising authority (223), a monopoly of legal coercion by violence (316), and the fusion of all bodies that had formerly engendered their own set of laws (666). These traits constitute the primary relays whereby the state increasingly determined the parameters of choice in all lifeworlds.

In its claim to universality, the state draws all the means of surveillance and coercion into itself, setting itself off as the most particular of all social instances. Indeed, before the modern period the state for itself did not exist. Previously the state as such shared coercion with other institutions and practices. For instance, Foucault noted that in Europe "up to the end of the 18th century, three major explicit codes . . . governed sexual practices: canonical law, the Christian pastoral, and civil law" (*History*, 1:37). Religious groupings, professional and social organizations, families, schools, and so on all continued to have some ability to coerce, whether through shame, blacklisting, or exclusion. As the modern state came to function for itself, however, by virtue of its monopoly on violence and the attendant expansion of legitimacy, these other forms of coercion had to rely on a voluntaristic acceptance of their power.[18] In the modern world citizenship is the only requisite form of association, a rule that the miserable lot of the stateless does not undermine but rather bears out. All other forms of affiliation (even familial) become subordinate to the state, determined by its law.

If, as Adorno observed, the totality of the universal failed to provide freedom to the particular, the state nevertheless cannot forgo claims to prove freedom in itself:

> Due to its hypostasis as spirit, the subject, the substrate of freedom, is so far detached from live human beings that its freedom in necessity can no longer profit them at all. This is brought to light by Hegel's language: "As the state, the fatherland, makes out a community of existence, as man's subjective volition submits to the laws, the antithesis of freedom and necessity disappears." No amount of interpretive skill would let us dispute away the fact that the word "submission" means the opposite of freedom. Its alleged synthesis with necessity bows to necessity and refutes itself. (Adorno, *Negative Dialectics*, 350)

All other lifeworlds come to experience this coercion. Under the modern condition of pervasive control, the truth of freedom lies in repression.

4. *The state assumes an expected pattern of relation to economy, over which it supposedly presides. The rationalization of law and administration allowed for a certainty of calculation that in turn facilitated rational enterprise. The state defines its relation to economy through a conscious policy of free trade, laissez-faire, partial regulation, or central planning.*

Hegel distilled and refined the discourse of *bürgerliche Gesellschaft*. All subsequent discussions bear his imprint. The English translation of this term splits it into two competing and equally influential directions: bourgeois society and civil society. Through Hegel we can recognize that civil society, as a system of needs, is the realm of the economic. We can recognize as well that the economic of bourgeois society is immediately the political economic, always inseparable from regulation and ethical determination, subsuming the individual into the mass.

Of course, this assessment of civil society sets off Hegel from his "liberal" contemporaries Smith, Ricardo, and Mill. The liberal view of civil society makes it the site of bourgeois emancipation, the realm of freedom and autonomy. For Hegel, the state is the last instance,[19] and of course in the area of national economies, Hegel was right. Were it possible to institute the wildest fantasies of the most ardent free-market liberal, even this market form would be at base politically directed.

As Hegel defined it, political economy is the science of civil society par excellence. "*Political economy* is the science that begins with the above viewpoints but must go on to explain mass relationships and mass movements in their qualitative and quantitative determinacy and complexity.—This is one of the sciences which have originated in the modern age as their element" (*Elements*, §189). The route to the totality of the state passes through the stage of civil society that subsumes "the *particular* person, as a totality of needs and a mixture of natural necessity and arbitrariness" (§182). In civil society the particular person becomes conditioned to other individuals in "a system of all-round interdependence" (§183).

The "natural laws" of political economy identified by Smith and Ricardo provide insight into the rationality of economic relations, but the state provides reconciliation of opposition. "To recognize, in the sphere of needs [civil society], this manifestation of rationality which is present in the thing and active within it has, on the one hand, a conciliatory effect; but conversely, this is also the field in which the understanding, with its subjective ends and moral opinions, gives vent to its discontent and moral irritation" (Hegel, *Elements*, §189). The state does not withdraw from civil society's economic contradictions. More precisely, it supersedes the economic sphere altogether. The subordination of the economic to the state is not opposed in principle to a free-market, noninterventionist system, nor is it opposed to planned economy. Neither "hands-off" nor "hands-on" systems contradict the Hegelian understanding of the autonomy of the economic. Thus contemporary free-market-oriented political claims about the wisdom of respecting the "autonomy" of the economy have no bearing on the relationship Hegel posited between the economy and the state. Indeed, in the historical progression Hegel charted out, the state preceded this economy of civil (i.e., bourgeois) society: the Oriental and Greek worlds did not recognize such a sphere, the Romans gave rise to it, and the Germanic world brought it to fulfillment.

Democracy constitutes one way that civil society is brought into the state as an institutional form. When this happens, however, or when we try to set democracy against the Hegelian state, we can see that they do not overlap. Democracy as a form of governance must be distinguished from the form of modern governmentality. As the representation of individual wills, the democracy of eighteenth-century political theory does not interest the modern state. Participatory democracy has never been practiced at anything more than the local level. Rousseau had already identified the failure inherent to representational democracy. Institutionalized representation of the individual is not the same as an expression of individual will or agency. Democratic representation only provides a sign of the recognition of legitimacy and mass assent to centralized coercion. Institutions such as the U.S. Electoral College or the German republic's parliamentary 5 percent rule bear witness to this. As "extra steps" in the electoral process, they remove government a bit further from having to be responsible to a "daily plebiscite." Democracy becomes generally signified as a certain form of economy. The freedom of political will finds expression in the freedom of the middle-class consumer. The commonwealth becomes literally the average purchasing power of citizens.

5. *Private autonomy becomes signified chiefly by the family as an institution of heteronormativity.*

Referring to figure 4 (see p. 71) we can recognize that in the ethical realm Hegel positioned a stage before civil society, the stage of the family. Hegel defined civil society as "the stage of difference which *intervenes* between the family and the state" (§182; emphasis added). It is important to note the term *difference* here. The household and the economy are in not a dialectical relationship but a relationship of difference. At first there appears to be a smooth dialectical transition between family and civil society. "The family disintegrates, in a natural manner and essentially through the principle of personality, into a *plurality* of families whose relation to one another is in general that of self-sufficient concrete persons and consequently of an external kind" (*Elements*, §181). But civil society as the realm of economy is not understood as an extension or cooperation of households. As an intervening form, it ruptures the transition to the state. The individual leaves the family, the household, and moves into an economic world. This intervening difference is a public/private division. Civil society becomes an (intervening) public sphere in which individual subjects act as agents. The family attains its dominant position in the representation of the private.[20]

The distinction between civil society and the family marks a dramatic transformation of the socius during this period. The Greek *oikonomia*, which contained both household and economy, is sundered. Hegel's distinction describes how a historical break or rupture of household from economy, found already in small urban pockets in the early modern period, accelerated at this time in Western Europe, rose to preeminence as social philosophy, and sublated all other family forms. Hegel's family differs from the family as conceived by Kant, who just a few decades earlier had still written of the *Haus*, the household. Having lost any extended structure denoted by Kant's use of the image of the *Haus*, Hegel's use of the word *Familie* designated a modern middle-class man-woman, mother-father, parents-children kinship structure.[21]

A century after Hegel Weber identified this separation of the *oikonomia* into household and economy as one of the foundational features of the "modern rational organization of capitalistic enterprise" (*Protestant*, 23). He described how the regularity of the capitalist exchange and labor form relied on the separation of personal and corporate property. The separation of household and place of business allowed private property protection from the possible devastation of failed investment, speculation, bankruptcy, foreclosure, and so on. We can move further from Weber to social historians to chart the development of this family form.[22]

In the early modern period the bourgeois nuclear family structure had competed with other kinship structures. The shape of the family in individual homes had varied and continued to vary throughout the German territories. Current statistical work has sought to show that preindustrial family structures were defined by the form of production in which the family engaged; where work was centered in the family and could sustain more people, the family was larger. At the same time there was a diversity of family structures unknown in the present period. Recall that for Kant, households consisted of various forms of kinship structure, as well as servants and workers. Agrarian families, families working in the putting-out system, families of tradesmen, and merchant families all had their own characteristics related to the method of production in which the family engaged. Eventually capitalism removed the household from the center of production, ultimately resulting in uniformly smaller families. This change in the locus of production and subsequent reduction in family size allowed for further ideological expansion as more families became incorporated into this model. Industrialization caused this separation of household from economy to cross class lines, moving from the bourgeoisie to pull the new proletariat into the same form, if for entirely different purposes.

Given the predominance of this family model across class, national, and ethnic lines in the industrializing and industrialized economies of the twentieth century, it makes little sense to continue to use the appellation *bourgeois*, except that the bourgeois model of the family was fundamental to the success of bourgeois hegemony. In Hegel's early nineteenth-century Germany, however, there was no real proletariat. Its mercantile capitalism was still caught in the putting-out system, which kept Silesian weavers' fingers busy in their cottages rather than in centralized factories. Hegel's definition thus reflects the triumphal entry of the bourgeois nuclear family onto the stage of world history. Hegel's incorporation of this family form marks his astuteness in identifying the rising actors on the world stage. If it were not for the fact that he could look to models in France and England, one might even accuse him of shoving a protégé amateur onto that stage.

Hegel discussed the family as a filiative group that provides the individual with his or her first experiences of society and its mores—that is, the ethical realm. Such a conception of the family as primary point of socialization is now commonplace, but Hegel's work was critical of other competing strands. Consider, for example, Rousseau's famous statement regarding the reason for public education's significance: "Families dissolve, but the State remains" (149). Hegel, however, basically ignored other points of socialization; schools, professions, the military, and so on receive at best a cursory glance in his texts. The significance of the family is thus elevated with Hegel—paradoxically, for it is ultimately sublated in the state. As the immediate substance of Spirit, the family provides the base for the state's ethical totality. "The expansion of the family, as its transition to another principle, . . . becomes a people or *nation*" (*Elements*, §181).

Once again his description of social philosophy shows that Hegel acutely recognized transformations in gender and sexual roles. He incorporated these transformations into his conception of the social totality. The removal of the center of production from the family altered sexual and gender dynamics sociohistorically, further limiting the means whereby femininity and femaleness could act as trajectories for power. This appears clearly in Kant's discussion of heteronomy, which places women as a category outside rationality. Patriarchal institutions were certainly part of the socius well before the modern period. It is necessary, however, to recognize that such institutions are not necessarily tied to domination; rather, in the modern period the patriarchal institutions became aligned with the public sphere of civil society in new ways that allowed for a dramatic increase in their ability to exercise coercive force.

Industrialized economies and Christian symbolic economies tend to value women's production less highly than other economies do.[23] In premodern Europe's farming communities and communities of manual laborers, the daily struggle for existence was precariously based on the total contributions of all members of the family unit. This situation left women to perform a diverse set of tasks crucial to the vitality of the unit. Women were excluded, however, when the source of livelihood relocated outside the home, to a public sphere dominated by patriarchal institutions. Cut off from sources of livelihood, women saw their work devalued, their movements restricted, and their options for work curtailed.[24]

At the heart of Hegel's ethics of the family and hence, as its supersession, the nation lie particular gender and sexual norms that draw on and support the social transformations of the modern period. I already discussed how this began. The difference reflected in the distinction between family as the private sphere and civil society as the public appeared in Hegel's highly elaborated essentialization of gender distinctions, marking two types or characters that primarily inhabit these distinct spheres. Complementary characteristics make logical the apportionment of the social sphere into two interrelated spheres: the house as the feminine sphere of activity and the world outside the house as the masculine. "Man therefore has his actual substantial life in the state, in learning [*Wissenschaft*], etc., and otherwise in work and struggle with the external world and himself. . . . Woman, however, has her substantial vocation [*Bestimmung*] in the family, and her ethical disposition consists in this [family] *piety*" (*Elements,* §166). Such oppositions reveal an intensification and rupture of Kant's distinction between inclination and understanding, the characteristics of women and men within the household. Following Hegel's split of the household into the two aspects of the ethical realm, distinctions such as man/woman, active/passive, scientific/intuitive, and objective/subjective aligned within the totality of the state, where they were to remain as part of its very nature. Gender distinctions defined oppositions that are *not* dialectical. Even though they represent positive and negative determinations on individual existence, Hegel did not understand them as contradictions that would drive the dialectic. Defined as essential, the gendered difference gave rise to heterosexuality as one of the first signposts of the ends of history.[25]

It is thus crucial to recognize that *heterosexuality is not simply a preferred form of sexuality,* one among many. Instead, it provides the prototype for the kind of social homogeneity that stood at the heart of Hegel's positive social totality. Heterosexuality here is not simply a compulsory form of sexuality. Rather, it ascends to the ethical norm that pervades the entire nation-state. It is the knot that binds the totality together. Without heteronormativity the social structure of modernity falls apart into contingencies, particularities, and accidents of desire.

In the heteronormative husband-wife relationship Hegel charted out a system whereby the posited natural, essential characteristics of masculinity and femininity complement each other to produce a harmonious social order. This harmony thus offers a vision of a perfected dialectic. The heterosexuality of the family suffuses the entire social order with ethical form.[26] The eighteenth century had witnessed marriage for love replace marriage as economic union. This love marriage was not solely a spiritual experience, however. Certainly even now, where go-betweens have been replaced by computers and newspaper ads, many couples continue to "fall in love" with each other's economic value. But the romantic emphasis on a love bond universalized marriage as an ethical principle for even those without wealth.

For Hegel, the family originates in love, confirming its position in a private sphere of emotions distinct from economic and political interests. "Love means in general the consciousness of my unity with another, so that I am not isolated on my own [*für mich*], but gain my self-consciousness only through the renunciation of my independent existence [*meines Fürsichseins*] and through knowing myself as the unity of myself with another and of the other with me" (*Elements*, §158). Hegel's conception of love differed from that of his contemporary Friedrich Schlegel, proclaimer of bourgeois love marriage. Hegel's distinction allows us to identify the anxieties of the proclaimers of totality and to recognize a significant threat to the promotion of heteronormativity. Like Kant, Hegel denied a solely procreative function to marriage. The purpose of marriage is *not* to produce children but primarily to check the natural drives of husband and wife. Marriage creates a unity, according to Hegel, that transcends individual drives and needs for the sake of an all-encompassing totality. Hegel, however, expressed only disdain for Kant's definition of marriage as contract for the mutual use of each other's sex organs (see *Elements*, §75). Whereas Kant began with marriage—not the family—as one form of contractual law, Hegel began with the entire family as the love bond sublated into ethical mores (*Sittlichkeit*). Marriage, "the *union* of the natural sexes," went beyond this union to bring private property and the socialization of children into the basis of the ethical realm. Here was the moment in which civil society superseded the family—that is, when ethics superseded love.

In the *Philosophy of Right* Hegel identified the family as the place where individuals come to recognize the common good at the heart of civil society. "The Family thereby makes [the individual] a member of a community which prevails over and holds under control the forces of particular material elements and the lower forms of life, which sought to unloose themselves against him and to destroy him" (§452). Without the family civil society would consist of only such destructive forces. It is in the family that the individual becomes aware of the ethical order and the destructive forces of civil society are reined in; civil society becomes community. Interestingly for our understanding of heteronormativity, Hegel does not locate the inculcation of ethics in the process of familial socialization. If it were the locus, the particular family form would not be so significant. Indeed, there might be room in the state for all sorts of filiative structures, and Rousseau's vision of public education might prevail as the center of state totality.

Although he discussed the inculcation of ethics that takes place in the family, Hegel made the union of husband and wife bear the weight of totality. Here the natural union of the contradictory elements wrought by love achieves the reconciliation of totality, representing Spirit:

> But among the three relationships, of husband and wife, parents and children, brothers and sisters, the relationship of husband and wife is in the first place the one in which one consciousness immediately recognizes itself in another, and in which there is knowledge of this mutual recognition. Because this self-recognition is a natural and not an ethical one, it is only a representation, an image of Spirit, not actually Spirit itself. A representation or image, however, has its actual existence in something other than itself. This relationship therefore has its actual existence not in itself but in the child—an "other," whose coming into existence is the relationship, and is also that in which the relationship itself gradually passes away; and this alternation of successive generations has its enduring basis in the nation. (*Phenomenology*, §456)

This reasoning, which must struggle to identify the husband-wife relationship as more determining or more ethically primary than other filiative relationships, makes clear how the tenuous nature of heteronormativity requires an input of coercion through its sublation into "ethics," since heteronormativity is the foundation for nothing less than the *nation*.

Further, Hegel still supported a modified form of planned marriage over the marriage of "passion," which can provide the basis of an affiliation of desire. Hegel would have none of that. He recognized the freedom to determine the object of one's affection as a move into a pure subjective reason for the union. He understood this move to characterize the modern world, but he viewed this insistence on self-determination with all its contingency as having no "importance *in itself*" (*Elements*, §162). In itself it made no contribution to any of the successive stages of totality that culminate in the state.

Hegel stopped short of sex because, we might recognize dialectically, the chief institution of heteronormativity—bourgeois marriage—carries within it its own negation. The physicality implicit in the marriage of passion would, once recognized, open the floodgates of discourses on sex and sexuality that have the potential to reveal uncontainable variety rather than an orderly teleological progression toward a high order of totality. For the progression to be truly orderly, it requires a preemptive designation of sexuality as singular in nature, thus predictable in outcome. Thus, as a bourgeois bedroom with its heterosexual coital activity came to constitute a new private place, it also became ideologically the *sole* legitimate center of sexuality. For all those other, "illegitimate" sexualities, however, the bourgeois marriage of passion also set the stage for an ethics of affiliation based on self-determination.

6. *Individual independence becomes replaced by communal interdependence. Freedom becomes antithetical to pleasure.*

Coercion appears to establish limits that restrict freedom and remove autonomy. It therefore seems to bring unpleasure to the individual. And yet many individuals appear to be content to live as good citizens, to imagine their desires within the limits of the state alone. Hume observed that no discernible principle entails that we will always seek pleasure and avoid pain. For Kant this observation proved highly significant in his formulation of the law. For us, however, Hume's observation returns us to our examination of lifeworlds and the question of coercion.

Hume's claim notwithstanding, a naïve line of reasoning continued to portray repression as opposing pleasure (especially libidinal). In chapter 4 I look more closely at figures such as Reich, Fromm, Marcuse, and Adorno and the developments in social psychology that followed this line, which construes repression as the negation of pleasure. These writers supposed that unpleasure would lead directly to attempts to undo its cause. The pleasure principle, libidinal force, or pent-up orgasms were to provide the energy to break through the alienation and domination of the economy. Late capitalism keeps getting later, however, and we are still waiting for this breakthrough to occur.

Taking a different line, Foucault's theory of power invites us to understand that resistance does not spring from repression. Although coercion and repression are not entirely the same experience, they overlap here, at least. Still, resistance does not necessarily exist in a direct relationship to coercion. It does not follow that the more coercive lifeworlds become, the more resistance individuals will display. Nor does coercion stand in direct relation to unpleasure. Lifeworlds need not offer less pleasure or more pain as they become increasingly coercive. Like repression, coercion bears a relationship to pleasure and resistance, but it is neither a direct nor a constant relationship.

The microhistorical level shows how the relationship varies widely. Coercion may have brought great pleasures to figures as diverse as Joseph McCarthy, Catherine MacKinnon, Clarence Thomas, and Bruce Bawer. Pleasure may incite to great resistance, as demonstrated by Ulrich Zwingli, Pierre-Joseph Proudhon, Daniel Bell, or Danièle Straub and Jean-Marie Huillet. Given this variance in the sociohistorical matrices of these episodes, there is nevertheless an underlying connection, and the individual stands at the center of it. Can we, then, identify certain principles that make the individual as subject in various lifeworlds amenable to pleasure in coercion or even prepared to find it there? To answer such a question requires a closer examination of the psychology of the modern subject.

Kant's transcendental ego may have been a necessary component, but the truth of modern psychology emerges in Hegel's subject. Hegel's recasting of the relationship between the universal and the contingent retains much of the impetus of the Kantian subject but refines this sociable ego structure to cohere within a state conception not by a process but by being. It removes any voluntarism of the categorical imperative as "an external and formal universal" and ultimately removes considerations of "the will of the single person [*des Einzelnen*] in his distinctive arbitrariness" (*Elements*, §29). Any praise that Hegel offered Kant's moral philosophy lies in its emphasis on the significance of duty.

In his definition of subjectivity Hegel proceeded from a position Kant made familiar. He began through similar distinctions by defining will. "The will contains the element of *pure indeterminacy* or of the ego's pure reflection into itself, in which every limitation, every content, whether present immediately through nature, through needs, desires, and drives, or given and determined in some other way, is dissolved; this is the limitless infinity of *absolute abstraction* or *universality*, the pure thinking of oneself" (*Elements*, §5). In the second step of this process, however—the emergence of the subject out of will—Hegel immediately deviated from Kant. The will as indeterminacy can remain here in the "freedom of the void," fleeing all limitation, engaged in the religious "fanaticism of pure contemplation" or the political "fanaticism of destruction"—or existing in a state of antisocial psychosis. As a definition basic to Hegel's psychology, the ego emerges first by a recognition of a limitation on will. "In the same way, ego [*Ich*] is the transition from undifferentiated indeterminacy to *differentiation, determination,* and the *positing* of a determinacy as a content and object.—This content may further be given by nature, or generated by the concept of spirit. Through this positing of itself as something *determinate,* ego steps into existence [*Dasein*] in general—the absolute moment of the *finitude* or *particularization* of the ego" (§6). A consistent theme in the modern understanding of psyche is an ego above but still at odds with "its own" desires. In the Kantian ego structure the social individual consists of two elements at odds with each other: the will comprising indeterminate desires and a rational moment that places limits on and directs desire. In Hegel's psychology the individual develops from the first level of subjectivity—the state of pure indetermination—to the next level, natural will, through the determinations of "drives, desires, and inclinations" (§11). The act of self-reflection then moves the will a step further, to free will, where the "rational" act of self-reflection takes the will as its own object and determines will and desires.

Indeterminacy should not be confused with heterogeneity. Hegel recognized a heterogeneity of will. He admitted a multitude of drives at work in the will, including a drive to morality, to property, and to the state (*Elements,* §19). Indeed, there are as many aspects of will as there are objects to desire or directions to drives. To restore the "philosophical shape" to this empirical psychological discussion, however, Hegel liberated objects of will from acts of willing. "Man finds within himself, as a *fact of his consciousness,* that he wills right, property, the state, etc." (§19). This "purification of the drives" separates their material forms or objective existence from a substantial essence.

In the development of the desiring individual, the psychological discourse of will followed this path by increasingly limiting the drives that shape the will. By the turn of the century psychological discourse posited a singular essence of drives, desires, and inclinations. This substantial essence eludes material determination. It increasingly avoided conscious determination by the will, and with Freud it was split into three essential qualities: the *Trieb*/libido, the object, and the aim.

For Hegel, however, this essence, the fact of consciousness, is itself the rationality of the will, "thus rational [*vernünftig*] in itself" (*Elements,* §11). The determinations of drives, desires, and inclinations are not the will but only its contents: one enters into the ego conscious of this fact. Freud's "wo es war, muß ich werden" ("where id was, there ego shall be") echoes Hegel when he says that "the drives should become the rational system of the will's determination" (*Elements,* §19). And Hegel echoed Kant's conception of reason when he defined consciousness of the will as consciousness of the role of determination in the will or determination as content of the will. Reason remains opposed to a heterogeneity of desire.

In its determination the subject's will is prepared for coercion. Coercion differs from determination only in its source: determination and the will are internal to the subject; coercion is external. But there is no reason to assume that because it is external, the will is somehow predestined to opposed coercion. Is there some component of subjectivity that makes it amenable to external determination? Indeed, the discussion of Kant suggests that this modern ego might include a component that brings external and internal determination to overlap.

For Hegel this consciousness is the first step in the dialectical development of ego. It is the move from an unreflective state of being-for-itself to a conscious subjectivity. Hegel used the shorthand "I" = "I" to designate this point, at which the ego becomes conscious of its own existence (see figure 4, p. 71). Hegel's story of consciousness is, however, a story of an ego in society. Indeed, "I" = "I" is only the first state of consciousness; self-consciousness occurs only when the ego looks around and realizes a world beyond this autistic totality. The ego proves itself immediately to be psyche prepared to assume a position in a socius.

Hegel first elaborated the story of the "I" = "I" in *The Phenomenology of Spirit* as part of his narration of the individual psyche, a sort of *Bildungsroman* of individual ego. There the story of subjectivity truly begins when a determinateness in the being-for-itself of consciousness comes forward as "antithesis to the universal substance" (*Phenomenology*, §171). The ego is confronted by objects outside itself, the "not I." To restore the idyllic totality of consciousness, the ego might seek to destroy this object—a truly radical individualism. But the *self*-conscious ego comes into being only through the "not I," even if it seeks destruction of this not I. The ego as self-consciousness requires its object. "Thus self-consciousness, by its negative relation to the object, is unable to supersede it" (§175). Confronted with an object as negative, unable to supersede it without loss of self, self-consciousness might become bound to this not I in desire. The negating object, as an organic self-consciousness, has its own independence and becomes a "You." The "You" is more than consumable inorganic material. This other presents itself to self-consciousness as an independent life. It is both object and ego for the subject, which literally finds itself in the other. This confrontation with the objective other is a mutual process and propels the subject into society and economy. We might give to this stage the somewhat paradoxical shorthand designation "I" = "not You." The *not* here presents a problem for totality; it is a negation that must be overcome. It must be removed for the sake of sociation, and it is at this point that the ego proves itself amenable to coercion. "What still lies ahead for consciousness is the experience of what Spirit is—the absolute substance which is the unity of the different independent self-consciousness which, in their opposition, enjoy perfect freedom and independence; 'I' that is 'We' and 'We' that is 'I'" (§177).

By recognizing the individual's position as object in a social system and becoming aware of cultural laws and precepts, traffic and trade, the individual ego finds its place in a community of egos and thereby enters the level of universality. In a shorthand form, these levels can be described as "I" am "I," "I" am "not You," "I" am "We." Sadly, the happy end of Hegel's story lies in the nation-state. There must be negative determinations in the "I" / "not I" if the ego is to exist, but on the path to a morality of will that passes through duty and conscience, the ego arrives at a state of being-for-another (*Phenomenology*, §646). And the supersession of objectification is present in the ethical order. Duty is transformed into a state of immaterial emotional desire—love (§787).

Kant's categorical imperative, with its reliance on individual reason, is replaced by an experience of community in the ethical order. The Kantian system described the nascent capitalist reality: a state of individuals in competition with one another. In the "I am We" of the nation Hegel offered up the antidote to the inherent atomization of the economy. Paradoxically ethical order guarantees freedom to a society's members by actually *preventing* a civil society, based on contingency or particularity, from assuming the finality of Spirit.[27] The recognition of the "I am We" comes at the exclusion of an "arbitrary" individualism. The ethical order as a homogenizing moment guarantees social cohesion by negating a heterogeneity of desire. For Hegel as for Kant, members of society are protected from others' desires by the loss of particular desire. For Hegel, however, they have achieved their "destiny" in the state: "*Union as such is itself the true content and end, and the destiny [Bestimmung] of individuals [Individuen] is to lead a universal life*" (*Elements*, §258).

In his insistence on universality Hegel made a great leap from the possibility of the local and contingent to the totality. The insistence on the nation-state as the epitome of the universal overlooks the fact that lifeworlds of different kinds possess their own universalizing aspects that their individual members may find far more exciting, fulfilling, or harmonious. As Simmel's insights on the individual's relation to social form imply, although not all individuals are truck drivers, anyone who seeks to become one must undergo a universalizing experience: sixteen weeks of night school, union dues to the Teamsters, a CB out on the open road—however you wish to designate it, some universalizing experience transforms the individual into a member.[28] At the same time, this universalizing experience does not prevent the individual from becoming more particular within that universality. Having become a truck driver or a lesbian, the individual is more differentiated. Being a truck-driving lesbian . . . neither designation presupposes the other—or requires more overarching universalities, for that matter. Not all individuals are truck drivers, and it would be absurd to insist on attendance at truck-driving school as a universal requirement.

When Hegel made the leap to the nation-state, then, he required everyone to be something like a truck-driving lesbian; that is, he required everyone to reduce truck-driving lesbianism into a mere particularity, a footnote to a higher pursuit of ethical universality. Of course, my ironic equation here threatens to overlook the finesse of Hegel's work and the service it grants to freedom, and of course there are historical and social processes at work in the rise of the nation-state. Indeed, it is the fact that Hegel's work distills these processes of the modern state that makes it so significant. For the modern state to come to act for itself, it had to follow the trajectory that Hegel set forth. When the nation-state appeared as universal in his work, when citizenship became a requirement, the modern subject became bound into not only universalizing experiences but totalizing ones as well. Individual subjects were coerced by a universal that may or may not have had anything to do with the lifeworlds they traversed. Some of us *are* truck-driving lesbians, but without recourse to the local lifeworld and its universalizing pleasures of commonality, the particular individual must submit to the state and its totalizing freedom of the universal. We all became citizens. In the same way that "gool" (or "home") is the central reference point in all the lines traveled in a game of tag, the nation-state became the central reference point of all lifeworlds. This totalization could not have succeeded without various types of coercion, some gentle and others not so gentle.

Arbitrariness, indeterminacy, and heterogeneity threatened the Hegelian ego and the constitution of the socius at all levels. It dissolved the ego into psychosis and the social order into terror. Neither the modern psyche nor socius can exist in a state of heterogeneity. In place of a plurality of drives there is a substantial essence of drive. In place of a plurality of willing there is a substantial essence of will. And when this will is transformed by the ego's self-consciousness, it becomes determination for itself, *"self-determining universality, the will, or freedom"* (Hegel, *Elements*, §21). "The commonest idea [*Vorstellung*] we have of freedom is that of *arbitrariness.* . . . When we hear it said that freedom in general consists in *being able to do as one pleases,* such an idea can only be taken to indicate a complete lack of intellectual culture; for it shows not the least awareness of what constitutes the will which is free in and for itself, or right, or ethics, etc." (§15). Such arbitrary choosing is not freedom; choice is determination, while the ability to choose (i.e., the will as faculty) is freedom. Yet here we might recall Adorno's observation on Hegelian freedom as having disappeared into submission and necessity.

Hegel no longer found it necessary to distinguish between need and want. The particularity of the individual contained in this distinction—individual need and want as external necessity, inner contingency, or arbitrariness—is undone by the social nature of humans. Hegel recognized certain universal needs for "food, drink, clothing, etc." as natural and common to animals and humans (*Elements*, §189), but the human relation to such needs develops a social means to fulfill them; humans share the responsibility for satisfaction. The socius, as mutual dependence and source of new means, opens up new needs that lead into ever more complicated relations; "everything particular takes on a social character" (§192). Thus human beings move through their means to a level of social need in civil society. That move liberates them *from natural need to a state of interdependent desire* (§195). In modern governmentality the paradox of freedom in necessity is resolved by robbing freedom of the thrilling possibilities of arbitrariness. Independence reveals itself to be interdependence. And totality, instead of developing as aggregate of difference, expresses itself as coerced universal. "The selfish end in its actualization, conditioned in this way by the universality, establishes a system of all-round interdependence, so that the subsistence [*Subsistenz*] and welfare of the individual [*des Einzelnen*] and his rightful existence [*Dasein*] are interwoven with, and grounded on, the subsistence, welfare, and rights of all, and have security only in this context" (§183).

In the modern state Hegelian freedom becomes an experience of universal determination. Subsistence, welfare, and rights (as the true grounds of freedom) oppose pleasure and desire (which are the grounds of arbitrariness). The individual continues to derive a little love from the family, but not in the community of the state, for love has little to do with freedom as determination. As Hegel described it in the *Philosophy of Right*, the state knows no emotions: "Love is a feeling, that is, ethical life in its natural form. In the state, it is no longer present" (§158). The ethical unity of the state is cold, bureaucratic, instrumental, determining, totalizing.

In Hegel's dialectical procedure the "I" = "We" features of the feminine female, as antithesis to the active, transformative, and ego-bound masculine male, was taken as the model of stable totality. Here the contradiction of male and female ascends from a not I relationship through love to the "I am We" of the family. No room is left in the totality of the nation-state for the desiring individual in other forms. And yet the indeterminacy of desire is anxiously acknowledged in social philosophy as the essential human form. Such indeterminacy can result only in the presence of "other forms." In this case the desiring individual experiences the life-worlds established by social institutions as coercive. In conflict with the universal, the arbitrary desiring individual is not superseded by the "I am We" but is caught in an aggressive relationship: "You" are not "We." The desiring individual is closed off from love and exposed to the domination of a universal that hates it as the asymptotic limit to its own totality.

Notes

1. The Second Reich adopted paragraph 175 from the Prussian penal code. It then read: "An unnatural sex act committed between persons of male sex or by humans with animals is punishable by imprisonment; the loss of civil rights might also be imposed." The National Socialists changed the law in 1935 to read:

> Paragraph 175: A male who commits a sex offense with another male or allows himself to be used by another male for a sex offense shall be punished with imprisonment. Where a party was not yet twenty-one years of age at the time of the act, the court may in especially minor cases refrain from punishment.
> Paragraph 175a: Penal servitude up to 10 years or, where there are mitigating circumstances, imprisonment of not less than three months shall apply to: (1) a male who, with violence or the threat of violence to body and soul or life, compels another male to commit a sex offense with him or to allow himself to be abused for a sex offense; (2) a male who, by abusing a relationship of dependence based upon service, employment or subordination, induces another male to commit a sex offense with him or to allow himself to be abused for a sex offense; (3) a male over 21 years of age who seduces a male person under twenty-one years to commit a sex offense with him or to allow himself to be abused for a sex offense; (4) a male who publicly commits a sex offense with males or allows himself to be abused by males for a sex offense or offers himself for the same.
> Paragraph 175b: An unnatural sex act committed by humans with animals is punishable by imprisonment; the loss of civil rights might also be imposed.

The Federal Republic of Germany adopted this version, so that some of the men who had been persecuted in the Third Reich were reimprisoned in the new republic. This version remained on the books until 1969, when the parliament reverted to an earlier form from the Weimar era that criminalized sexual acts between a man over twenty-one and a man under twenty-one. In 1973 the age was again reformed to eighteen to parallel a similar law for heterosexual relations.

2. The initial concentration on the state gave way to an expanded address to economy, family, and self. See the ground-breaking study by James D. Steakley (*Homosexual Emancipation*). The 1980s brought significant contributions to the history of this period; see Faderman and Eriksson. For works focused beyond Germany, see Weeks; Duberman, Vicinus, and Chauncey.

3. Cindy Patton employed the term but as a tool that owed no debt to Foucault's work. Patton's work makes a distinction between the modern state and postmodern governmentality that actually does not draw on the rich connection between governance and bio-power. This usage overlaps more closely with the general term of gov-

ernance or even government. In a related fashion Michael Warner has drawn upon governmentality as a tool. Michael Warner edited Patton's work and was understandably influenced by her usage. See Warner, "Something Queer"; Berlant and Warner.

4. Among Western industrialized countries, this particular exercise of sovereignty, the execution of criminals, is practiced only in the United States. This shared technique of power links the "most advanced" democracy with the "most primitive" theocracies, such as Iran.

5. As further clarification, Foucault wrote that "the things with which in this sense government is to be concerned are in fact men, but men in their relations, their links, their imbrication with those other things which are wealth, resources, means of subsistence, the territory with its specific qualities, climate irrigation, fertility, etc.; men in their relation to that other kind of things, customs, habits, ways of acting and thinking, etc.; lastly, men in their relation to that other kind of things, accidents and misfortunes such as famine, epidemics, death, etc." (*Foucault Effect*, 93).

6. The regularity of the capitalist exchange and labor form relied on the separation of personal from corporate property signified in a separation of household from place of business; see Weber, *Protestant Ethic*. This same distinction becomes for Foucault a question of governance that subordinates the economy, kicking it out of its role as social base or motor of history.

7. Where Foucault invoked the term *life*, it should not be confused with a random, chaotic *nature*. Rather, this term demonstrates Foucault's debt to Nietzsche. Here life appears more in line with Nietzsche's discussion: life that is a trajectory of the will to power. Foucault's term *bio-power* fleshes out the notion of the will to power.

8. For extended discussions of the specific German context, see Lütge 345; Allen 18–22.

9. Old but still compelling and rich in information is the book by F. W. Coker.

10. Judith Butler's early work *Subjects of Desire* concentrated on Hegel's *Phenomenology of Spirit* and surveyed its influence on French poststructuralism. Her book is of interest for this study and recognizes the significance of desire in Hegel's work. For more information on Hegel, see Beiser, esp. ch. 8; Rockmore; Kaufmann; Marcuse, *Reason and Revolution*; Adorno, *Drei Studien*.

11. Hegel began lecturing on the philosophy of right in 1817 and repeated these lectures throughout his life. Just before he died he had again begun lecturing on the topic. This topic thus provides the systematic elaboration to his other works, defining their relationship to the social order.

12. To clarify this distinction, Hegel wrote: "If, then, religion constitutes the *foundation* which embodies the ethical realm in general, and, more specifically, the nature of the state as the divine will, it is at the same time only a *foundation*; and this is where the two diverge. The state is the divine will as present spirit, *unfolding* as the actual shape and *organization of a world*" (*Elements*, §270).

13. A point of clarification: for Hegel, such stages must be understood as diachronic *and* synchronic. That means that there is a developmental accumulation of forms that sublate earlier forms. With respect to Freud's discussion of sexuality, for example, the developmental story relates how the drives move from oral and anal stages to genital and libido, progress through the Oedipal conflict, disappear in the latency stage to re-emerge in puberty, and so on. But there is also a synchronic story. The adult is still a subject of drives that have now been configured as libido across the oral, anal, and genital stages, bearing the weight of all the trauma of Oedipus. For Hegel, political development charts a similar path: whereas a Greek adult would never arrive at statehood, a German adult would pass through all the stages that the Greek did but then move on to the state form.

14. For a recent discussion of the problem of civil society in a comparative and historical perspective, see Trentman.

15. Burke already understood universal rights as guaranteed in belonging to a state. Hannah Arendt would pick up on this point much later.

16. Altruistic behavior stands a chance of reward from the state, as in the soldier who throws himself on a hand grenade. Freedom riders or those Germans who harbored Jews could expect only persecution from the state. They acted according to a higher instance of freedom, taking the laws of the state "to be violence and wrong" (Hegel, *Phenomenology*, § 470). The ethics of masochism should be understood broadly as deriving pleasure from the expressed pleasure of others. The pain of masochism here would be connected to going against the expressed wishes of legalities, a project that has the potential to invite punishment. The ethics of masochism can present a challenge to the state on the basis of desire and act as an emblem of noble behavior according to a higher instance.

17. Schopenhauer frequently unleashed his characteristic wit and venom against "Hegelian tomfoolery" (2:34). "But the greatest effrontery in serving up sheer nonsense, in scrabbling together senseless and maddening webs of words, such as had previously been heard only in madhouses, finally appeared in Hegel. It became the instrument of the most ponderous and general mystification that has ever existed with a result that will seem incredible to posterity, and be a lasting monument of German stupidity" (1:429).

18. Regardless of the elaborate mechanisms through which family members can coerce one another, the family is nevertheless subordinate to the state. Of course, the sovereign had always enjoyed the ability to intervene in the affairs of the family. See the discussion of early modern family politics in Hull; Koselleck; Perrot.

19. For an extended discussion of Hegel's political philosophy especially vis-à-vis the state, see Weil.

20. Lauren Berlant recently wrote about the conditions in the United States.

21. The German *Familie* and the English *family* both derived from the Latin *familia*, which designated the entire household including "servants," hence the word *famulus* ("servant" or "slave"). By the mid-seventeenth century the term had come to focus on offspring to the exclusion of other members of the household. By the early nineteenth century the term had taken on its contemporary meaning.

22. For lengthy discussions of family structures, see Michael Anderson; Laslett; Mitterauer.

23. For a detailed discussion of the transformation of women's work and family form, especially in Germany, see Frevert; Rosenbaum. For an insightful discussion of the transformation of women's work in the symbolic economy, albeit outside Europe, see Gailey.

24. Even in the new proletarian class, where women worked out of necessity, their work was devalued, forcing women to accept low pay for dangerous and monotonous tasks.

25. There have been extensive discussions of essentialism and particularly of the significance of Hegel for the proposition of essentialism. For a brief and insightful discussion of Hegel and gender, see Benhabib.

26. This point is an important point and stands as a corrective to Butler's discussions of Hegel. In *The Psychic Life of Power* Butler again focused on the lord and bondsman relationship that she had addressed in her earlier work. In *Psychic Life* she concentrated on Hegel's first attempt to resolve that negation, where the individual (male) subject turns his desire into material production. This is indeed an important step in Hegel's understanding of the emergence of the bourgeois citizen. It is doubly significant be-

cause it installed a gendered distinction between production and reproduction. But-ler, however, remained caught in the (historical) failures of consciousness Hegel had addressed in the *Phenomenology*. She did not follow the entire narrative of Hegel's story of the subject to its happy heteronormative end. It is important to underscore that in the *Philosophy of Right* Hegel made clear that it is the act of marriage, not birth into a family or the act of reproduction, that gives rise to the ethical realm and civil soci-ety, where the bourgeois citizen finds fulfillment. Thus, beyond production, heteronor-mativity in itself, not a reproductive imperative, marks the resolution of unhappy consciousness and the emergence of the ethical citizen-subject.

27. Hence England receives his critical dismissal as bound into civil society with a weak state.

28. Žižek uses the phrase *Universal-in-becoming;* see *Abyss of Freedom* (51).

3   Marx and the Limits of Emancipation

> Then things will go badly enough for poor frontside
> people like us, with our childish penchant for females.
> —Friedrich Engels

Political Emancipation Is Progress . . .
in the Present Order

The struggle has been long and difficult, and despite successes in the United States and Europe, sexual minorities have not yet attained even the political form of emancipation—that is, full citizenship
in the state. While efforts in this arena deserve our support, political
emancipation has its limits. Marx stated, "Political emancipation is, of
course, a big step forward. True, it is not the final form of human emancipation in general, but it is the final form of human emancipation within
the hitherto existing world order" (Marx and Engels, 3:115).

As the preceding chapter revealed, there are fatal/fateful limits to
"political progress," especially a political emancipation that proceeds
through integration into existing state structures—in Marx's terms, the
present world order, and in Foucault's terms, the modern forms of governmentality. These critics invite us to consider how striving for full
citizenship might bring representation in the juridico-political system but
leave the form of that system intact. Political emancipation as citizenship actually legitimizes the institutions of the nation-state. It is almost
paradoxical that without having to change its institutions, the nation-

state can draw the desires of all its queers into it precisely by withholding rights.[1] Vis-à-vis the state, what difference does it make if the movement invests its financial and theoretical resources in articulating an antimilitarist position rather than in struggling to end discrimination in the military or in articulating requests for inclusion in the contract of marriage rather than seeking the expansion of inheritance, property, and health-care rights? What difference does it make if the movement invests its financial and theoretical resources in articulating the worthiness of the minority as citizens of the state?[2]

We must continually pose a series of critical questions to practices of emancipation. What is the political nature of the movement? Is the movement focused on local, quotidian, and tendentious tasks, or does it participate in a larger project of political emancipation? How can individuals exposed to a coercive queering state apparatus successfully struggle against such coercion? To what extent can a movement oriented toward the emancipation of a minority become an agent of universality; that is, can it participate in any further form of human emancipation?

In his critique of Hegel and his fellow Left Hegelians, Karl Marx introduced the term *human emancipation* as a step beyond political emancipation, thereby holding out a certain possibility beyond the integration of "life politics." Marx was the first great social philosopher of the modern period to oppose the practice of governmentality. Following Marx's concentration on civil society and political economy, the subsequent development of Marxism as social philosophy envisioned a radical transformation of governance. Marxism was, of course, not the only critical direction in social philosophy to emerge in the nineteenth century. The foundation of the modern state brought about other directions, but these contained more inchoate articulations of opposition, such as the political emancipatory goals of the homosexual rights movement. Marxism, however, can be considered a systematic critical articulation because it sought the full transformation of all lifeworlds, a fundamental supersession of the coercion at the heart of modern governmentality. Significantly, Marxism promised a universal liberation of desire in this transformation.

Nevertheless, Marx and Marxism have proven inadequate to the task. Like his mentor, Heinrich Heine, Marx may have advocated an "emancipation of the flesh," but it was a heterosexual emancipation, and like Heine, Marx and Engels were not above a puerile satire of same-sex desire. In 1869, after having read Karl Ulrichs's work, one of the foundations of the modern homosexual emancipation movement, Engels wrote to Marx:

These are extremely unnatural revelations. The paederasts are beginning to count themselves, and discover that they are a power in the state. Only organisation was lacking, but according to this source it apparently already exists in secret. And since they have such important men in all the old parties and even in the new ones, from Rösing to Schweitzer, they cannot fail to triumph. *Guerre aux cons, paix aus* [sic] *trous-de-cul* [war to the cunts, peace to the assholes] will now be the slogan. It is a bit of luck that we, personally, are too old to have to fear that when this party wins, we shall have to pay physical tribute to the victors. But the younger generation! Incidentally it is only in Germany that a fellow like this can possibly come forward, convert this smut into a theory, and offer the invitation: *introite,* etc. (Marx and Engels, 43:295–96)

In this chapter I trace Marxism's promise as well as its inability to fulfill that promise.[3] The account follows three lines of analysis. (1) It begins with an analysis of liberation versus emancipation, starting from the distinction between political and human emancipation. This insightful distinction challenged liberation efforts in the first half of the nineteenth century, and it continues to pose significant challenges to contemporary lesbigay political efforts at the outset of the twenty-first. It then moves on to look at the way human emancipation exceeds the vision of the primacy of the state as the point of address and arbiter of conflict in the socius. Such a relationship to the state represents a path very different from that assumed by emancipatory groups since the 1960s. Civil rights, gay rights, women's rights, and so on rely on the state to perform as arbiter and advocate.

The distinction between human and political emancipation actually opened up a new space for an analysis of the desiring individual within Marxist social philosophy. Thus (2) the account then turns to subjectivity in Marx, particularly the vision of the liberated subject as an indication of Marxism's goals. Marx understood the subject of human emancipation to be not the speaking subject but the *desiring subject.* At the same time, however, Marx and the general development of Marxism also accepted the limits that the hetero-coital imperative imposed on the desiring individual, thereby limiting the movement's radical critical potential. I therefore then turn to the paradigms of gender, sex, and sexuality in Marx and Engels's writings to illustrate this point. Marx and Engels used the term *sex love* to describe their commitment to the particular morpheme of heterosexual activity or their own response to the emergence of the homosexual emancipation movement; this awkward term marks a general trajectory in Marxist social philosophy that undermined the analysis of the desiring individual.

(3) Finally, this chapter addresses the possibilities for a queer materialism and stresses the need to strive for a full liberation of humanity, not an emancipation of a particular lifeworld. One subsection in particular looks closely at the theoretical insights that developed from the intersection of Marxism and gay studies, especially the view of the gay subject as revolutionary subject. The concluding sections seek to further this work by analyzing queer conflict and the mode of desiring production.

Political and Human Emancipation

To begin to understand what distinctions underlay the forms of political and human emancipation, we can turn to Marx's essay "On the Jewish Question." Particularly apt when thinking about the relationship of gays and lesbians to political emancipation, this essay addresses the issue of a minority group seeking emancipation within the emergent modern state, guaranteeing the essay continued significance for an analysis of oppositional and critical groups within liberal political systems today.[4] Marx drew the distinction between political and human emancipation in this essay.

Around the time that Marx wrote the article (1843), certain critics were attacking Jewish attempts to secure religious emancipation—that is, the freedom to practice Judaism in the Christian state—as a form of special rights. The Left Hegelian Bruno Bauer demanded a route of assimilation that required the loss of all "Jewishness" for the sake of the "German" or "human" struggle; that is, Bauer demanded emancipation on the basis of integration into existing structures, a suppression of "Jewish" particularity, and a sublimation of specific desires for the sake of sociability. Marx likewise rejected what amounts to a direct "closeting" of religious particularity. The immediate route he charted required a change not in the minority but in the state's relation to the minority. Outside Germany he found a state model in which he could recognize the basis of positive political emancipation: "Only in the North American states— at least in some of them—does the Jewish question lose its *theological* significance and become a really *secular* question" (Marx and Engels, 3:150). North American nations as secular states removed the minoritizing term *religion* from the state's domain of regulation. Without a state religion to define citizenship, the state lost its ability to determine religious form and define human religious identity. The minority ceased to be recognized as a *minority* by the state, with a parallel result for all similar (religious) majority groups. Jewish political emancipation here does not mean that religion ceases to have the ability to determine group identity. The distinguishing term, however—*religious difference*—was moved outside the influence of the state. Religion became a secular question played out in civil society.

Marx found political emancipation precisely in the inversion of the Hegelian relationship to the state. Prior to Marx political emancipation signified the integration of individuals into a (Kantian) state of "independence from the compulsive arbitrary will of an other" (Kant, *Metaphysics*, 314). Hegel had anticipated political emancipation through the individual's ever-increasing subsumption into the structure of the state as a result of the supersession of difference and desires. Marx's transformation reveals the degree of his critical relationship to Hegel. *Political emancipation* occurs through a withdrawal of the state's limits or jurisdiction. Minority (e.g., religious, racial, or sexual) groups achieve political emancipation neither by getting the state to recognize them and grant them rights nor by seeking recognition and protection from the state as a minority group but rather at the point where the state relinquishes its power. From this position the burden of emancipation is removed from the minority group and placed on the state. The oppositional factor is not the minority group but the negating force that emanates from the state itself. To paraphrase von Praunheim, it is not the homosexuals who are perverse but the heteronormativity of the state in which they must live.

In contrast to Kant, Hegel, Bauer, and others espousing a liberal paradigm, Marx did not end with this form of emancipation. Instead he conceived of freedom not as state-granted freedom from the harm of others—a monadic conception designed only to protect private property—but rather as a passage beyond the state into a reformed civil society. True freedom is based on the "union of man with man" within civil society. Thus Marx established a critical distinction between political emancipation and human emancipation. Political emancipation is a process of integrating the individual into a state structure as a moral citizen alienated from the egoistic self of civil society. Human emancipation is a process of integrating the individual into a civil society as *Mensch*,[5] not into the state and "laws." Human emancipation is the supersession of the state but also the supersession of a certain form of civil society.[6] Whereas Hegel designated the state as the goal of all human striving, Marx located it as a penultimate form, a state to both seek and overcome. The direction of contemporary gay emancipation moves according to the Hegelian map, not the Marxist.

In the case of religious groupings (here Jewish and Christian), the state withdrew as a determining moment for religion. Yet as Marx and many others have pointed out, the United States is the land of religiosity par excellence. If the United States as a modern state came to have a "political attitude" toward the religion of its citizens, citizens as members of civil society still had (and have) a "theological" attitude toward the state and one another. This attitude means that for the United States and all those states that followed this model, political emancipation from religion as a point of coercion proved doubly incomplete. First, political emancipation shifts the structures of coercion from the state to civil society. Second, the displacement of the minoritizing term *religion* from the state to civil society does not complete emancipation for all individuals. As equal citizens they must still contend with a displacement of inequality onto civil society. In this model of emancipation (religious) inequality is not overcome, only displaced. The state developed according to the Hegelian map should not be understood as distinct from this displacement. As the previous chapter showed, the negation inherent in the modern state, the coercive totalizing whereby the equal citizen comes into being, is inextricable from the exclusion, reduction, and coercion of lifeworlds associated with civil society.

The State of Sex

Such observations on political emancipation are especially significant for queer studies; although the modern state may have retreated from the terms of religion, it clearly never lost its ability to define sexuality. Why does sexuality maintain a role in the techniques of power that religion does not? In my discussions of Kant and Hegel I have shown how, historically, sexuality came to occupy a fundamental role in modern forms of governance. Sex was a much better relay of power than were the police. When Foucault described how the exercise of power through sex resulted in regulatory mechanisms that exceeded the law, he did not suggest that familial norms and self-regulation do not serve governmentality. Indeed, sex is intimately bound to modern governmentality in a way that facilitates new and significant forms of regulation.

In the modern state the enforcement of heteronormativity is taken to be so natural that for those whose desires are enfolded within it, social philosophy has ascended to the level of common sense—or rather, to an ideological determination of consciousness. But those whose desires are excluded can take heart that, like the "commonsense" role the state once occupied vis-à-vis religion, its role vis-à-vis sexuality will also fade. The first step will require abolishing antihomosexual laws, such as Germany's §175 and various antisodomy laws in the United States. This is only a first step, however, since the state retains the further trappings of heteronormativity. Article 6 of the German constitution or "defense of marriage" legislation in the United States reserves to the state the right to control marriage and families, one of the chief sites of sexual legislation. Human emancipation means that the state would have to withdraw entirely from this domain of legislation.

Let me illustrate what I mean. A number of years ago the Cambridge Lavender Alliance addressed the question of gay marriage. The group successfully promoted an initiative in city council, with the councillors agreeing that "the state shall enact no legislation to interfere with the ability of lesbians and gays to marry." Such a statement obviated having to advocate "moral" imperatives for gay marriage. In fact, it made no argument for gay marriage at all but rather attempted to promote moral minimalism with respect to the state. It required the state to cease regulating marriage, thereby allowing for a de facto expansion of civil society's ambit.[7] Otherwise homosexuals remain a sexual minority within the state, an oppositional subgroup constantly soliciting rights that the state should never be expected to dispense. In such a state homosexuals share their incomplete emancipation with other subgroups of sexual dissidents, including nonreproductive heterosexuals.

Moreover, repealing laws that constrain sexual dissidents is not the same as promoting such subgroups to full equality. To undo the overwhelming enforcement of the heterocoital imperative, the state would have to get out of the business of determining sexuality and family structure altogether. Absent such a withdrawal of the state, each sexual dissident subgroup is left to scrabble for itself, seeking certain separate rights and protections. The state that would be conducive to human emancipation is *not* the mediator to which the sexual dissidents transfer all their human liberty.

Were we to achieve the dream of political emancipation within the state, we would still have to contend with the question of civil society, the lifeworld of the economy. Heteronormativity permeates all spheres of modern governmentality so thoroughly that even in a state that recognizes all citizens, the heterocoital imperative continues as the spirit of civil society, the family, and the self. The incompleteness of political emancipation reveals itself in such forefronts of emancipation as the Netherlands, Denmark, and Germany: even after the state repealed laws criminalizing homosexuality, gay activists had to return to the state to request new laws that would protect and regulate equality in civil society. Activists in these countries now see support for bourgeois gay and lesbian families as their primary concerns. Marx seems to have commented directly on this condition when he stated: "Where the political state has attained its true development, man—not only in thought, in consciousness, but in reality, in life—leads a twofold life, a heavenly and an earthly life: life in the political community, in which he considers himself a communal being, and life in civil society, in which he acts as a private individual, regards other men as a means, degrades himself into a means, and becomes the plaything of alien powers" (Marx and Engels, 3:154). Being a plaything for alien powers, along with all the other aspects of being a private person, seems highly erotically charged and to promise a great deal of pleasure, at least for certain configurations of desire. This pleasure is an individual pleasure, however, not a universal configuration, and certainly not what Marx had in mind.

In Marx's analysis the split between the state and civil society—the site also of his rejection of Hegel—results in a limit to political emancipation. Marx recognized that striving for political emancipation in the liberal paradigm will lead only to unlimited reformism. Full human emancipation must be sought elsewhere, beyond the state. Queer theory can develop the full ramifications of this analysis and a critique of Marx by exploring two directions: first, who is this "human" to be emancipated, and second, where do we go beyond the state?

The Subject of Human Emancipation

Marx's philosophy seeks to unfetter the economy, that is, the aspect of the lifeworld that Hegel located within the authority of the state. Marx's philosophy leaves only civil society as the site of governance. The ethical and moral developments that for Hegel define civil society and state give way in Marx to material determinations by which unalienated individuals approach one another on truly human terms. According to Marx, however, such conditions are possible only after revolution, and this investment in revolution caused problems that will always haunt Marxism. Although Kant's and Hegel's systems of social philosophy rested on a series of revolutions (the industrial, the French, the bourgeois, the national, etc.), they do not rely on revolution. The strength of liberalism as emancipatory struggle is that it is not inherently revolutionary. Liberal philosophy has always been willing to work within its present order.

The point of Marx's philosophy is not to interpret the world but to change it. For Marx, human emancipation is a step beyond the political emancipation of liberalism. It is a condition fundamentally incompatible with existing state and civil society. The politics of human emancipation that replace the ethics of the liberal state are not possible in the existing order. Thus revolution, as the not here and now, marks the necessary route to a there and then. Later in this afterward, a different time and space, such politics will be possible. In the meantime Marxism refuses the ethics of a "true socialism." Marxism remains restricted to the critical position, the self-conscious negation of capitalism, but is not itself the negation of the negation. Marxism is not the revolution. Until the revolution it remains critical philosophy. Only afterward can it ascend to social philosophy.

The role of revolution imbues Marxism with a sense of futurity that is ultimately as irrefutable as the Second Coming. The fact that it has not yet happened does not mean it never will. A portion of the revolution will always remain safe from critique. A portion of human emancipation will always be energized by faith. Marxism's promise of human emancipation remains a principle of hope.

As significant as revolution is for Marx, he rarely discussed the postrevolutionary society. He thereby retained the critical potential of his writings and avoided transforming his work into utopic socialism. This is not to say that Marx did not anticipate a state of full human emancipation to involve a paradisiacal end of history. He nevertheless focused on political economy, an analysis of the conditions of capitalism that in stages would lead to this end, and he saw capitalism's productive forces and their contradictions as the vehicle to this end. His concentration on the economy immediately undid the Hegelian hierarchy. It broke apart the distinctions of modern governmentality and paved the way for a reformulation of the system of lifeworlds.

On rare occasions, however, Marx did provide a glimpse into the structure of governance he envisioned, the reformulated relationship of lifeworlds: "Whereas in a communist society, where nobody has one exclusive sphere of activity but each can become accomplished in any branch *he wishes*, society regulates the general production and thus makes it possible for me to do one thing today and another tomorrow, to hunt in the morning, fish in the afternoon, rear cattle in the evening, criticise after dinner, just as *I have a mind* without ever becoming hunter, fisherman, cowherd, or critic" (Marx and Engels, 5:47; emphasis added). The pastoral quality of this oft quoted description from the young Marx might not attract the hardcore urbanite, but the description certainly leaves open myriad possibilities in social arrangement that presumably could accommodate all interests. The inhabitant of this pastoral setting is not a monad isolated in a rural idyll but a particular member of a social-economic organization, an individual defined not by social function (i.e., position within the division of labor or in sex or gender roles) but by a uniqueness that is inherent to the simple statement "he wishes." The contingencies of desire define as such the freedom of this subject, the experience of a "freedom *to*" rather than a "freedom *from*." Without such contingencies there would in effect be no "mind" to direct the individual toward any one particular sphere of activity.

Marx was one of Hegel's boys. Engels, too, started out in the circle of the Left Hegelians.[8] In his essay "On the Jewish Question," a review of Bauer's work, the younger Marx revealed his Left Hegelian origins by using terms such as *civil society* and *species-being* (*Gattungswesen*). These terms clearly evoke German idealism, the language of Hegel and Feuerbach, but Marx adds his own inflection to them. Human emancipation, or liberation that would allow all to become truly human, to manifest the essence of their species, relies on transformative liberating strategies (i.e., revolution) that undo the divisions of political emancipation: state and civil society. As liberation, human emancipation promises to invert Hegel's totalizing state. This rejection of an integrative political emancipation in favor of revolutionary liberation accelerates in the subsequent texts.[9]

Soon after he wrote his review of Bauer, Marx, along with Engels, wrote *The German Ideology*, where he moves away from Hegelianism considerably if not decisively. Here Marx put forth the basic principles of the social construction of humanity. These principles revolve around the recognition that human existence (or existence as humans) is bound to the interlocking development of needs and means of meeting needs. Development as humans rests on social development, which is interconnected with a material technological development of the means of production. Each new form of production brings with it new needs, which in turn not only allow but require further development of humanity. Such development does not take place in isolation. Although individuals experience it, it is not an experience of individuals. It is a social historical activity. At the heart of this vision of humanity is, thus, very real human need.

This understanding of social construction is not a step into a purely descriptive relativism. In the same text Marx and Engels developed a vision of a fully human society based on the unfolding of the individual in self-activity not dominated by material *need*. (Note the significance of need as that which Marx's pastoral promises to fulfill.) In a world without a division of labor, a world they identify as a precondition for fully human society, such unfolding would allow for a universal social development of the individual. Unlike romantic notions of *genius*, a trait of the individual artist, the development of *all* talents would be the self-activity of *all* people. In such a socius individual consciousness realizes the universal human, the state referred to in Marx's earlier work as species-being. This process occurs, however, not through a Hegelian self-consciousness as "spirit of the spirit" but through technological transformations of material conditions that make possible such self-consciousness. This society is populated by the liberated human, and it is located on the terrain of Marx's pastoral.

Such a conception of the nature of the human subject remained into the late period of the economic writings. It echoed in the "Critique of the Gotha Programme" (1875) when the old Marx put forth his oft-cited formulation of human society. "After Labour has become not only a means of life but life's prime want; after the productive forces have also increased with the all-round development of the individual, and the springs of co-operative wealth flow more abundantly—only then can the narrow horizon of bourgeois right be crossed in its entirety and society inscribe on its banners: from each according to his ability, to each according to his needs!" (Marx and Engels, 24:87). This new horizon set the direction toward which the critical apparatus of late Marxism steered. Only those who would benefit from denying the humanity of others would not want to fly these banners on their shores. There are of course many ways to benefit from denying the humanity of others.

Need is not desire. Marx does not promise that all desires will be fulfilled. Nor, for that matter, does he promise fulfillment to wishes or demands. As I have shown, however, desire has been a primary means for denying the humanity of fellow humans. Thus, however appealing this pastoral scene may be, we should examine more closely who inhabits its shores, because the move from ability to need postulated here presents a paradox: the limits Marx set to the universal. What can such human subjects need, and what can they not desire?

Sex-Love and the Limits of Human Emancipation

Marx and Engels remained Hegel's boys when it came to sexuality and gender. They held fast to a "natural relationship of the sexes" where "the direct, natural, and necessary relationship of person to person is the *relation of man to woman*" (Marx and Engels, 3:295). The rest of their work avoids claims of such a natural relationship. Nowhere else is nature so "natural." Nowhere else did they rely on such a fundamental essentialism. Even their description of species-being is not about human nature but about the construction of humanity. Their material, sensuous world is a historical product, a result of industry and intercourse, not an eternal given but a part of a dynamic process of human activity.[10]

Suddenly, however, in a passage drawn straight from the *Phenomenology of Spirit*, a gender essence delimits the form human desire can take.

Engels's book *The Origin of the Family, Private Property, and the State* was written in the spring of 1884—one year after Marx's death. As the first significant work to address questions of gender and sexuality from a *Marxist* perspective, it can be counted as Engels's most significant individual contribution to Marxism—indeed, the beginnings of a discourse of Marxism distinct from the texts of Marx. At the same time, the spirit of Marx haunts the text, making it well-nigh a collaborative work. For this study Engels drew information from Marx's extensive comments on Morgan's *Ancient Society, or Researches in the Lines of Human Progress from Savagery through Barbarism to Civilization* (1877), along with his own reading of Bachofen's *Mutterrecht* (1861).

The book's sweeping critique of the patriarchal family structure initiated a historical understanding of the family, gave theoretical impetus to two waves of feminism, and became a mainstay of scientific Marxism.[11] Engels set matriarchy as synonymous with an originary communism (*Urkommunismus*) where everything, including sexual relations, is held in common. Positing this promiscuous origin, Engels argued that matriarchal kinship is more originary than patriarchal because the act of birth is a remarkable event, whereas the act of fathering in a promiscuous society is not.

Patriarchy emerged through a system of legal rights that replaced the blood ties and familial duties of matriarchy, resulting in "the *world-historic defeat of the female sex.* The man seized the reins in the house too, the woman was degraded, enthralled, became the slave of the man's lust, a mere instrument for breeding children" (Marx and Engels, 26:165). This observation, a beautiful description of the historical collapsing of sexuality and reproduction, carries significance for queer theory.

Engels may have sought to move away from a reproductive imperative, but he could not escape a heterocoital imperative. Considering only (bourgeois) heterosexual relations, Engels further observed that in the establishment of patriarchy, the monogamy necessary for clear lines of inheritance extended only to women as wives, creating a double standard. Men did not have to control their heterosexual desires to promote patriarchy. Thus sexuality for women as wives became synonymous with biological reproduction, and sexuality for men became bifurcated into reproduction and nonmonogamous predatory behavior. "Our bourgeois, not content with having the wives and daughters of their proletarians at their disposal, not to speak of common prostitutes, take the greatest pleasure in seducing each other's wives" (Marx and Engels, 6:502). Marx and

Engels, however, were not cultural or historical relativists. They posited history as not just progression but rather progress. In critiquing the origins of patriarchy, Engels did not seek to reinstate matriarchy, and he clearly rejected any idea of nonmonogamy. Engels argued that the historical development of monogamy in patriarchy "created the possibility for the greatest moral advance which we derive from and owe to monogamy—a development taking place within it, parallel with it, or in opposition to it, as the case might be, namely modern individual *sex love*, previously unknown to the whole world" (Marx and Engels, 26:177; emphasis added). Arguing through a notion of dialectical progress, Engels suggested that the negative oppression of patriarchy carries with it a positive potential for the moral freedom in the monogamous relationship of a heterosexual couple. In his support of this notion of sex love, Engels echoed bourgeois feminist reformers who opposed the double standard applied to male sexuality while supporting an explicitly heterosexual conception of desire.

Engels's focus on monogamous heterosexuality intensified as he, following a path similar to Hegel's, turned his attention to the history of the family. His initial incentive for examining family history is found in its relation to production—the motor of historical change. In his analysis Engels presented changes in biological reproduction as being dependent on changes in production. The family, both as the initial source of material production and the source of "the production of human beings" (Marx and Engels, 26:132), acts as site of these changes. This proposition has been at the heart of all subsequent research on the history of the family. In analyzing how the various historical forms of reproduction were due to the forms of production, Engels elaborated the materialist position put forth decades earlier in *The German Ideology*. Yet he shut down the radical critical potential of that moment by reinforcing the idea of historical progress in terms of sex love, collapsing production and reproduction into one overdetermined, homogeneous system of desire.

Clearly Engels never called for or attempted to understand (sexual) desire as heterogeneous. And the sex of sex love should not be confused with an open acceptance of forms of (mutual) pleasure(ing) that are hinted at in even Kant's definition of marriage: "a contract for the [married couple's] mutual use of their sexual attributes" (Kant, *Metaphysics*, 280). Sex love was based on a privileging of heterocoital breeding. And ultimately Engels's collapsing of production and reproduction led him to denounce "nonreproductive" sex. He attacked homosexuality and lesbianism in his discussion of ancient Greece, twisting and contorting his argument so as to be able to both explain and condemn the sexual economy of the ancients. And he laid the blame for Greek male homosexuality on the "degradation" of women that resulted from the Greek's enforced patriarchal monogamy. Homosexuality indicated the decay of ancient Greek culture. "But the degradation of the women recoiled on the men themselves and degraded them too, until they sank into the perversion of boy-love, degrading both themselves and their gods by the myth of Ganymede" (Marx and Engels, 26:173). Sex love reveals itself here to be incapable of containing sexual difference. The moment of heterogeneity in sexual desire is assessed through a moral framework in line with this period's pathologizing models of sexuality.[12] Sexual difference sinks into sexual perversion, and a utilitarian theory of desire/love consistent with Marx and Engels's basic materialism emerges. Thus one goal of a queer reading of Marx must be to explore the possibility of a queer materialism.

Overall the analysis in Engels's treatise addresses only gender difference, an analysis that relies on an understanding of gender as a point of stable role and identity. Even if technology undoes the import of the physical differences between the genders in regard to labor, it does not undo the physical difference or, perhaps better phrased, the double vision of physical difference. The German term *Geschlecht*, on which Engels relied, contains and collapses gender and sex, masking the performative aspects of gender. Nevertheless, at this point we can recognize that men and women, masculine and feminine, remain the essentialist correlated polarities posited by Hegel. Sex love as a trope is nothing more than the bourgeois ideal of Hegel radicalized as a utopic antithesis to the everyday of bourgeois lived experience. Engels's logic allows the ideal of bourgeois marriage to be realized even in the absence of the economic constraints imposed by the sexual division of labor. In refusing to distinguish sex from reproduction and in keeping sexuality imbricated in gender, Engels retained sexuality as a sphere of social control, a justifiable point of incursion into individual experience, the site of sex panic. It is hard to comprehend Engels's commitment to monogamy and reproduction, however, given the complicated "domestic arrangements" of the Marx and Engels households—hardly havens of the moral advance of sex love.[13]

The understanding of reproduction fits into Marx and Engels's materialist analysis whereby reproduction is "elevated" to a status equal with production. While this elevation still maintains certain problematic distinctions (reproduction with nature and species, production with culture and needs), it opened up space for eventual discussions of domestic production. Thus their approach to gender proved productive in inquiries regarding women's labor, domestic labor, the history and sociology of the family, prostitution, and so on. Following Marx and Engels, however, these studies have tended to subsume issues of sexuality under gender, equating sexuality with women's issues.

What happens to Marxism if we think sex, as Gayle Rubin enjoined us to do over a decade ago? The discussion of sex love betrays a certain Nietzschean nihilism. Sex love did move the discussion away from a Hegelian presumption of the family as morally immanent and substantial form. It also certainly opened up our ability to think of patriarchy in a more differentiated form than that described by Bachofen. The analysis of *The Origin of the Family* presents a model of analysis at the heart of contemporary discussions of male homosocial organization. Of course, sex love focused attention on reproduction, setting it alongside production and putting forward a two-spheres model of gender. Moreover, to recognize gender relationships and sexual dynamics as shaped historically frees us from the trap of the natural, giving rise to a dynamic perspective that Marx himself had certainly begun to envision. "Therefore, *human objects* are not natural objects as they immediately present themselves, and neither is human sense as it immediately is—as it is objectively—human sensibility, *human* objectivity is directly given in a form adequate to the *human* being" (Marx and Engels, 3:337). Knowledge of the past and recognition of the transformations of history—knowledge that things were once different, that the objective world will not remain the way it is, and that things will be different again—return to us a desiring individual. Marxism confronts us with the recognition that there is no essential subject whose form is cast by nature. Wherever such a natural "cast" is invoked, it proves itself to be not the artless mold outside human construction it claims to be. Rather, this invocation of nature appears under the Marxist lens as ideologically wrought fetters binding and restricting the possibilities of material form.

Beyond Heterosex Love

In the light of sex love, what had once appeared to offer the individual freedom in human emancipation proves to do otherwise. Marx may have overturned the Hegelian dialectic, but he did not lose the Hegelian totalized subject; for both Hegel *and* Marx, fully emancipated civil society relies on a radical equality that erases not just difference of status but also subjective difference—namely, difference of desire. The desiring individual turns up here, but Marx's pastoral seems to portray a gated community closed to differences of desire. Individuals marked by heterogeneous, untotalized desire hang out on the margins, looking in, sensing, oddly enough, that there ought to be room here. The earlier assertion that the subject of the pastoral is an individual defined by an inherent uniqueness embodied in the phrase "he wishes" must be modified. The promise of a "freedom to" rests on a conception of all subjects as inherently unified, as particularly like-minded. The contingencies of desire that define the freedom of such subjects can take place only within a limited terrain. Yet the problem of desire evokes all the keywords of Marxism: *conflict, economy, materialism, production, labor,* and so on.

The terrain of the pastoral scene is formed within the proletarization inherent in capitalism, within which process Marxism, from the *Communist Manifesto* to *Capital,* sees the promise of the revolution. For the revolution to work, proletarian consciousness—a unification, a proletarian "identity"—must form: "the proletarian movement is the self-conscious, independent movement of the immense majority, in the interests of the immense majority" (Marx and Engels, 6:495). Proletarization, however, has not proved successful at universalizing interest—a revolutionary proletarian consciousness. On the one hand, this process constitutes perhaps the most fundamentally radical promotion of affiliative politics to emerge from the nineteenth century. On the other hand, Marxist discourse established limits to affiliation by simultaneously promoting a radical "filiative" politics that offset any affiliative potential in Marxist-oriented governance.

In Marx's work the revolution and the unchaining of the desiring individual's productive forces require first a move from the existence of the vast majority, or class in itself, to a self-conscious movement, or class for itself. Marx invoked a paradigm of science that requires a performative to accomplish this transformation. Lenin observed that left on its own, the working class is capable of organizing only through unionism. Having observed this "failure" of the working class to behave properly, to make the full transition to class for itself, Lenin and subsequent Marxist revolutions relied on a performative in the form of the party, transforming it into the site of performativity and in effect a radical filiative politics. The "dictatorship of the proletariat" thus lost any of the affiliative potential it contained when Marx coined the term. Indeed, without a fundamental awareness of the dynamic of performativity here, we are left no affiliative possibilities in the practice of Marxist governance, no real way out of the prospect of Hegelian totality.

Queer materialist considerations suggest routes to universality other than that of totality. First, we must reject the paradigm of science in the discourse of proletarization. The transition from class in itself to class for itself, as with other forms of identity, proceeds via a performative.[14] Second, we must reexamine how material conditions determine subjectivity and consciousness. Pauperization certainly plays an objective role in capitalism and establishes similar material conditions for an otherwise disparate group, yet a union of the interests and desires of the vast majority does not follow from this experience. This dual union cannot be achieved as a result of the heterogeneity of lifeworlds I have already explored. A heterogeneity of determinations precludes a homogeneity of desire. And third, we should follow Hegel in recognizing that desire gives rise to subjectivity. The subject exists only when there is desire. Pace Hegel *and* Marx, however, the more differentiated and *uncontained* this desire is, the more intense is the subjectivity. It is not the universal (e.g., the state) that unites desires. Rather, it is desire that compels the universalizing process, drawing the subject simultaneously into commonality and into particularity.

There is little desire or pleasure in thinking sex with Marx and Engels; in truth, few people have tried.[15] The analysis of sexuality has simply not had the same effect. Sexuality remains a blind spot for Marxism, subsumed under discussions of gender, women's oppression, and bourgeois family structures. While sexuality is partially constitutive of these structures, identities, and oppressions, it is not solely attendant on women or the family. The struggle for gay and lesbian liberation invited Marxism to examine how the capitalist mode of production, the heterocoital imperative, and heteronormativity are interconnected. That struggle challenged Marxism to recognize sexuality in itself as constitutive of material relations—much as the struggle for women's liberation did for gender. Here we can find the beginnings of a queer materialism.

The Political Economy of Homosexuality

Beginning in the 1970s a number of gay Marxists sought to apply the terms of political economy to their analysis of their own sexuality as one of the negating forces to capitalism. Following on Engels's work in *The Origin of the Family*, they focused on the antagonisms established by the bourgeois nuclear family and its enshrinement of not just a heterosexual but also a reproductive imperative.[16] In this work the family operates according to the dictates of economy and state superstructure defined by Engels. Gay Marxist work of this period overlooked Engels's claim that homosexuality originated as a degeneration brought about by the patriarchal family. Instead, they identified the family as the source of homophobia.

In an analysis reminiscent of work from the 1970s, John D'Emilio undertook a dialectical analysis of capitalism's relationship to gay identity.[17] D'Emilio, however, recognized capitalism to encompass forces that both require and supersede the bourgeois family form, forces that negate and support gay identity. D'Emilio suggested that "capitalism has created the material conditions for homosexual desire to express itself as a central component of some individuals' lives; now, our political movements are changing consciousness, creating the ideological conditions that make it easier for people to make that choice" ("Capitalism," 474). D'Emilio opened up a more elaborated discussion of political economy. He moved away from viewing homosexuality as simply an object of persecution and oppression. Dialectically D'Emilio recognized capitalism as generating conditions both for the possibility of homosexual identity and for the negation of homosexuality. Indeed, the previous chapter showed that homosexuality emerged with heterosexuality as the negation necessary for the very substantiation of heterosexuality. Proceeding dialectically, however, D'Emilio also identified how capitalism weakens the nuclear family, making possible the supersession of this antagonism: "Capitalism has led to the separation of sexuality from procreation. Human sexual desire need no longer be harnessed to reproductive imperatives, to procreation; its expression has increasingly entered the realm of choice" (474).

Even in the 1980s, when gay politics focused on minority emancipation instead of human liberation, D'Emilio continued to assert the liberatory role of the gay community. "Our movement may have begun as the struggle of a 'minority,' but what we should now be trying to 'liberate' is an aspect of the personal lives of all people—sexual expression" ("Capitalism," 474). Ultimately, to accomplish this goal queer materialism must withdraw from assessing homosexual emancipation as negating the fetters on desire. To further a positive human emancipation, any contemporary discussion of gay political economy must take into account the flexibility of capitalism. Even if capitalism required the bourgeois nuclear family, and this family required capitalism, this is an historical contingent truth, not a permanent universal one. Filiative form and economy are interrelated. Beyond the role of reproduction and homophobia, however, queer materialism can attend to the structure of the market. In seeking to escape the crisis of overproduction, capital has historically followed two routes: further exploiting existing markets and breaking open new ones. Precisely because they are outsiders, lesbians and gays form such new markets.

Indeed, the homosexual market, under prohibition as closet market, created a resource for the extraction of labor and value within nineteenth-century capitalism.[18] Homosexuality created a cottage industry for an informal economy supported and extorted through blackmail and hustling, as well as through protection rackets targeting bars and other gathering places. As Hirschfeld pointed out a century ago, such economic activity would not have been possible without the state's prohibition of homosexuality. With the removal of the prohibition, however, a new exploitable market is made available to the more formal capitalist economy.

Following waves of domestic partner legislation beginning in the 1980s and attempts at gay marriage legislation in the 1990s, it appears that private property has broken the fetters that bound it to the bourgeois nuclear family.[19] Private property can now equally accommodate serial heterosexual and serial homosexual monogamy. Further, consumer capital requires precisely the choice that D'Emilio located outside the family. Indeed, the 1990s witnessed a wave of marketing designed to create product loyalty among gays and lesbians, joining consumerism to sexual identity.[20] Annoyingly to the gay left, capitalism has incorporated gay emancipation as a marketing technique. And many lesbians and gays have accepted this position, offering the fundamentally anti-Marxist proposition that economic emancipation can provide the route to political emancipation.[21] Having once been bound into oppositional status, they may well perceive the new objectification by the market as emancipation. It definitely intensified the integrationist impetus of lesbian and gay emancipation, propelling gay emancipation more fully into bourgeois concerns. Whereas once their exclusion of homosexuality marked the state and civil society as oppressive and perverse, integration into the market led many to understand state and civil society as "cured."

Marketers have even attempted to present gays and lesbians as having larger disposable incomes than do those in other demographic segments. This strategy did not represent the full lesbian and gay community but brought to the fore only an "untapped" gay middle class. At the same time the far right capitalized on this "information" by using it to support their position that gay rights are special rights. The logic goes something like this: parents, proving themselves responsible and upstanding family types, have to support families with their income. Gays and lesbians irresponsibly avoid family obligations, live the high life, and still beg for more "freedoms."[22]

For a queer materialism, perhaps the strongest insight to emerge out of gay political economic analysis was the identification of the nexus of desire, economy, and identity. In a provocative statement designed to explode traditional forms of economic analysis and to appropriate political economy for queer studies, Richard Cornwall defined the foundation of political economy as "the concept of each person's tastes or preferences, i.e., desire" ("Queer Political Economy," 89).

Queer Conflict

According to the preceding analysis, capitalism established the material conditions for homosexuality. Capitalism's reliance on the bourgeois nuclear family as the foundation to its mode of production also positioned homosexuals as a site of conflict. Nevertheless, over time capitalism also recognized in the gay subculture a fettered market into which it could expand. As the gay liberation movement becomes increasingly bound to the capitalist mode of production, entwined in homosexual integration, and committed to liberal tolerance, it becomes increasingly bound to the present political order. The gay role in the project of human emancipation that D'Emilio identified becomes more distant. Marx's understanding of human emancipation requires a break with this present order.

Those who advocate gay emancipation through capitalism, who find their liberation in their existence as a market, who experience their desires as represented in ads for scotch and automobiles, might wonder why a break with the present order is necessary. At the same time, those advocates who denounce current trends and rally around the slogan "it's a movement, not a market" run the risk of promoting a politically romantic notion of self-fashioning. If it were a matter of a simple romantic call to become our better selves, then a break with the present order would be not just unnecessary but impossible. Providing a response to both groups, Marx indicated that the problem with the present order is that it contains certain kinds of contradictions, certain kinds of negations and conflicts that limit the desires of the vast majority. Furthermore, these conflicts and negations propel the present order toward its own undoing. With or without the gay liberation movement, the move to human emancipation must and will happen.

Certainly lesbian and gay men will play a role in any project of human emancipation. But what role? As subjects of negation in the modern period, gays and lesbians continue to provide a self-conscious energy in the rebellion against the negation of desire. Of course, they will never constitute the vast majority required for a radical break. They can do so only ideationally, in coalition with other groups in conflict, other groups whose desires are negated by the present order. Indeed, the present order reveals others existing as negation, a larger field of queers beyond gays, lesbians, bisexuals, nonnormative straights, S&M practitioners, fetishists, transgendered people, chubby chasers, bears, raunch lovers, kinksters, WSers, CBTers, and so on. What positions them as queers is not the acts in which they engage but rather the coercive norms that place their desires into a position of conflict with the present order.

A queer materialist analysis must take care in its assessment of any of these groups. Marxism sets us to look for the "class with radical chains." Those in such a group must have their desires fettered by the mode of production in such a way that the inevitable breaking of those chains will transform the entire mode of production. The analysis of the political economy of homosexuality indicates that any of these queer groups could likewise present themselves as a market. And indeed there are already scotch ads directed toward trannies and trannie chasers. Nevertheless, sexuality maintains a significant but problematic radical potential in the present order. The problematic derives precisely from the mechanisms of conflict described by Marx, and an exploration of it offers a critique and extension of Marxism along three lines.

First, queer sexuality challenges and is challenged by the dialectic of conflict in Marx. Marx drew from Hegel his dialectical understanding of conflict: two terms exist in a state of conflict, one term acting as the negation of the other. For Hegel, the state of antagonism is resolvable only through a synthesis of the terms. Hegel's discussion of the lord versus the bondsman provides the quintessential account of this understanding. Marx retained the basics of this account of conflict while focusing more firmly on class conflict (e.g., feudal aristocracy vs. bourgeoisie and bourgeoisie vs. proletariat). Marx, however, relied not on synthesis but on the total negation of one term as the resolution of the antagonism. The negated term had to assume the position of a universal positive term for the dialectic to resolve; thus the proletariat could come to the fore not through reformist synthesis with the bourgeoisie but only through a revolutionary negation of the bourgeoisie.

Subsequent analyses of non-class-oriented oppression have relied on an understanding of antagonism that follows Hegel more than it does Marx. Binary patterns of oppression based in those essentialist identities that emerged in the nineteenth century—for example, masculine versus feminine, male versus female, or heterosexual versus homosexual—or even race oppression could not accomplish the total form of negation required by the Marxist revolution. There are few theorists who, from within essentialist paradigms, have even flirted with this idea of total negation.[23] Binary essentialist models of oppression, following a Hegelian trajectory, bound themselves either to reformist state-oriented measures or to a politics of negativity of the type promoted by Adorno and Sartre.

To circumvent this impasse, queer disruptions of essentialism must necessarily undo the stable identity relationships of these models of oppression and open up other possibilities of analysis that move away from binary models. Explorations of sexuality's discursive relation to gender, class, race, vestmentary habits, religious practices, zoning laws, kinship structures, medical practices, and so on can remove sexuality from the essential identity-based models established in the nineteenth century. These analyses, however, must also attend to possibilities for agency. Political subjectivity is determined by existing structures. And we must thus attend to the mechanisms and structures that cause queer conflict. The nineteenth century still provides the primary classifications in contemporary politics. Thus, for queer theory it is important to recognize how the nineteenth-century designation *homosexuals* structurally and discursively places individuals as threats to heterosexual desire. At the same time, it is important to recognize that the conflict that resides in sexuality is not proper to lesbians or gays (or heterosexuals, bisexuals, transsexuals, zoophiles, etc.). This conflict results from particular, historically determined antagonisms of individuals placed into the position of negation. It is furthermore important to recognize that the conflict that resides in sexuality is not the same as the conflict that resides in desire as such.

Second, Marx's structural analysis of conflict challenges and is challenged by queer sexuality. Marx's radical shifts and revolutions are distinct from idealist romantic self-fashioning in that his analysis remained material, identifying structures distinct from consciousness that gave rise to "the class with radical chains." The analysis of surplus value locates the structural source of negation in the mode of production. It is the cause of pauperization, creating a vast majority of propertyless workers, wage slaves, thereby causing a material form of universality. Furthermore, surplus value is a necessary mechanism of capitalism and therefore also its mechanism of destruction. Consider the following much simplified account of Marx's analysis of surplus value. The worker sells her labor to the bourgeois in order to answer bio-needs. The employer contracts with her, however, for a period of time that exceeds the worker's own interests. She must work longer than simply meeting her needs requires, yet her pay only just meets those needs. This time spent laboring in excess of individual need becomes profit for the employer and returns nothing to the worker. This extracted profit always goes to the employer, meaning that all the worker can hope to do is meet biological needs, while the employer is able to fulfill increasingly elaborate desires. This mode of production sets the worker against her interests; her labor serves only the interest of the bourgeoisie and can in no way allow for the elaboration of her human desires.

As understood in these terms, the problem of conflict is not with the bourgeois fulfillment of desire. The bourgeois increase of possible material desiring is not the problem. This increase in desire is not directly bound to a bourgeois desire for the limitation or decrease of the worker's ability to desire; it is bound directly to the structure of surplus value. It is a subtle point but significant. For Marx, the goal never was—and, for queer materialist analysis, never should be—to limit desire. In fact, the problem is the limitation placed on desire. The employer can increase her ability to extract wealth from the worker and therefore her ability to desire based on the surplus labor of the worker. Surplus labor limits the desires of the laborer structurally, not as a result of the employer's desires as such.

This analysis of surplus labor identifies a queerness that is distinct from sexuality but relates to sexuality through the common term *desire*.[24] The result of surplus value is an ever-increasing army of laborers whose desires are ever further cut off from the wealth of the material world they themselves produce. Their desires become queer to this world and to their own interests. They have only limited means to experience their own desires, but they can witness the expanse of material wealth through which the bourgeoisie desires. Thus their desires are at odds with their material existence, which leads them to want to transform their conditions. Queer desire thus presents itself as the universalizing term in Marxism.

Third, a queer materialist critique challenges and is challenged by the Marxist understanding of ideological conflict. The commonality of desire identified between sexual and labor queerness encourages queer materialist analysis to attend to that common term and collapse the two forms of desire. Yet there is reason to distinguish the two. On the one hand, sexual queers are aware of their negation and seek to act in their interest, to fulfill their desires. They are aware of their conflict with heteronormativity, although they might not be aware of heteronormativity's relation to the mode of production. On the other hand, the vast majority of workers do not experience their queerness. An experience of their negation remains distant, even absent. According to Marxist analysis, they do not know or act according to their own interests.

Capitalism establishes its own universalizing claims that seem to offer wealth to all. Capitalist discourse holds that the general production of capital should raise wealth for everyone, so that the buying power of the rich "trickles down" to those who have less wealth. In the history of capitalism the borders between classes have come increasingly to appear porous and indistinct, making it seem that all can pull themselves up by their bootstraps and, through industry and hard labor, enter the bourgeoisie. The analysis of surplus value, however, indicates that the vast majority can never realize either of these universalizing claims. These claims and their supporting analyses can therefore be oriented only toward the successful reproduction of the capitalist mode of production itself. Keeping these three points of queer conflict in mind, in the following section I explore in more detail how capitalism connects desire to sexuality and production.

The Mode of Desiring Production

As was discussed in the first chapter, Kant distinguished bio-needs and contingent wants from essential sexual desire. Hegel returned to this distinction, recognizing bio-need as a universal and elaborating its significance in relation to contingency. "There are certain universal needs, such as food, drink, clothing, etc., and how these are satisfied depends entirely on contingent circumstances" (*Elements*, §189). Contingency here establishes a dialectic of biological necessity and material possibility. When seeking to answer their needs, humans have relied on immediate material possibility but have also had to confront material shortages. Human historical-technological development rests on this contingency. What humans had to produce to answer bio-need and how they produced it resulted from the material conditions in which they found themselves. In his analysis of material conditions, Marx radicalized Hegel. Picking up from Hegel's observations on technology, society, and progress, Marx allocated the production of needs a primary place in historical development. "The satisfaction of the first need, the action of satisfying, and the instrument of satisfaction which has been acquired, leads to new needs; and this creation of new needs is the first historical act" (Marx and Engels, 5:42). Expanding needs and their satisfaction becomes the stuff of material technological change and therefore of history. Such a position resonates only at the point when the historical period dominated by biological need was giving way to a different mode of production.

The history of human development is the progress from bio-need to liberated desire. Such a condition of "need" or desire permits displacing a morality of subsistence with a relativism of the contingencies of desire. Need made multiple presents the individual with choices. Choices presume a decrease in necessity. That is, the (original) choice between being clothed or naked was made in the face of extreme necessity. The choice between a rainbow T-shirt with nifty slogan, a fab designer tank top, or a 100 percent cotton V-neck is made in such a low level of necessity that only want and opinion seem to be left. This does not mean that desire is autonomous, but it does mean that when bio-need drops out, only materially manifested desire (i.e., choice) is left. The tremendous increase in production resulting from industrialization let humans emerge from under the sway of bio-need, and thus contingent desire came to supersede need. When the issue is no longer whether one has enough food but which type of food to choose, when fear of famine disappears, the distinction of need no longer obtains.

The transformations of the means of production and thereby the transformation of what is produced likewise result in a transformation of the possibility of choice, opinions, and wants. Marx observed that the commodities of capitalism answer wants equally, and whether "they spring from the stomach or from fancy . . . makes no difference" (Marx and Engels, 35:45). Desire is liberated so that individuals can pursue their humanity in the development of their desires as tastes, preferences, and opinion. The possibilities for desiring as such expand. In truth, these observations mark the transition from a need-based production to a desire-based production.[25]

It might surprise those who understand Marx as a critic of capitalism to find that the economic writings reveal a real sense of hope in the manner through which labor is transformed in these conditions. Indeed, Marx identified labor's liberation from need as a distinguishing characteristic of the truly human: "man produces even when he is free from physical need and only truly produces in freedom therefrom" (Marx and Engels, 3:276). The lack of need transforms the conditions of production; labor, too, is freed from necessity. Once unencumbered, labor takes on the character of play and pleasure.

> Economizing . . . does not mean the giving up of pleasure, but the development of power and productive capacity, and thus both the capacity for the means of enjoyment. The capacity for enjoyment is a condition of enjoyment and therefore its primary means; and this capacity is the development of an individual's talents, and thus of the productive force. To economize on labour time means to increase the amount of free time, i.e. time for the complete development of the individual, which again reacts as the greatest productive force on the productive force of labour. (Marx and Engels, 30:383)

Or at least it has the possibility. Although capital-driven industrialization brought about such great positive progress, it also established specific forms of negation. This economy of enjoyment, this pastoral utopia, could exist only after capitalism.

Indeed, Marx's description, based in aspects of the present, discerned only as if through dark glasses the vague outlines of a possible future based in a certain humanist hope. The present, however, was and continues to be dialectically fraught. As I discussed regarding the second point of conflict, the possibility to desire is not evenly distributed in capitalism. More important, the inequity of distribution resulting from surplus labor is structural to capitalism and actually accelerates inversely, so that an increase of the desiring possibilities of a minority decreases those of the majority. In full exclusion this majority could only desire the possibility of desire. Capitalism proves more dynamic, however, more flexible. The mode of production must step back from full exclusion. The laborers must be left some experience beyond bio-need, for otherwise the objects produced by their labor would have no consumers.

We can add to this conflict another dynamic of desire identified by Marx. This dynamic assists in the reproduction of the relations of production, tying the limited desire of the worker to the flow of capital itself. Marx recognized that the economic cycle of capitalism requires individual desire to be directed to individual commodity consumption. In this commodity fetishism the material construction of desire subsumes all forms of desire, directing them toward commodities. According to Marx, this process turns our desires away from a mode of human production, averting human wants from their greatest resource, their fellow humans. Desire becomes object desire, and fellow humans are desired as fetishes, not as humans. We no longer desire each other in a "human" fashion. The limits of my abilities are demarcated not by the nexus of others but rather by the buying power of my take-home pay. We degrade ourselves to a means and become the playthings of alien powers.

Even if capitalism had caused productive capabilities to expand to a point where needs were subsumed in desire,[26] Marx suggested a second tendency in this development. Whereas desire supersedes biological need in capitalism, commodity production requires that desire become needs. Contemporary consumer capitalism, dependent on desire for the consumption of commodities, turns desiring itself into a need. Thus the capitalist mode of production on the one hand makes desiring production possible, and on the other hand it prevents that desiring production from producing human desire.

In their critique of consumer capitalism, Adorno and Horkheimer charted a development of capitalist desiring production that Marx could have only vaguely recognized. They approached the production of needs in this mode of production with suspicion. Consumers whose needs once provided the rationale of production are now caught in a "circle of manipulation and retroactive need" that projects new needs retroactively back onto the consumer (Horkheimer and Adorno, *Dialectic*, 121). The masses are *deceived* about their needs, and the culture industry can offer them only deception. Here we enter into a mode of desiring production that is not a break or outlet for desire but rather the production of desire for the sake of production itself.

Horkheimer and Adorno would have us understand the needs produced by the culture industry as instilling false articulations of desire in the individual. But how can desire in itself be false? This presents a central problem for queer materialism. It is certainly easier to describe how desire operates than to adjudicate its truth. For example, desire may be positive or negative, a flight to or a flight from. It may lead to action. It may focus singularly on an object. It may migrate wildly, leaping from object to object. It may be directed at no object at all but at an idea or a concept. And then it may not. Nevertheless, if we follow Horkheimer and Adorno, the rationale for the determination of desire as true or false must lie in the term *retroactive* and not in *manipulation*. Marx showed that desire is part of a process of material manipulation. Historical activity is based in the production of the material means to answer a desire and thereby, in answering that desire, creating new ones. Material activity manipulates desire as much as it manipulates matter itself. Each time one reaches out to fulfill a material need, the grasping leaves the individual with hands full of new desires.

Material technological advancement, the general improvement of the human condition, proceeds in this manner. At the same time, retroactive manipulation, like the relationship of surplus value that underlies capitalism itself, breaks with Marx's process of human production. Instead of engaging in material activity as a means to improve production, we labor to acquire new objects. In this relation desire does not drive material activity to improve the human condition; rather, desire is directed to material objects divorced from further production. Now material objects are produced to incite desire, and desiring itself becomes a need for the next object.

The discussion of the culture industry, however, shows that desire is caught up in a system of material supply and demand, where it appears as "natural" that desire is unfulfillable. In supply and demand, moreover, desire appears only as need. Desire as need leaves us with only an impoverished, passive, reified awareness of our social bonds. Instead of experiencing desire for others, we need the objects that materially bind us together. Capitalism thus leads us away from human emancipation. This mode of desiring production renders enjoyment of consumer goods unavailable, leaving us only desire for them. The new dinette set or the trip to Majorca does not even pretend to sell itself as offering the experience of transcendence that Schopenhauer hoped to find in music.

Consumerism can offer nothing closer to transcendence than satiety, and satiety is, at least for consumerism, the death drive itself. Lack of satisfaction is guaranteed. Satiety must constantly be overcome to produce ever ready consumers. Yet the ache of lack, that apprehension of desire's unfulfillability, must be forestalled. Easy credit revs up the economic appestat, inducing commodity binges. It provides consumers with the illusion of equality. Metaphoric equality masks real economic difference. The "have-nots" may, if they use enough of their credit potential, live like the "haves," but only by amassing debt that transforms them into "have-even-less-than-nots." And lack continues to drive desiring production, so that the bankrupt consumer would do it all again, as "e-z-credit" institutions know.

Although Adorno and Horkheimer's insight about objects offered as artifacts of the culture industry continues to resonate, and although the mode of production they described expands in quantity and advances in quality, most readers are left suspicious of the consciousness they describe as inhabiting this mode of production. Probably no consumer is so passive and so ill informed. What if we proceed from the position that most (if not all) consumers recognize that the freedom offered by the choice between fifty different brands of soap or thirty-five different brands of toilet paper is no real freedom in itself? In fact, we may recognize that consumption is not about freedom at all but about a maximization of (purchasing) power. The consumers in the culture industry are constantly forced into a situation of reading and calculating so that their desires can be supplied in the best way possible for them—the desiring individual becomes devoted to maximizing purchasing power. Although the image this mode of production presents as ideal is one of an individual consuming in peace, this is not the experience of the vast majority. Indeed, if advertisements for easy credit, worry-free financing, and convenient purchasing indicate anything, it is that consumer desire is bound up with anxious debt, fretful calculation, and forced consumption. The "have-even-less-thans" are aware of their indebted status, and they often calculate on an ability to replicate the threat of states such as Mexico or Brazil: the threat simply not to pay your debt.

The problem of the culture industry and of consumerism is of course not simply commodities or consumption. It is the mode of production and consumption. Just as liberal theorists once contemplated the danger in democracy, the majority's tyranny over the minority, Horkheimer and

Adorno contemplated the tyranny of the lowest common denominator over the entirety of society. Horkheimer and Adorno explain that the schematism, standardization, and massification of the artifacts held up in the culture industry as necessary objects of desire all result from a "false identity of the general and the particular" (121), the "heroization of the average" [die Heroisierung der Durchschnittlichen] (156).[27] Capitalism's tendency toward monopolization becomes a tendency toward homogenization not simply of the commodities offered as objects of desire but of the desiring individuals themselves. Individuals as subjects desire and make choices, but subjects as individuals must increasingly make those choices in a homogeneous field. And this homogeneity limits rather than liberates the desiring individual.

If we accept this diagnosis, we still might consider the result if this tyranny of the least common denominator, the tendency toward homogenization, is experienced consciously. The image of the Eastern bloc, with no consumer goods and a gray, deadened, desireless citizenry, was always the terrifying fascination of the Western bloc. Such a point of fascination certainly suggests an unarticulated anxiety on the part of the subject—namely, that this is actually his condition. And if it is experienced consciously, why does it not result in action against it? Why does Marx's promise of revolution remain unfulfilled? Why do homogenization, anxiety, and dread not generate revolutionary consciousness?

In its liberal form capitalism contains mechanisms to confront this awareness and put brakes on revolutionary consciousness. The welfare state is of course the biggest brake to the full experience of a "pure" capitalism. This shoddy Bismarckian demagoguery appeals to the anxieties of the people, masquerades as socialist practice, and simply keeps citizens sutured to their state form. Further, to sublimate the awareness and anxiety of coercive homogeneity on the desiring individual, consumer capitalism increasingly mobilizes heterogeneous lifeworlds. Sexuality and gender, for instance, once limits to material desire and sites of heterogeneity, no longer need be deployed to contain material desire—they can unleash it. In the earliest forms of consumer capital, gender became the vehicle for new forms of consumption. Herbert Marcuse (for a while a force in the Frankfurt School, along with Horkheimer and Adorno) showed perhaps better than anyone else how sexual freedom became "a market value and a factor of social mores" (*One-Dimensional*, 74; see also Breines). Here the third point of conflict outlined previously comes to play a role in the development of the mode of production.

In the middle stage of consumer capitalism sexual desire was removed from the distinct position to which Kant and Hegel relegated it and brought within the flow of capital. Sexual desire does retain a certain distinction, but it now operates alongside material desire.[28] Marketing strategies in consumer society employ sexual desire to motivate material desire. Marcuse described this freeing of sexual desire in industrialized society as repressive desublimation, thereby describing a paradoxical effect. Sexual desire is not freed; it is bound up tightly into the mode of production.

Sexual desire now acts as means to make contingent commodity-oriented desire appear as need. Commodity capitalism relies on this bridging position of sexuality, the experience of a real, urgent need for commodities, to keep distribution fettered. Sexuality as a conduit of desire now becomes bound up with the commodity form itself. And sexual desire as a significant form of incitement in capitalism is increasingly coerced into homogeneity. That is not to say that everyone observes the heterocoital imperative, but it is to say that homosexuals are incited to consume just like heterosexuals. On an immediate and superficial level, heterosexuality has long served as a conduit for desire, inciting the consumption of everything from cars to bananas. More recently capitalism has recognized the possibility of tapping into homosexual desire as incitement to consume commodities. Sexuality in itself becomes a mechanism of the means of production.

To continue to sublimate the experience of coercive homogeneity, new (still heterogeneous) lifeworlds must be drawn into the totalizing activity of capitalism. They must be tapped, opened up, and expanded into, and they lose their heterogeneity in this process. For instance, since the success of the "We Are the World" project, consumer spending has been spurred on in new directions by tapping politically oppositional lifeworlds. The culture industry has realized that it can sell consumer products through the activation of the social or spiritual desire that once was a repository of anticapitalist activity. Now consumers are spurred on by promises that their purchase of everything from compact discs to refrigerators will improve the world, the environment, the conditions of the starving children in Africa, *and* their own personal appearance and sex appeal. Indeed, in advanced industrial society capitalism and political emancipation need no longer be in opposition. Capitalism can continue its necessary expansion through the relentless opening of markets by relying on the elimination of exclusions from political emancipation.

The suggestion, then, is that the culture industry and consumer capitalism will foster the process of homogenization, and there appears to be no way out. We have reached the end of history, as Francis Fukuyama has suggested. And unless we can identify some aspect of desire that remains surplus to the totalizing force of capitalism, we must accept such a diagnosis. We might ask, if people are supplied from a homogenized field, how can they desire outside it? Can they know what *else* they may desire? Horkheimer and Adorno answered no, suggesting that such subjects are robbed of their imagination. I disagree. After all, why do we have discontented consumers? If we briefly look away from the suggestion that consumer capitalism incites us to consumption, we can ask why there is not "contentment" in consumerism in itself.

Within advanced industrial societies distribution can support only individual and not human emancipation. While the means of production have advanced to answer bio-needs, very real fetters on distribution still prevent the full supersession of need, because new needs are constantly generated. We do not need to focus on the "Third World" for examples. We live in a historic juncture when, even in the midst of "boom economies" in the most highly industrialized country on earth, record numbers of citizens suffer from hunger, homelessness, disease, incarceration, and psychic traumas. Yet in this mode of desiring production bio-need exists alongside desire for consumer commodities. And understandably sometimes such desire takes precedence over bio-need.

While capitalism draws sexual desire into its totalizing activity, sexual desire has never entirely lost the special status Kant accorded it. It now tenaciously straddles the divide between bio-need and contingent desire, bridging them, yet not fully drawn into the coercion of capital. Sexual desire retains a transformative relationship to the mode of production, foremost because it retains both a form outside the heterocoital imperative and a function distinct from commodity consumption. A portion of sexual desire remains outside heterosexuality or homosexuality, outside regimens of sexuality altogether. And it remains outside the capitalist mode of production. Marcuse suggested throughout his work that sexuality, in its special status, remains a desire that everyone experiences and that everyone can, at least temporarily, satisfy. Further, it is in sexual desire that a glimpse of the possibility of real human emancipation remains. This analysis tended to confuse sexual activity with human emancipation. The influence of Marcuse and Wilhelm Reich on the sexual liberation movement set sexual activity as a goal in itself. Marcuse's focus, however, was not on the identification of sexual activity as a goal but rather on the consciousness that arises from this material, physical activity. Sexual activity remained a form of activity that reminds us of a cycle of desire outside the capitalist mode of production and consumption.

The portion of sexual desire that remains outside the mode of production becomes a subversive or queer desire. Within Marxism revolutionary activity ultimately arises from an ontological position, albeit a historically and socially contingent one. A form of revolutionary consciousness, queer desire results from the mode of desiring production itself. Desire itself is not a motor of revolution. Desire might propel the transformation of the means of production, but it does not guarantee a transformation of the mode of production. Yet capitalism itself gives rise to contradictions out of which queer desire emerges.[29] Any attempt to transform the mode of production must attend to the political potential of sexual dissidence, subversion, queerness.

I distinguish queer desire from considerations of the status of sexual minorities within the dynamic of desiring production.[30] Sexual minorities might appear to provide the basis for subversive activity in relation to capitalism, but we should not confuse rebellious behavior directed at political emancipation with Marxism's larger historical, transformative project of human emancipation. The leadership of sexual minorities has been primarily concerned with political emancipation and not their role as agents of human emancipation. Sexual minorities organized as such have primarily sought communicative recognition from the state. The subversion of queer desire does not emerge from assuming a minority status. Such a conception exceeds homo/hetero oppositions, and in that sense it is *as antigay as it is antistraight*.[31] Unlike the antigay homonegativity inherent in the heterocoital imperative, however, a liberation of desire leaves no room for homophobia.

The Marxist promise of human emancipation is not simply an impossible utopian projection, a longing for an unrealizable harmony and transparency of subjectivity, or a subject who knows and can articulate his or her proper desires. (The following chapter examines how the longing for transparency gave rise to a diametrically opposite discourse, one of latency systems.) Nevertheless, despite Marx's identification of the unchaining of the desiring individual as the goal of human emancipation, Marxism has never yet broken with the basic essence of Kantian and Hegelian subjectivity: the reliance on an autonomy based in self-mastery. Nor has it broken with the heteronormative means to coerce social homogeneity. Within Marxism it has been possible to acknowledge capitalism as a system of desiring production, but the significance of the desiring individual has not been recognized. Self-mastery rather than queer desire was taken as the ontology of revolution. In the next chapter I examine as a case study a particular instance of the way the desiring individual came to haunt the party, the revolution, and the general critical discourse and how self-mastery in the discourse of liberation drove it toward domination and totalization.

Notes

1. For a reflection on how the gay rights movement has bound itself to expansions of state authority, see my essay "Political Organizing."

2. This is not to say that being gay or lesbian should automatically make one immune to patriotism or even nationalistic jingoism. The point is the curiously heavy *emphasis* the U.S. media and the movement have placed on the military as a symbol of acceptance and legitimacy, even though it affects far fewer people than do such issues as hate crimes, tax benefits, health care, adoption, and discrimination in general.

3. The relationship of Marxism and feminism was similarly explored in Haraway, 127–49.

4. For a related discussion of this essay, see Brown.

5. *Mensch* is the German and Yiddish word for "human being," "man," or "person." In the context of the Enlightenment, *Mensch* took on a connotation of universalism, commonality, education, and rationality that stood in opposition to class privilege. For a discussion of this term and its relationship to the project of tolerance and the Enlightenment see, Grell and Porter; Vovelle; Hubschmid.

6. The title of the *Declaration of the Rights of Man and Citizen* displayed a certain attentiveness to the division of human and political emancipation, striving for emancipation in both civil society, the realm of man, and state, the realm of the citizen. But the *Declaration* did not recognize these as dialectically related and in its attempt to regulate both could guarantee only a "freedom from."

7. For a complete discussion see Halle, "Political Organizing."

8. Marx and Engels are perhaps the best known of the Left Hegelians, but they were certainly not the only ones seeking to keep Hegel's corpus animated. Significant essays of the other members of this circle, including Ludwig Feuerbach, Bruno Bauer, and Max Stirner, have been collected in a useful introductory anthology; see Stepelvich.

9. Louis Althusser, out of his desire to (re)assert Marxism as science, would perhaps compulsively designate this process as the unfolding of Marx's problematic. Whatever the reason, Marx quickly leaves behind discussions of species-being and becomes more of the Marx of Marxism. Nevertheless, Marxism has already taken shape in this critical moment. See Althusser, *For Marx.*

10. For explorations that exhibit an antiessentialist dynamic, see, for instance, the discussion of nature and industry in *The German Ideology* (Marx and Engels, 5:38–41) and *Economic and Philosophical Manuscripts* (Marx and Engels, 3:270–83). For a discussion of Marx's approach to gender, see Di Stefano.

11. Engels's book, however, had little immediate effect on the male-oriented homosocial organization of the German Socialist Party (SPD). For a discussion of the structure of the socialist women's movement and its relationship to the "broader" socialist movement, see Frevert; Herve.

12. The most significant publication of this type during the period is Krafft-Ebing's *Psychopathia sexualis.* The book was frequently revised and reissued well into the middle of the twentieth century. Also significant is the work by Carl Friedrich Otto Westphal, who coined the term *inversion* in 1869. For influential works that followed, see Weininger; Bloch. While not a matter of a pathologizing model of sexuality per se, Darwin remains of interest for the Marx and Engels of this period.

13. The Engels and Marx households had a complicated interweaving that included not only financial exchanges but possibly also exchanges of one "illegitimate" child. The embarrassment that would have motivated the swap seems odd coming from the authors of the *Communist Manifesto,* with its diatribe against the predatory nature of bourgeois males on *all* females. Now in their older years, this might serve to illustrate how biography is more estranging than fiction. For a discussion of the problems of paternity that developed between the two, see Siegel.

14. Donald Morton argues that "for queer theory, class conflict turns out to be just another set of problems, marginal at best, which have no determinate relation to sexual politics. Admittedly queer theory opposes some aspects of bourgeois life: what it opposes, however, is only the oppressiveness of homophobia as a set of attitudes and discourses. By neglecting to address and attack homophobia . . . as a structure of oppression inextricably bound up with class structure, queer theorists/critics become 'sex rebels' rather than revolutionaries committed to radical social transformation" ("Review," 475). It is rather absurd and reductionist to suggest that queer theory addresses only homophobia. This criticism evokes those that suggest homosexuals to be narcissistic, concerned only with self-interest. Morton rejects queer theory as a bourgeois theoretical undertaking, in the same way that the Marxist orthodoxy of the "good old days" rejected Weber, Simmel, the Frankfurt School, Brecht, Lukács, and so on.

In general Morton adopts a dogmatic Marxist approach that is better oriented toward finding shortcomings in the works of others. He has yet to accomplish himself what he demands of others. Morton is not simply encouraging considerations of class conflict; he insists on its primacy. Morton's dogmatism leads him further to suggest broadly that "postmodern discourse" rejects class struggle, and it prevents him from considering that the problematic of class struggle brought forward by postmodern discourse is that class consciousness has not emerged in the manner anticipated by Marx. Alternative explorations are therefore in order. There is no structural reason that precludes queer theory from relying on class conflict, but there is every reason to accept that class consciousness is determinate in only a small minority, at best. And without this consciousness, the promises of Marxism can never be fulfilled. I do not want to go into a lengthy discussion of Donald Morton, having learned that critical engagements elevate the object of critique and that debates seem to establish an equality of discussants. Rosaria Champagne has initiated a critique of Morton's "(anti-)queer Marxism."

15. See Haraway, 127–49. For a more traditional Marxist approach to questions of gender, see Mutari, Boushey, and Fraher.

16. See McCubbin; Escoffier, *American Homo;* Raffo; Penelope; Marshall.

17. D'Emilio's positions have changed over the years. For more recent perspectives, see D'Emilio, *World Turned.*

18. For further discussion of the homosexual market, see the work of Escoffier, especially *American Homo.*

19. Recognition for domestic partner arrangements continues to be a central point of gay and lesbian political activity. For U.S. media discussions of varying domestic partner agreements and legislation, see Richardson, et al.; "Domesticated Bliss."

Further, the Human Rights Campaign Fund maintains a list of cities, colleges, and private employers with domestic partner laws; see <http://www.hrc.org/issues/workplac/dp/dplist.html>. For an organizers discussion, see R. Anderson. May 1999 saw the first city-sponsored domestic partner registration in Germany. Hamburg followed the model of many U.S. cities, allowing same-sex couples to register with city hall.

20. For a discussion of the history of lesbians and gays in consumer capitalism, see D. Clark; Gluckman and Reed; Field; Lukenbill. See also Albelda et al.; Amott and Matthaei.

21. The collection Martin Duberman edited, *A Queer World*, contains a number of essays in the "Homo-Economics" chapter that consider capitalism as the proper vehicle for lesbian and gay emancipation. Michael Piore's essay in the volume, "Economic Identity/Sexual Identity," is critical of such developments but can do no more than hold up a notion of there being no "one single way to be a human being" (506) as a naïve ethical basis for opposition.

22. In the United States this line of analysis is prevalent in groups such as the Family Research Council, Focus on the Family, and the National Legal Foundation. It has been used in voter initiatives throughout the nation, spearheaded by groups such as Colorado for Family Values, the Oregon Citizens Alliance, and the Maine Christian Civic League. Bob Dole issued a rejection of "special rights" in his 1996 presidential campaign.

23. Consider, in this regard, the works of figures such as Monique Wittig, Franz Fanon, or Catherine MacKinnon. In general, although these theorists might recognize a need for total negation, they step back from the full consequences—Fanon into national separatism and MacKinnon into despair and state authoritarianism.

24. In this vein Rosemary Hennesy defined the project of a materialist queer critique: "While it acknowledges that sexuality is always discursively constructed, it simultaneously insists that the materiality of sexuality is not *just* discursive. This perspective shift encourages us to address how the normative discursive construction of sexuality as heterosexuality has been implicated in divisions of wealth and has helped organize state relations and formations of citizenship" ("Incorporating," 273–74).

25. The term *desiring production* was central to the work of Deleuze and Guattari in *Anti-Oedipus* and to a certain extent in *A Thousand Plateaus*. My own usage is indebted to but distinct from this deployment. In *Anti-Oedipus* they wrote explicitly, "The truth of the matter is that *social production is purely and simply desiring-production itself under determinate conditions*" (29). Desire might transform social conditions, but not according to material conditions chosen by the desiring individual. We need to maintain a distinction between socius and psyche or risk falling back into idealism.

Further, Donald Morton has broadly distinguished between need production and desiring production, where the latter is mainly the form of analysis of queer theory. This, he has suggested, is a nonmaterialist approach. Morton's distinction between need and desire is specious. It devolves into an oddly monistic materialism with an idealist form of analysis, evincing a limited relation to historical materialism. This may be because Morton spends a great deal of time in a critical rather than a productive mode. Moreover, Morton seems to suggest that queer theory and the analysis of desiring production is inherently non- or even antimaterialist. Now even if desiring production has been discursively deployed in queer theory as a nonmaterialist form of analysis, this deployment would not be a necessary aspect of queer theory but one open to critique. And certainly in my own considerations desiring production is understood as a central aspect of the mode of production as such.

26. Marx relied on this development for the possibility of a successful revolution. It is the line of analysis developed throughout his work from the *Communist Manifesto* to the economic writings. The supersession of biological need combined with the proletarization of the majority meant that for the first time in human history, the ruled majority could overthrow the ruling minority and achieve a society oriented toward the rational/human distribution of resources.

27. Cumming's translation, "the idolization of the cheap," actually misses the sense of the original (155). I provide my own translation here.

28. At the advent of modernity, however, capitalism had not yet taken on this form, lacking its present supply and demand of consumer goods. The example of the Dutch

Republic, where charges of sodomy helped to contain material desire, illustrates a different relation of sexual to material desire. See, for example, Simon Schama's discussion of the Dutch Republic in the Golden Age. For the way in which sodomites as dandies became the target of persecution, marking the end to the Golden Age and the new limited means of the republic, see also Rey.

29. In this regard Stanley Aronowitz has similarly suggested that "desire is the ontological need that becomes *surplus* in relation to capital (remember Marx's formula that capital is a surplus in relation to *necessary* labor time). Thus desire is the surplus of the surplus, and the social order is condemned to define itself in terms that undermine the normative structures of imposed discipline and repression" (95). This passage from a previous decade now resounds with too much faith in inevitability, especially at a historical juncture when employees, in periods of record corporate profits, "understand" their forced downsizing "for the sake of the company"; when sexual minorities beg for the "rights" to uphold bourgeois marriage and family forms; and when liberal, gay, and women's political action committees support conservative candidates in electoral politics.

30. In his now classic assessment of the "crisis" of historical materialism, Stanley Aronowitz wrote rather hopefully about the role of desire and sexual subversion in capitalism. "Capital is constantly conflating desire and need in order to insure the conditions of its own reproduction. The counterlogic is to maintain their separation, to define desire as that which goes beyond need and is unrecuperable by the prevailing structure. This is the basis for the subversive content of sexuality in those groups that have been forced or place themselves on the margins of social life, and the communities that are established informally by working people on the shopfloor and in the neighborhoods whose existence limits the accumulation process" (249–50). Aronowitz's attention to sexually subversive groups *and* to labor-based forms of organization is an insightful gesture toward coalition politics. His language does not rely on a promotion of gays and lesbians as possible coalition partners. Aronowitz avoids attributing an inherently progressive status to sexual minorities. Rather, he recognizes a mutual goal shared by sexual subversives and shop-floor activists—a commonality of desire.

31. This statement must be understood. I do not want to set up gay identity as the problem or set up some delusion of freedom from contradiction. Nevertheless, gay identity as a product of negation must be exceeded if we are to find positive terms with which we can exceed heteronormativity. This is a difficult proposition to negotiate. Recall how Nietzsche's position as anti-anti-Semite did not turn him into a "philo-Semite." Did his antifeminist or his antisocialist positions make him the opponent of women and workers? We can also recall how in the 1980s Monique Wittig, in the face of certain strands of feminism from the period, adopted the rather bold position that, from a lesbian perspective, the switch from patriarchy to matriarchy would result only in the exchange of one system of domination for another. Before this "antigay" position may be mistaken for some repulsive "postgay" nonsense, recall also that Wittig left the term *lesbian* intact as a position from which political negotiations could take place.

4 Reich, Fromm, Adorno: Latency Paradigms and Social Psychology

> Before its birth, the child is . . . appointed as a subject in and by the specific familial ideological configuration in which it is "expected" once it has been conceived. I hardly need add that this familial ideological configuration is . . . highly structured, and that it is in this . . . more or less pathological . . . structure that the former subject-to-be will have to . . . become the sexual subject (boy or girl) which it already is in advance. It is clear that this ideological constraint and pre-appointment . . . have some relationship with what . . . Freud registered by its effects as being the unconscious. But let us leave this point, too, on one side.
>
> —Louis Althusser

Let us return to that point Althusser put to one side in the passage I've used as an epigraph. Its goal being not simply to interpret but to change material conditions, Marxism focused on the socius, neglecting the psyche. I have used the terms *socius* and *psyche* throughout this study, but here I employ them to accomplish two tasks. The first is to obviate the debate in Marxist discourse about the relationship of the base to the superstructure.[1] When Marx initiated his discussion of base and superstructure in *The German Ideology,* he compounded two concerns. He sought to move away from idealist conceptions of consciousness to a materialist understanding. In doing so he used *superstructure* to designate the first concern, the political, legal, aesthetic, educational, and so on—in short, the institutional aspects of the material world. He also used it to designate the second concern, the separate problem of consciousness. Few have had difficulty understanding the base's relationship to the institutional aspects. It is consciousness that presented the most difficulty. At its most interesting this debate has always been about the status of consciousness. I maintain that for Marxism, consciousness is a separate question and should be treated as such. With the terms *socius* and *psyche* I seek to shift the discussion more directly to the question of consciousness. With *socius* I designate the terms of the base and the first aspect of superstructure—in short, the material world. With *psyche* I seek to encompass various aspects of the individual: social being, unconsciousness, consciousness, and subjectivity.

The second task I seek to accomplish flows from the first. With socius and psyche I pick up the discussion of earlier chapters. I turn to terms that are sufficiently broad and encompassing to serve as structural designations. They can and will take on historical specificity. At the same time, they allow for an intersection of multiple discourses—discourses that have often been at odds. In this chapter I specifically focus on such a problematic. The concentration on the socius in Marxism led to a neglect of the psyche. Freud's concentration on the workings of the psyche produced a science that neglected the socius. In the interbellum a number of prominent theorists began seeking to join the two sciences. Many hoped that Freud might offer a corrective to Marx, a way to draw together socius and psyche. They saw the divide between socius and psyche as problematic, limiting their ability to confront the crisis of fascism. As the masses seemed to drift further from the transformation of the socius described by historical materialism, the psyche or the desires of the masses became increasingly opaque. A science of socius *and* psyche, it was hoped, would give clear direction through the crisis of fascism.

I begin this chapter by turning to a particular development in the discourse of social philosophy, the emergence of the field of *social psychology*. Seeking a response both to neoidealist psychology, with its singular emphasis on the psyche, and to determinist materialism, with its singular concentration on the socius, various figures in 1920s Germany began to explore more flexible models of relations between socius and psyche. Social psychology continues to find practitioners in the United States as well as Germany, but this earlier work has now taken two forms. The first was the basically liberal work of Kurt Lewin (1890–1947). Lewin brought his work into exile in the United States, where it has continued to exert influence as a quantitative project.[2] The second, operating outside liberal confines, was Freudo-Marxism. I examine the latter here. The social psychology of the Freudo-Marxists knotted the socius and psyche together, but this form of social psychology failed to take hold. In this chapter I examine why it failed. What is significant is that the discursive threads of this knot continue to be drawn into the present. Freudo-Marxist social psychology may have failed, but its concerns present a still-current problematic of modernity.

The initial examination of these social psychologists will reveal that they suffered from a dread of the homosexual that limited the critical potential of their social philosophy. This limit marks the starting point of a queer critique. Their queer dread will indicate why their social psychology failed. In the section entitled "Latency, Repression, and More Contemporary Debates" I explore the legacy of this psychology's paradigms. I introduce the concept of *latency systems,* which I then explore in detail in the next two sections. The second half of this chapter then returns to the discussion of fascism and sexuality to set out new directions for social psychology. To this end the section "A Return to the Repressive Hypothesis" picks up the question of repression—neglected since Foucault's critique—to distinguish between primary and secondary repression. The goal in the final section is to reinvigorate this discourse, freed of the paradigm of latency.

Antihomosexuality and Antifascism in Social Psychological Paradigms

In reflecting on the problems of contemporary social philosophy, Axel Honneth in effect identified it as a discipline without a task. Too broadly defined in Germany and too narrowly defined in the English-speaking world, social philosophy needs a new direction. Thus he writes, "It is imperative for social philosophy to find a determination and discussion of those developmental processes of society that can be conceived as processes of decline, distortions, or even as 'social pathologies'" (370). Honneth redraws the line between social philosophy and social psychology. Queer theorists should jump to inspect any mention of social pathology, whether it is in quotation marks or not. My interest, however, lies not in Honneth's work but in the discourse whereby such a connection is drawn. Honneth is one of the leading inheritors of the tradition of critical theory and the Frankfurt School, which makes it both understandable and surprising that he should identify this as the direction of social philosophy. It is understandable in that it was the Frankfurt School in particular that first established the examination of social pathology as the purpose of social philosophy. To this end its members developed a specific project of social psychology. It is surprising in that Honneth offers this "rather traditional" determination without reflection (370). And as I will show, the ongoing ability to retie this knot is an indication of the urgency with which queer theory must engage critical theory.

Social psychology and fascism emerged at the same time. Indeed, the former sought to define the latter, to describe its effects on the socius and the psyche. Further, this social psychology was not content to interpret these effects. It also sought to develop methods to transform the conditions of the masses subjugated by fascism. To accomplish this task, this description of the socius and psyche, this social psychology sought to suture together the insights of Marxism and psychoanalysis. Unfortunately, this attempt resulted in an untenable equation of fascism and homosexuality. Homosexuality became the psychological source or origin of a socioeconomic structure. In this construction the homosexual is the site of governance out of control: a hyper-regulation of the self, homosexual repression was seen as mirroring a hyper-regulation of society, fascist oppression. Let me rehearse an argument briefly and follow the development of this position.[3]

In Wilhelm Reich's early writings, homosexuality functions as a threatening demon of the oppressive double standard of sexual morality. In a move reminiscent of Engels's work in *The Origin of the Family*, Reich framed homosexuality as the outcome of the restriction of women's sexuality: women, afraid of getting pregnant, become frigid and reject men, thereby forcing them to become homosexuals. In subsequent work homosexuality continued to appear as a negative foil to "healthy" heterosexuality. Homosexuality became a specter haunting every aspect of male sexuality, conscious and unconscious.

In Reich's analysis "On the Specific Nature of the Forms of Masturbation" (1922), heterosexuality formulates the categorization of acts and establishes the valuations of health. Reich described four masturbatory types (all male), with various subcategories, and judged their healthiness on the basis of their relationship to a perception of heterosexual behavior. Ideal is the decidedly heterosexual type 1, who engages in "pelvic thrusting." Reich described the pelvic thrusting as symbolizing "alloeroticism" ("Über Spezifität," 142).[4] He understood these thrusts as representing a heterocoital act, as if such thrusting does not accompany acts other than coitus. Reich did identify the "active homosexual" type 4, special form 1. More interesting is type 3, which consists of men who lie on their backs without thrusting their pelvises. They were designated as exhibiting a "feminine mindset." Recognizing in their masturbation a pathology, Reich judged their prognosis to be "not very favorable" (142). The image of thrusting as an indication of a masculine mindset clearly relied on, and promoted, cultural images aligning activity and passivity with masculinity and femininity. The third type's likely homosexuality is a latent threat, unknown to the masturbator but not to the clinician. Actually, throughout Reich's work the judgments of (hetero)sexual health resorted to material drawn from the self-identification of the individual. The analyst's observations and diagnosis then appeared as superior to any form of self-knowledge or self-disclosure.

In *The Mass Psychology of Fascism* (1933) the homosexual took on a new role. Speaking of the Greek patriarchal order, Reich stated, "The male rule of the Platonic era is thoroughly homosexual." To which he then added, "The same principle controls unconsciously the fascist ideology of the male leadership" (*Massenpsychologie*, 139). Here Reich drew the first direct discursive connection between homosexuality and fascism. This line moved from the state of the individual psyche—the "principle" that "controls unconsciously" and, as homosexual, is determined as negative—to the mass form of a socius governed by fascist ideology. It turned the negative, violent, oppressive structure of fascism into a surface effect, the true source and meaning of which was located at a deeper, latent level of a homosexual psyche.

As the development of psychoanalysis diminished the significance of conscious processes and self-knowledge, the analyst's diagnoses became able to identify causes, effects, and ultimately psychic truths unknown to the patient. Of course, physicians perform a similar role in other clinical settings, revealing to a patient, for example, that the truth of a pain is cancer. The patient understands the diagnosis and undergoes treatment. In psychoanalytic work the diagnosis should likewise reveal a truth that can guide the patient's treatment. The type of mass clinical diagnosis in which Reich engaged, however, displays little concern that the patients find themselves identified by the diagnosis. There is a move here toward a concern with latent truths of character unknown to the subject but observable by the trained analyst.[5]

A different twist to this work appeared with Erich Fromm, who concentrated in particular on the role of latency in his own elaborations of social psychology, especially in discussions of the connection between homosexuality and fascist authoritarianism. For Fromm no sexual act signified the homosexual—at least no homosexual act. The individual who submitted to fascist authority was homosexual because of his character. Character acted as a sort of psychic base. Again, as with Reich, homosexuality marks the site of a negative psyche, both a product and producer of a negative superstructure, fascist authoritarianism. "From a physiological perspective the average authoritarian man is heterosexual. From a psychical perspective, however, he is homosexual" ("Sozialpsychologischer Teil," 126). Still, Fromm did leave open the possibility that the homosexual psyche might express itself through homosexual acts: "In a number of individuals, this component of homosexuality will also transform itself rather frequently into manifest homosexuality in the more narrow sense" (126). Such manifestations of homosexuality did not interest him, however, nor did they present themselves as a solution to authoritarianism.

Fromm's colleagues in the Frankfurt School supported the thesis of a latent base to mass social effects. After the Holocaust became public and the horror of the genocide began to be felt, Max Horkheimer and Theodor Adorno sought to describe the psychological source of the anti-Semitism underneath it all. Finding the locus in a forbidden act, the desire for which had to be converted to find expression, they explained that "the forbidden action which is converted into aggression is generally homosexual in nature" (*Dialectic*, 172). Their analysis followed "the psychoanalytic theory of morbid projection" (172). This theory of morbid projection led them under the surface of the Holocaust, under the surface of the individual subject, and into the construction of the unconscious. The psychoanalytic map they employed took them to the source of this abnormal prohibition: "the homosexual character" (172).[6] In this understanding homosexual desire appears not so much as latent but as inherently repressible—the desire that cannot be named. There is no discussion of a social component of repression. It is presumed that the id of the homosexual, naturally unable to express homosexual desire, found release elsewhere—in anti-Semitism. Clearly no desire to liberate this repressed psyche from the social constraints that lead to anti-Semitic aggression is expressed here.

In the now famous study *The Authoritarian Personality*, in the section entitled "Submission, Passivity, and Homosexuality," R. Nevitt Sanford analyzed "Mack" as a particularly clear example of the authoritarian personality. Sanford stated: "Even without this piece of evidence we would be led to hypothesize repressed homosexuality in order to explain some of the outstanding features of Mack's personality development. The material is replete with manifestations of authoritarian submission" (Adorno et al., 798). The evidence of which Sanford spoke was Mack's fear concerning a picture of a hypnotist. Here as elsewhere the analyst's diagnosis outweighs the subject's self-identification. Latency and repression come to explain why this self-knowledge is unavailable to the subject. And authoritarian submission was regarded as a consequence of homosexuality.

Confronting mass political and cultural developments that seemed beyond their control, the previously cited theorists sought to develop social psychology as a tool of analysis. Yet they could speak of a mass psychology only by positing universally shared natural drives. The idea of these drives, as part of a teleological character development, also allowed the belief in the possibility of a harmonious social order. A society that fosters full development of its members' drives will guarantee the harmonious coexistence and satisfaction of those members. Such a conception challenges a Hobbesian or Nietzschean understanding of the foundations of social organization, which sees individuals by nature in a state of conflict and competition. It also challenges a Hegelian or Heideggerian conception, according to which individuals are naturally harmonious in their filiative spheres (*Volksgemeinschaft*). In the various directions mass psychology took, however, the control of desire continued to be the purpose and goal of social organization. Desire was understood only as sexual desire. All forms of desire other than sexual desire were excluded or constituted as secondary. And within sexual desire only one form was admitted as healthy: heterosexual desire.

On his own, however, Adorno could not leave the topic of homosexuality alone. In his article "Freudian Theory and the Pattern of Fascist Propaganda" (1951) he attended to the question of mass behavior. There he noted that Hitler "was well aware of the libidinal source of mass formation through surrender when he attributed specifically female, passive features to the participants of his meetings, and thus also hinted at the role of unconscious homosexuality in mass psychology" (122). In a footnote to this remark, Adorno made clear that for his analysis, the borders between overt and repressed, conscious and unconscious homosexuality were fluid. The fact that homosexual love is far more compatible with group ties, he said, "was certainly borne out under German fascism where the borderline between overt and repressed homosexuality, just as that between overt and repressed sadism, was much more fluent than in liberal middle-class society" (177–78). Here Adorno explicitly drew a direct connection between repressed and overt homosexuals. The connection between homosexuality and sadism and the disregard for a more careful analysis of manifest homosexuality are reminiscent of Fromm's work. The assertions of a homosexual fluency in fascism that exceeded the fluency of liberal society is surprising given the information on the persecution of homosexuals that was available at the time. This was certainly a difficult and problematic position to maintain at that point in history, yet it was in keeping with the general position that kept the Nazi version of §175 on the books until 1969 and that refused to treat gay survivors as victims of Nazi persecution until the late 1990s.

Adorno figured prominently in the sexual reform movement of the postwar period. Even as he called for a more tolerant position vis-à-vis homosexuals, however, he sharpened his critique of homosexuality. In his article "Sexual Taboos and Law Today" (1963) he sought to support arguments being made in postwar Germany to decriminalize abortion and homosexuality. Adorno's "sympathetic" essay did acknowledge that many homosexuals can sublimate their desires into good art (the essay is so ridden by cliché, he could have added hair dressing) and therefore make positive contributions to society. It is significant that he offered an escape from repressed homosexuality other than aggression or authoritarian submission. The phenomenon of homosexuality continued to disturb and fascinate him, however. He may have held open the possibility of some positive social function for homosexual artists (such as his friend Thomas Mann) who sublimate their desires in their art, but not all would attain this positive social function. The negative repressed homosexual continued to exist. This homosexual haunted and threatened the fundamental masculinity of the heterosexual male. The man (he considered only men) who consciously understood himself as heterosexual and actively behaved as heterosexual could reveal himself as living a lie, a pure surface form of bad faith, a hidden source of negativity. In precisely what Adorno understood to be the positive masculine ideal then promoted by the culture industry, he spotted the negative opposite, the latent homosexual. I quote at length.

> *Tough baby.*—There is a certain gesture of virility, be it one's own or someone else's, that calls for suspicion. It expresses independence, sureness of the power to command, the tacit complicity of all males. Earlier, this was called with awed respect the whim of the master; today it has been democratized, and film heroes show the most insignificant bank clerk how it is done. Its archetype is the handsome dinner-jacketed figure returning late to his bachelor flat, switching on the indirect lighting and mixing himself a whiskey and soda: the carefully recorded hissing of the mineral water says what the arrogant mouth keeps to itself: that he despises anything that does not smell of smoke, leather, and shaving cream, particularly women, which is why they, precisely, find him irresistible.
>
> If all pleasure has, preserved within it, earlier pain, then here pain, as pride in bearing it, is raised directly, untransformed, as a stereotype, to pleasure: unlike wine, each glass of whiskey, each inhalation of cigar smoke, still recalls the repugnance that it cost the organism to become

attuned to such strong stimuli, and this alone is registered as pleasure. He-men are thus, in their own constitution, what film-plots usually present them to be, masochists. At the root of their sadism is a lie, and only as liars do they truly become sadists, agents of repression. This lie, however, is nothing other than repressed homosexuality presenting itself as the only approved form of heterosexuality. (*Minima Moralia*, 45–46)

While it might be easy to identify here a dim recognition that heterosexuality arises through a disavowal of its negative opposite, its alterior, homosexuality, this is not the case. Rather, Adorno puts forward, with the schoolyardlike taunt "Tough, baby," the assertion that virile heterosexuals are truly repressed homosexuals. He seems to want to produce a cleansed heterosexuality here. Adorno disavows the sadistic, repressive, lying, virile, arrogant, despicable, irresistible traits of heterosexuality. These become the traits of the homosexual. In an Orwellian inversion, suddenly the heterosexual appears as the threatened and beleaguered position. The heterocoital imperative does not regulate society, the strong are weak, the active are passive, the positive are negative, and oddly, the liberated are repressed. And Adorno, presumably identifying himself with purified heterosexuality, is left where? Disavowing homosexuality and discarding his dinner jacket, his virility, and his "irresistibility to women"? Might this explain why a few years later, the sight of the naked flesh of his female students would be enough to kill him? Adorno's heterosexuality certainly seems a shaky proposition.

The vision of homosexuality common to all these theorists is unrelentingly impervious to the discourse of the German homosexual emancipation movement. These figures grew up and were active in an era of insightful political arguments articulated by various homosexual rights organizations. The petition to repeal §175 was well known and had a lengthy list of signatories from within their intellectual and social circles, yet they never turned to these sources. Hirschfeld's work on sexual heterogeneity and the concepts already presented by Westphal or Ulrichs left no impression on their work. Even if they took exception to Hirschfeld's theoretical work, they should have recognized the heterogeneity of desire he documented instead of remaining purposefully oblivious to it. They found it appropriate to speak about the homosexual rather than with homosexuals, to reveal the truth of homosexuality rather than listen to the way homosexuality is experienced or lived out. The knowledge of homosexuality thus generated is fundamentally oblivious to the truth of homosexuals yet widely influential, and as such it is a good example of the coercive force of heterosexual lifeworlds. There is not a queering heterogeneity of desire but rather a singular queer lifeworld into which heterosexuals can project their own fantasies, a world populated by feminized males passively and latently submitting to the dictates of fascism.

As the preceding quickly makes obvious, the homosexual as social philosophical phenomenon provided the deep-structural source or base of a "surface" social, superstructural phenomenon. We should not wonder. Sexuality often served and continues to serve as a theoretical concept that marks the connection and source of widely disparate phenomena. The discourse of sexuality serves as a substitute for direct discussions of economy, power, taste, education, clothing, same-sex relational possibilities, and so on, condensing them into this single, albeit not simple, "deep-structural" phenomenon, as when homosexuality condenses and displaces discussions of fascism. These concepts of latency and repression of homosexuality also point to a discursive surface quality of masculinity. Masculinity inhabits the same surface as fascism in the previously quoted passages; it is not the cause of behavior but the result of some deep structure. Adorno's anxieties reflect how deep structures problematically relate to surface. The perversion or degeneration of homosexuality haunts the surface of masculinity. This structure versus surface relationship entails that the discourse of latent or repressed homosexuals forces *all* heterosexual men into the position of being *seeming* heterosexuals, men whose "real" desires might lay hidden to the world and even to themselves. Heterosexuals look like "real" men. They behave like "real" men. But they might not be real men. Indeed, if we could get beneath the surface of masculinity, we would recognize many heterosexuals for what they "really" are: active homosexuals. Social psychology in the Frankfurt School set out to reveal this truth—an unsurprising development, given that along with the "Red scare" we always had the homosexual scare.[7] Disappointingly, the reds were themselves scared of the homosexual.

I am not seeking to deny or endorse the existence of deep structures at this point, although I have clearly tried to reserve some space for desire that is distinct from rationality or consciousness. What concerns me is the coercive use to which deep structures are put. Philosophically we have too often been confronted with the false choice between surface and depth: either there is no deep-structural source to a surface material phenomenon, or there is only psychic deep structure, and the surface is only appearance. Obviously we must find some other form of description, but my goal here is to discredit this description of the homosexual origins of fascism.

To understand fascism we might turn to what Simmel referred to as *"Vergesellschaftung"* (sociality or sociability) and specifically to what Eve Sedgwick has referred to as "homosociality." Sadly, Simmel's much earlier term runs the risk of being forgotten, even though his work constitutes a large and elaborate opus. Sociality points to relational possibilities, filiation and affiliation, and not to sexual identity, especially not to a hidden one. In such a paradigm social form and consciousness do not present oppositions but are mutually constitutive. This paradigm suggests that fascism, anti-Semitism, and so on have nothing to do with (homo)sexuality and everything to do with (homo)sociality. The objects of my critical analysis here, however—Western Marxists in general and the members of the Frankfurt School in particular—confounded these two, setting up untenable paradigms. We could certainly place sexuality as one phenomenon of fascism, although a neither deep- nor superstructural one. Given that social psychology as developed in Frankfurt am Main was not the only place of such theoretical work, however, I find it necessary to stay focused on my critical object and put forward a more pointed rejection. The real conditions of real *homosexuals* have nothing to do with any of the previously identified phenomena. *Homosexuality* as discourse, however, appears to have everything to do with them.

Latency, Repression, and More Contemporary Debates on the Status of the Homosexual

The figures involved in the project of Freudo-Marxist social psychology went on to become the central theorists of the sexual revolution. They all rose to great prominence, Reich even achieving a sort of cult status. This prominence might partially explain why critiques of the connection between homosexuality and fascism/authoritarianism/anti-Semitism/sadism are extremely limited.[8] In fact, this connection has only recently been recognized. It should be clear that the homosexual as conceived in these works had no connection to our current vision of openly gay men.[9] Yet it should also be clear that the critical attention to this discursive deployment of the homosexual derives in part from the current manifestations of lesbians, gays, and other queers in state and civil society.

Some have objected to a queer reading of the Frankfurt School as a false or inappropriate imposition of a sort of political correctness on a group of theorists who had no knowledge of manifest political homosexuals. There are a number of responses to provide. We do not need to invoke contemporary paradigms of gender and sexual dissidence. The social psychologists under examination here not only seem to have been oblivious to the model of homosexuality promoted by the highly visible and theoretically articulate German homosexual emancipation movement of the prewar era, but they also ignored the more complicated understanding of homosexuality that Freud deployed in his own psychoanalytic paradigms. The active homosexual as such does appear in Fromm's work and in *The Authoritarian Personality*, but only to act as a visible and outward sign of a more significant and pervasive threat. Furthermore, the queer readings I have undertaken have sought to pay attention to historical context, to understand the historical period *wie es gewesen ist*. Such historicization does not mean, however, that an event or paradigm is over, part of the rubble heap of history. In fact, my own reading of this particular paradigm of the homosexual seeks to diagnose a symptom of modernity, one of the crises of common sense that has structured the social philosophy of modernity.

Note that even as "manifest" homosexuals came to have a more prominent position in state and civil society, this paradigm of the homosexual psyche did not disappear, and contemporary queers continue to confront it. The homosexual continues to be identified as the source of many of society's ills. The Christian right currently promotes a "pink swastika" explanation to fascism. Well-intentioned "liberals" and progressives also continue to point accusatory fingers at homosexuality, denouncing it as the source of fascism. Under their veneer of tolerance, they evince an ability to align themselves with Christian conservatives and the very far right radicals. In *Male Fantasies* Klaus Theweleit's discussion of "homosexuality and white terror" is filled with the word *homosexuality* in cautionary quotation marks as a gesture toward acknowledging that the social forms under examination have nothing to do with homosexuality, latent or manifest. Nevertheless, Theweleit does not leave the term behind and follows in the path of Reich and Fromm. Moreover, in his attempt to negotiate the fascist psyche, he remains bound to developing a type of homosexual practice that, as fascistic, should be denounced and medicalized.

In *The Mind of Stalin* Daniel Rancour-Laferriere expanded the social psychological paradigm beyond Hitler and fascism and identified a homosexual origin to Stalin(ism) as well. Homosexuality became the most advanced form of patriarchal oppression of women in the work of certain radical lesbian feminists and Marilyn Frye in particular. Not having sex with women (whom Frye argued do not want sex with men) is thus tantamount to reveling in all the privilege that patriarchy has to offer. Interestingly, Frye was speaking of manifest homosexuals, but her work inverted the paradigm, so that homosexual males serve as the paragon of masculinity, thereby transforming patriarchal heterosexual male desire into a sort of latent homosexuality. French feminism brought its own variation of the equation. Recall Luce Irigaray's discussion of hom(m)o-sexuality or Julia Kristeva's more complicated form of the equation, her invocation of the homological economy.

In the judicial system latent homosexuality came to provide a defense for criminal gay-bashing cases, as Eve Sedgwick's analysis of the so-called homosexual panic defense explored. Film theoretical forays into spectatorship from Laura Mulvey to Carol Clover delved into "the nature of the male sexuality that turns woman into an image of its desire and, crucially, the repression of homosexuality as one of the founding moments of that sexuality" (Mulvey, 59). Pat Califia's work on the politics of transgenderism productively explored how paradigms of latent or repressed homosexuality have haunted analyses of gender radicals.

Homosexuality functions as the central term in all these theoretical works, but the term is preceded by modifiers such as *latent, repressed,* or *pseudo-*. Here liberal invocations differ from those of the far right only in that the latter forgo modifiers. As a secondary term in these works, *heterosexuality* is preceded by modifiers that indicate dysfunctionality, for example, *misogynistic* or *fascist*. These writers draw the relationship among these terms to explain a greater social ill; the goal is rarely to remove the repression. Whether a source of anti-Semitism or a source of authoritarian submission, the homosexual functions within these critiques as the origin of pathological behavior. And all too often, the homosexual is inherently pathological, to be overcome, not liberated. This paradigm is further supported by a politics of coming out. When models of gay identity are based in a politics of coming out that relies on a narrative of coming to terms or coming to awareness of one's "true" identity, closeted existence takes up the function that latent or repressed homosexuality served in social psychological paradigms. To come out, one must accept and continually reiterate a term such as *homosexual* as defining the truth of a totality of existence. The outcome of all these models is to expose the individual to a coercion that is sometimes violent and sometimes willingly internalized. In any event, this review shows that what held true in the 1930s and 1950s holds true in the present. The real conditions of real *homosexuals* continue to have nothing to do with any of the previously identified phenomena. *Homosexuality* as discourse, however, continues to have everything to do with these phenomena.

From out of the gay wilderness Martin Dannecker's voice has risen to defend the Frankfurt School from "attack."[10] Dannecker set out to *defend* the Frankfurt School, and he began by placing Adorno et al. above critique, which meant that he had to approve their link between fascism and homosexuality. Dannecker then went on to take up the discussion himself, approaching this equation in the same problematic fashion; he forced the truth of homosexuality into deep structures and away from acts. I want to respond to Dannecker, but also to more than Dannecker; he stands here as a placeholder for all the other leftist and left-liberal discussions of homosexual latency already described, yet I take his more "seriously" in that it emerges from a figure who occupies a significant position within the gay rights movement itself.[11] In Dannecker's response all the problematic terms of the Freudo-Marxist social psychological paradigm of homosexuality came to the fore: *latent, repressed, unconscious,* and *manifest.*

To begin his defense of Adorno et al., Dannecker insisted that "with his reflections on homosexuality Fromm aimed, as did later Horkheimer and Adorno, not at a sexual but rather at a gender-related behavior, precisely stated at the relationship of heterosexual men among themselves that oscillates between power and submissiveness. The behavior of men among themselves was thematized by Fromm, to which thematization he lent a sexual connotation through this characterization as homosexual" (23).[12] In other words, the characterization as homosexual was metaphoric, with the tinge of sexuality an unintended result. A key aspect of his defense of Frankfurt derives from a suggestion of stylistic problems, a level of pure word choice. Fromm's poor word choice of *homosexual* resulted in an undesired sexual connotation. Are we really supposed to believe that theorists as prolific as Erich Fromm or Theodor Adorno were such sloppy stylists, that when they wrote about homosexuality, they really meant not homosexuality but rather a homosexuality without sexuality, a homosexual configuration that actually meant authoritarian submission? If they meant authoritarian submission, or male-male relations, why did they not simply use that phrase? Might wrestling or the military not have provided better sources to comb for metaphors of submission? In his uncritical defense of the Frankfurt School, Dannecker is unable to recognize how real (homo)sexuality and real (homo)sexual acts remain theoretically present in this supposedly sexless sexuality. If we accept from the start that Fromm, Adorno, et al. knew of the sexual "connotation" of homosexuality, the origin of authoritarian behavior they sought to identify was not only not sexuality but had everything to do with sexuality. Authoritarian submission was thus a surface phenomenon for which they sought the deep-structural source.

Going beyond the "metaphors" of Frankfurt, Dannecker then followed critical theory in his own analysis, positioning homosexuality as a deep structure and actually extending the analysis of Freudo-Marxist social psychology. Such homosexuality is not consciously available to the individual. Unawareness of its presence leads to what Dannecker defined as a "sexuality-less homosexuality" (22). Here Dannecker went one step deeper than Adorno et al. He did not speak about a sexuality that is repressed from expression. Dannecker put forward a paradigm of sexuality that is foreclosed from sexuality; it remains outside expression of any kind. It is *only* unconscious. In this paradigm homosexuality becomes an ontos or a noumena closed to the individual subject's perception. Not materially or consciously manifested in sexual acts, this sexual essence remains unknown until recognized in categories available only to the social scientist, not the individual subject: the truth of the being of the individual subject is discernible only to the analyst. Dannecker exhibited the phenomenological blindness typical of these paradigms of homosexuality.

Nevertheless, given Dannecker's insistence on both a connection between homosexuality and fascism and a disconnection between homosexuality and sexuality, what does homosexuality have to do with it? Theorists who identify homosexuality as *only* an "unconscious" homosexuality take distances from the violence of this analysis. When these theorists insist that the perpetrators of a particular social ill (e.g., fascism, Stalinism, or female masochism) are *really* homosexual, they resist examining other "suspects" closer to the surface and insist on the homosexual as a deep ontological perpetrator. The goal of a social analysis such as Dannecker's should at best result in the anagrammatic equation "sexuality – homosexuality = –homo," but a sexuality beleaguered by the foreclosure of same-sex cathexes is not the remainder of his equation. His "–homo" is a state of inescapable being.

Fromm's work on characterology left open the possibility that the practical direction of an individual's drive can turn to manifest homosexual behavior. Nevertheless, no sexual act signifies the homosexual— at least no homosexual act. The authoritarian submissive individual is homosexual because of his sexual desire. Fromm's understanding of character, an essentialist ontological state, derived from the individual's drive constellation and remains typical of this direction of analysis. In Fromm's failure to make a thorough and rigorous distinction between latent and manifest homosexuality, he gave the lie to Dannecker's assertion. The liberation of the homosexual was never the goal in critical theory or beyond. The homosexual as character, as individual drive constellation, as ontological state, is always understood as the problem.

There are lines of analysis where a discussion of the real repression of real homosexuals might prove theoretically possible, if not absolutely productive. Fascism, patriarchal masculinity, totalitarian persecution, and so on can be understood as emerging through a homosexuality taboo or rejection of male effeminacy. Such a taboo might act as a means to coerce mass behavior, that is, a discourse that promotes homosexuals as effeminate males and shames "real" men into rejecting homosexual attachments.[13] Here the rejection of homosexuality is tied to the rejection of femininity. But then the problem would be the deployment of taboo and effeminacy, and masculinity would be the problem, not homosexuality, and certainly not a –homo. Alternatively, a Dannecker-like proposal of a sexuality-less homosexuality that construes even repressed homosexuality as a source of fascism yet makes the problem be how to relieve the repression could then recognize homosexual liberation as antifascist practice. Like the other theorists, however, Dannecker did not follow this line of analysis.

One further reformulation of the equation remains available. The problem could be understood as one of homosociality and not of homosexuality. These social psychologists were familiar with Simmel's term *Vergesellschaftung,* but they did not explore its explanatory potential here. Dannecker seems vaguely to have recognized the concept's use value when he asserted that the discussion of unconscious homosexuality in critical theory designates "a desexualized and at the same time characteristic male-male relational modality" (19).[14] Even if we accept that a divide existed between the methodology of Simmel and the Freudo-Marxists, Dannecker's phrase "male-male relational modality" seems to suggest that a discussion of homosociality could follow in his analysis. It was from this very assertion that he set off in his discussion of sexuality-less homosexuality, deriving it from the "desexualized" modality. But let us step back from what threatens to become a too specific analysis of latent homosexuality. I want to shift this discussion to examine how the symptom or crisis of the paradigm under examination here does not lie with the term *homosexual.* I would like to explore how the problematic of social psychology is to be found in the term *latent.*

The Four Characteristics of Latency Systems

The terms *latent* and *latency* appear in widely disparate discursive settings. Nevertheless, these usages share certain structural characteristics. In psychoanalysis the term *latency* addresses various points, from the latent content of dreams to the latency phase. Such discussions are well known and theoretically compelling. In dream analysis it is not the manifest but the latent content that is the stuff of real interest. The manifest content is the obvious, remembered portion, but the latent is the hidden message, the real meaning of the dream, hidden by the mechanisms of repression. The latent content is not yet understood—but analysis offers hope that it might eventually be revealed. In the latency phase—between the resolution of the Oedipal conflict and the onset of adolescence—traumas experienced in childhood lie dormant. Neither repressed nor manifest, they await the surge of desire brought on by puberty to evidence themselves. They are there, but simply not yet manifest.

Certainly psychoanalysis is not the only discourse that employs a concept of latency. Francis Bacon relied on the terms *latent process* and *latent configuration* to describe processes beyond superficial observation. Robert K. Merton, the American sociologist famous for his research on deviance, identified the significance of latency for sociological thought, encouraging social observers to look beyond the avowed, manifest purposes of behaviors that remain unattained (he cites the Hopi rain ceremony as an example; we could recall the First Gulf War) to accomplish latent attained purposes (e.g., reinforcement of group cohesion). He further indicated how "the distinction between manifest and latent functions has been utilized in analyses of racial intermarriage, social stratification, affective frustration, Veblen's sociological theories, prevailing American orientations toward Russia, propaganda as a means of social control, Malinowski's anthropological theory, Navajo witchcraft, problems in the sociology of knowledge, fashion, the dynamics of personality, national security measures, the internal social dynamics of bureaucracy, and a great variety of other sociological problems" (63). While this extensive list comes from a now dated source, its breadth in both scope and influence lends it ongoing relevance.

In general latency pertains less to accounts of broad social behavior and more to discussions of subjectivity, where the latent appears as the true but as yet unmanifest self. The presence of a "true" self, however, means then that the manifest self becomes a mask, a sham truth, a lie. This latent self appears in Horkheimer and Adorno's vision of the culture industry. Here, unlike the sites of the latent homosexual, the latent is a positive term. Although it is never stated explicitly as such, in the culture industry the manifest self is deluded and out of touch with its real interests. It is a false self, a false consciousness whose desires are manipulated by media. The delusion of the manifest movie-going self refers us therefore to a latent, undeluded, truly enlightened self who is aware of the alienating processes surrounding it. In effect, there is a consciousness that objectively exists, in itself, yet does not subjectively exist, for itself.

A latent self is not coeval with the manifest. It is projected onto some place outside the present. The Nietzschean overman similarly requires a subject above culture, above three-dimensional time. In the case of the latent homosexual the latent corrupts the present and future of three-dimensional time with the threat of manifestation, of its very existence. The latent homosexual lingers, causing, for example, fascism. In Horkheimer and Adorno's discussion in *Dialectic of Enlightenment*, the true self, the truly human, is made latent by the culture industry in the present, and thus latency transforms the past and future into utopic possibility. It marks the present as a dystopia but manifest only to disgruntled crank critics adapting a protopunk affect.

Although not using the term *latent*, in *The Conquest of America* Tzvetan Todorov described a system of latency within religious discourse. The Inquisition brought to the New World its suspicion of the religious convictions of the convert. The priests of the Inquisition feared that the converts did not really believe what they professed they believed. We can understand this fear of false belief as a perception of a latent self. The priests of the Inquisition went as far as seeing heathen practice in the religious devotions of the converts. Watching a native offering flowers and ears of corn for the Nativity of Our Lady, the Dominican Diego Durán believed the worshiper did so "because through her an ancient pagan goddess [was] being addressed" (in Todorov, 205). Durán saw a latent paganism even in the manifest practices of faith.[15]

In the discourses of biology and nationalism, the latent marks a sort of dormant essence that has yet to be awakened. Additionally the latent appears in linguistic discourse. Linguistics was quick to identify and make manifest patterns on the phonetic, phonemic, and grammatical levels. The order of these levels was codified, and they now serve as the basic analytic tools of the discipline underwriting any claims to scientificity it makes. Semantic and semiotic intertextual meaning, however, has eluded such codification. The "final description" remains absent. One linguist, David Butt, observed that the semantic and semiotic levels of meaning are part of "the 'process' character of human speech," making them unavailable to easy structural resolution: "Patternings at the level of meaning . . . have not been so easy to explicate let alone formalize." Nevertheless, we do generate meaning, which "can only be the consequence of semantic and textual structure" (77). Thus within linguistic analysis, phonetic, phonemic, and grammatical patterns create a surface, while meaning lies in deep semantic structures as yet unidentified. Hence, while not immediately identifiable or identified, these structures are implicit. Alternatively, to paraphrase Freud, even if we could not prove their existence, we would have to assume them. In the analyses of figures such as Sapir, Sinclair, Coulthard, and Butt, semantic structures are latent structures. Butt's originality in approaching this problem rests in his efforts to incorporate chaos theory to address the linguistic dread of semantics. Chaos theory deals with the order implicit in systems otherwise perceived as chaotic, such as the system of semantics. Butt recognizes in this idea of implicit order a link to discussions of latent linguistic order initiated in the 1970s (see, e.g., Sinclair and Coulthard). The latent, like the implicit, is the unrecognized, "a part of a pattern which is yet to be articulated as order or pattern" (Butt, 81).

All these examples suggest a semiotics of latency. First, latency systems rely on a sense of futurity. Second, they necessarily lead to a theory of repression. Third, they rely on order as a meaning-bearing system. Fourth, in latency systems meaning becomes the key to coercive (even authoritarian) systems of knowledge.

1. Although the possibility of a hidden nature had long been accepted, latency emerged as a form of pathology only in the nineteenth century. This understanding of latency as a possibility for the subject stands in opposition to the transparent subject Kant proposed or the socially mediated subject in both Hegel and Marx. Where latency is pathologized, however, such a system also supports an understanding of the transparent subject as a goal or telos, the attainment of which is a desirable, healthy state. Latency may be a condition of the present, but it is not a permanent condition. A state of permanence and transparency becomes relegated to the future. Individual subjects may speak, act, and signify in ways that are not available to understanding in the present, but the meaning is not lost forever. It can later be revealed though a process; the latent or implicit can become manifest or explicit.

2. But why is it not transparent? The futurity of latency systems means, of course, that some block exists in the present. As latent, they involve some mechanism that hampers the full identification of meaning structures. Hence latency systems are led to identify sources or mechanisms that enforce latency, that suppress or repress meaning structures. Freud recognized in his neurotics, such as the Wolfman, the workings of repression, an active force that prevented the meaning of surface forms from being identified. Latency is distinct from repression, although it may rely on such a mechanism. The meaning of latency is not a "simple" message that must be revealed. In the case of the Wolfman or dreams, the surface behavior was understood as the subconscious trying to send a message (e.g., "I saw my parents doing it"). Rather, latency implies an underlying deep structure or ontos. The homosexuality that lies latent and the undiscovered structures of semantics are not repressed acts or undelivered messages. They are structures that the common sense of

science cannot (yet) identify. They are identities that exist outside political and social roles and organizations. Affiliation and poetic linkage play no role whatsoever.

The terms *repressed* and *latent* (as in homosexual) are often used indiscriminately. This perceived interchangeability or synonymy results from a confusion with the action of metonymy. We have seen how repression came to fulfill the same function as latency in the work of Adorno. To state it more precisely, because repression functioned as the mechanism of Adorno's latency system, repression became metonymically aligned with latency. As a key aspect of latency systems, repression came to stand for the whole. While latency systems cannot function without repression, the converse does not hold true. These two terms are not synonyms, nor is their metonymic relationship a necessary connection. Repression can stand as a distinct theoretical term, as it does in psychoanalysis.

3. Order is a constant to the production of scientific knowledge, but the order of latency systems, the deep structure or ontos presumed to be there, is elusive. It is sensed intuitively. Its presence is felt rather than observed. We know that meaning happens. We sense that homosexuals walk among us unbeknownst to us and unbeknownst to themselves. We might not yet have eyes to see or ears to hear, but those who know how to look will surely see. But what order underlies a latency system?

Having emerged as disciplines at roughly the same time, all the social sciences, linguistics and psychology included, equate order, predictability, and knowledge. Linguistics, along with psychology, economics, sociology, political science, and so on, recognized knowledge in the description of ordered, predictable systems. To reveal order and predictability was to know a system. The linguistic analysis of semantics has been confounded by this understanding of knowledge. Knowledge and meaning are not the same thing. Even if we could know how things mean, we would not know what they mean. Meaning has a relation to order that has eluded prediction. Thus Butt turned to chaos theory, a development in the hard sciences and a new model for scienticity itself. On a basic level chaos theory seeks to differentiate order from predictability. It retains its claim to science but abandons predictability, which might allow us to identify it as a different form of scientific endeavor, a postmodern science, for want of a better term. Complexity replaces predictability. Order, complexity, and knowledge become the basis for science. Yet replacing predictability with complexity still at best tells us how something means. What it means remains distant.

From its emergence psychoanalysis has always had an ambivalent relationship to predictability. The description of the Oedipal conflict never guarantees any individual outcome. The tools developed for the talking cure deal with existent structures, outcomes of already traversed trauma. They do not seek to describe how to help children pass through the Oedipal conflict, telling us, for example, "If you threaten to castrate your little boy at age four, then he will grow up to be a healthy heterosexual male." Psychoanalysis has operated as a postmodern science. Its knowledge claims are based in an ability to provide order and structure but not necessarily predictability.

When social psychology appropriated psychoanalysis, it did so to give order to a social setting that was experienced as chaotic. The German economic collapse, the political bankruptcy of the republic, the inability of the state to control violence and terror, the massification of culture, and so on created a surface that could only vaguely be known. Certainty of predictability was lost during this period. Not only did Germany's long-predicted revolution fail to materialize, but its opposite took place. In the face of these events Wilhelm Reich was forced to ask why the masses desired fascism instead of communism. It is thus small wonder that social psychology turned to latency systems in its search for order. This means, however, that the goal in Frankfurt was never to liberate the latent. The latent was the source of an effect; it was the order to the chaos; it manifested itself in ways that disrupted expectations; it gave structure to the unpredictable.

4. In latency systems meaning becomes the key to an authoritarian system of knowledge. Although produced by a subject, meaning is understood as not immediately transparent to that subject. The subject of speech, while uttered by a speaking subject, is not interpretable by that subject. Meaning becomes a property assigned to or interpreted by an outside figure. A parody of the principles of the talking cure, latency systems make the analyst an arbiter of meaning. The analyst draws to himself address unsolicited from the speaking subject. This analyst seeks to force the speaking subject to apprehend and confront the analyst, with the ultimate goal of the analyst's installing himself not simply in the subject of speech but in the speaking subject him- or herself.

The analyst is set up as arbiter through his knowledge of the deep structures. Self-knowledge is not the goal. Knowledge is imposed, read in, interpreted. The repressed or latent homosexual is a homosexual who is unaware of his own homosexuality. It is unconscious. Indeed, the analyst of latency systems displays a peculiar relationship to observed behavior and phenomenon. Real material activity ceases to signify as such and becomes a sign of false consciousness, a misshapen return of the repressed, or a masking of real need. For the analyst, the *absence* of homosexual behavior, for instance, becomes the sign of homosexuality. For the analysts of the Communist Party, absence of a communist revolution in Germany in 1933 became the sign of a latent preparedness for the revolution. The expressed desire to become a woman becomes a sign of a hatred of women (see, e.g., Raymond). Presence at fascist political rallies becomes the sign of a latent political need.[16] Enjoyment of a Hollywood blockbuster becomes the sign of having been duped by the culture industry, a making latent of real critical skills. The presence of antihomosexual behavior among gay bashers becomes the sign of a homosexual disposition.

In the case of Freudo-Marxist social psychology, the analyst is led to posit a homosexual origin to behavior even without evidence. (Dannecker should have spoken of a homosexuality-less homosexuality.) And because self-knowledge is not the goal, there is no mechanism for dealing with the latent. The analyst does not address false consciousness by making the real need manifest. Making it manifest does not solve the problem. To solve fascism the analyst does not advocate homosexual rights. To solve misogyny one does not advocate transsexual rights. This social psychology inverts Freud's goal of extending harmony, peace of mind, and full efficiency to the neurotic homosexual. It is no longer the goal of accommodating the individual psyche to the socius. Nor is it about transforming the socius to accommodate the "neurotic" psyche. Rather, those who find satisfaction in a particular social configuration are decried as perverts. Just as there is no room in the world for the social configuration they inhabit, there is also no room for them. In this paradigm, not only are homosexuals perverse, but so too are the conditions in which they live.

The Latency System at Work

Dannecker elided the difference between a latent and unconscious homosexuality in the first two-thirds of his essay, after which his own argument began to diverge from his support of the Frankfurt School argument.[17] The divergence began when Dannecker recognized that unconscious homosexuality, the sexless homosexuality of Adorno, Fromm, et al., "cannot be identified outside the psychoanalytic situation" (29). Only an expert analyst can reveal the meaning of the behavior of unconscious homosexuals. The psychoanalytic situation takes on the function of providing the knowledge of the subject.[18] Although he supports the equation of homosexuality and fascism that would provide the knowledge of the subject, Dannecker thus demoted the work of the Frankfurt School in terms of its use value. He clung to some absolute value of the Frankfurt School's work—perhaps a cultural value—but he found the fact that the Frankfurt paradigm is recognizable only within the psychoanalytic situation to be limited. Dannecker then moved on to develop his own understanding of latency.

Nonetheless, although the notion of the unconscious homosexual may have only limited usefulness, this proves not to be the case for the latent homosexual. Dannecker's aims could at best be described as a sociological psychology much more in line with an American version of clinical psychology than was the social psychology developed in Frankfurt. The latent homosexual is empirically identifiable and therefore has a great use value for Dannecker. In that respect his essay fails as an attempt to revitalize the discussion of Frankfurt-style social psychology. Dannecker therefore had to deploy order, structure, and knowledge to identify an ontos of homosexuality. And indeed, basing his project on a form of empirical clinical observation, Dannecker sought to disclose the essence of homosexuality.

This essence must retreat from observation of all "surface" phenomena to identify an ontological deep structure. Thus Dannecker turned from "crude sexual practice" to "the truth of sexual feelings" (33). "Decisive for the classification of a person under the positive concept of homosexuality are not his sexual activities but rather his sexual fantasies and wishes" (31).[19] Dannecker turned away from "crude sexual practice," what I suggest is the real of the real homosexual. He went in search of a more stable foundation on which he could build his definition of homosexual essence. Now the distinction of acts and desires is certainly productive and worth making. We should also distinguish acts from identifications, for some men and women happily engage in homosexual and homoerotic acts without ever identifying themselves as homosexual or gay.[20] Nevertheless, Dannecker's deployment of fantasy life as the essence of a homosexual disposition negates sexual acts. One does not know that one is a homosexual by what one does. This definition of the homosexual essence lowers the number of individuals Dannecker would characterize as "real" homosexuals: "As if behind the homosexual behavior, which [Kinsey] found as a mass occurrence, stood a mass-occurring homosexual disposition with its attendant wishes" (31).[21] It is not surprising that Dannecker turned to fantasy life and sexual wishes of individuals, because this move follows his support of a sexuality-less homosexuality. It is also not curious that he turned to fantasy life and sexual wishes in his search for stability, because latency systems require the search for the deep structure. Yet these moves take him ever further from the social, the material practice of individuals.

Dannecker set up a relationship of futurity between the latent and manifest homosexual. He wrote: "Latent homosexuality and conscious homosexuality [stand] in a complementary relation to each other, and both refer to the existence of a homosexual disposition" (33).[22] The latent and the manifest homosexual share an essence of fantasy life. They differ in the sense of futurity in the latent state. According to Dannecker, the latent homosexual has not (yet) cognitively integrated his "increasingly urgent homosexual wishes" (33).

While Dannecker proved himself unwilling or incapable of challenging the authoritarian structure of knowledge implicit in the judgments of Frankfurt-style social psychology, he went on to develop his own authoritarian structure. Self-definition plays only a slight role in his definition of disposition. The clinician is set above the individual in the ability to determine true identity. Without full cognitive integration, a latent homosexual would be able to recognize himself as such only through a clinician's assignment of a label.

The rigorous distinction of acts and wishes led Dannecker down a path of reasoning that nineteenth-century advocates of *pseudohomosexuality* had also trod. Retaining for the analyst the ability to detect "real" homosexuality, Dannecker's essay ends with the tone and quality of a conservative "sex reformer." Here we can recognize the full dismissal of the socius. Behavior, acts, and material practice cease to matter. "For a long time now humans have experimented with themselves, including sexually; that is to say, they have tried out for themselves whether or not certain sexual behaviors and practices, about which they have heard or read, might not be exciting to them as well. Even if a few of them have experiences of early sexuality that have an impact on the rest of their lives, in the case of the majority of the people engaged in sexual experimentation, including those experiments with partners of various genders, they are not motivated by an inner wish; rather, their actions are dictated by a social imperative for variation" (32).[23] Clearly this position rejects any possibility of bisexual existence. Bisexuality must give way to either homo- or heterosexuality. Bisexual existence becomes aligned with pseudohomosexuals, who are motivated by "a social imperative." The real homosexuals (and heterosexuals) are motivated by an "inner wish." There are a number of comments one can make at this point. The dread of self-experimentation expressed here supports the type of numerical surety necessary for quantitative endeavors in sociology, but it does little for promoting the fullness of lived experience. Moreover, I would need evidence of a social imperative for sexual variation that could counter the prevailing heterocoital imperative. The "inner wish" that Dannecker described speaks clearly not to the individual but rather to the psychologist. Given the categories of "real homosexuals" and heterosexuals who simply experiment with themselves and change the gender of their object choice while doing so, should we begin to worry about the influence of the "real homosexuals" on the heterosexuals? Should we worry about instituting fantasy life certification so that real homosexuals and real heterosexuals can be documented as such?

The wedge this latency paradigm drives between the socius and the psyche moves ever deeper, widening the gap ever further. Can we remove the wedge? We should certainly attempt to do so. Clearly something is not working here; some problematic makes itself felt. I would like to take up this project, but the development of a fully elaborated working social psychology is beyond the scope of this particular study. We can, however, explore the tools queer theory provides us to reinvigorate this debate.

The "Cause" of Fascism: Heterosexuality?

Picking up the exploration with the initial issue behind this problematic—namely, to identify the cause of fascism—we might think first about the motives underlying the search for a cause. Nietzsche suggested that cause and effect are myths imposed on recurrent events by a precariously positioned consciousness. Similarly Lacan suggested that we offer causes only when something does not work (see *Four Fundamental Concepts,* esp. 20–22). We move about the world with expectations that are usually met. When always met, these expectations form the field of common sense, the taken for granted. When they are not met, we are brought up short and must step outside our common sense and ask why. When Wilhelm Reich asked why the masses desired fascism, he posed the question out of a sense of an effect. Something was not working in the common sense of the Communist Party, and he set out to find a cause. The something that was not working was of course the revolution, or better stated, the party's expectation that the highly organized German proletariat would rise up and revolt against fascism and, in that revolt, end finance capitalism. This was the expected moment, the one a certain reading of Marx led party members to anticipate. When the expectations were not met, the Communist Party came up short. Reich was of course not the only one to pose the question, not the only one to set out looking for a cause. To answer the question, however, Reich et al. posited a deep-structural cause to this surface phenomenon: latent homosexuals are fascists.

How do we respond? Can we rebuild their project of social psychology? Can we remove the latency system that inhabits these paradigms? What relation would the socius assume vis-à-vis the psyche in such a social psychology? There are numerous directions in which to proceed. To focus on the immediate question of antihomosexuality and antifascism, we could assert that homosexuals are one of the groups persecuted by the Nazis, so they cannot be fascists. Such an assertion would have to rely on a form of existential purity and overlook the existence of gay Nazis past and present. We might simply reject the latency paradigm, denying the existence of deep structures or the effect of the unconscious on surface phenomenon. To do so, however, we would also have to deny that people become homosexuals in long, wearisome processes. We would have to turn away from the psychopathology of everyday life and reinstall a crass materialist vision of humans as behavioristic automatons, a position as untenable as the equation with which I began this chapter.

We could shrug off the question posed by Reich et al. and pose a question in response: why wouldn't the masses desire fascism? We can challenge the very break in common sense they experienced and suggest that the rise of fascism was determinate in a chain of events just as in the law of action and reaction. We can assume that the problem giving rise to their search was their original expectations, which were confounded by "surface" phenomena.

Of course the masses desire fascism. Fascism fascinates. Fascism gives the masses a chance to express themselves politically. Fascist Germany might have instituted police terror, but for the "innocent" that terror brought with it material prosperity. Fascist Germany might have instituted programs of positive racial eugenics, but for the "pure" those programs were incitements to sex. The very need to question why the masses desire fascism is a privileged heterosexual male question posed at a great distance from common sense. The need to question does not arise among homosexuals. All homosexuals know, or at least intuit, that people negotiate their oppressions, striving to maximize their benefits. The masses thus accept the terror of the fascists if material benefits result. The rights offered by communism, which await a transformation of the mode of production, become distant and abstract in comparison. That is why so many homosexuals will give up an abstract right to express themselves when presented with the concrete opportunity to change their financial status as subjects. That is why the closet is such a desirable place for many homosexuals. In the closet they can appear to follow the imperatives of heterosexuality. And why shouldn't they want to? The more interesting question, given all the benefits that accrue to participation in fascism or the heterocoital imperative, is why anyone would want to be a revolutionary. Why would anyone want to be a homosexual?

All homosexuals know, or at least intuit, that heterosexuality is the determinate of fascism. Just as effect flows from cause, genocidal violence flows from heterosexuality (see Crompton). It appears, however, that many heterosexuals do not know this, their own law. We could ask why heterosexuals do not recognize that they determine fascism, but the answer—that heterosexuality is repression is fascism—is too obvious; it is too much common sense.

A Return to the Repressive Hypothesis

Heterosexuality is repression, but what type of repression? Foucault's critique of the "repressive hypothesis" should not incite us to a blanket rejection of repression. Foucault himself was quick to acknowledge the presence of repression, restrictions, domination, and so on.[24] He directed his critique against a particular discourse of repression, especially the social psychological form developed by Reich and Marcuse. Foucault's critique of the repressive hypothesis is a critique of their fantasy of sociability without power and their promotion of a universal psychic health based in homogeneity. These are not necessary components of a theory of repression. Indeed, a closer examination of repression reveals the Marxist understanding of social being, the Freudian understanding of consciousness, and the Foucauldian understanding of subjectivity to be not antagonistic but rather reconcilable.

Both Marxist and psychoanalytic discourse incorporate two forms of repression, which we can designate simply as primary and secondary. Primary repression occurs in the process whereby an individual comes to consciousness. Primary repression is thus an act of psychic enclosure, while secondary repression is bound more firmly to activity and the entry into sociability, the process whereby an individual becomes a subject.

In Marxism primary repression is always understood as the moment of determination belonging to the socius. In primary repression the socius takes on an in-the-last-instance status of determination. Marx made this dynamic clear when, in his inversion of idealism, he insisted that it is social being that determines consciousness and not the converse. Primary repression in Marxist discourse then simply designates how each of us exists first as an object in a field of limited possibilities. For Marx, these limitations are based primarily on class and then on gender. To these two determinations we can add race, climate, language, vestmenting, representation, environmental pollution, time, weight, nutrition, health, and so on. Although its terms differ, psychoanalysis deploys an understanding of primary repression that closely resembles the Marxist understanding of social being. Julia Kristeva's work, for instance, which evinces a social psychological commitment, describes primary repression as a process of "objective *ordering* [*ordonnancement*] which is dictated by natural or socio-historical constraints such as the biological difference between the sexes or family structure. We may therefore posit that social organization, always already symbolic, imprints its constraint in a mediated form which organizes the *chora* not according to a *law* (a term we reserve for the symbolic) but through an *ordering*" (27). The term *chora* is specific to Kristeva and functions as a sort of placeholder for an experience that remains unrepresentable by any individual—the social being's preverbal, presubjective state of childhood. Kristeva has concentrated on this preconscious state. The chora is the articulation of "the drives, which are 'energy' charges as well as 'psychical' marks" (25). The starting point for her work resembles that of Reich and Fromm, who had earlier and in their own ways concentrated on the development of drives as a form of primal energy. Reich likewise envisioned our configurations of desire as stemming from a batterylike source always seeking discharge. In fact, we could go back through a series of tropes employed to describe this energy, the source of desire: the spark of life; the mysterious life force; Kant's plethora of wants, wishes, needs, desires, and lusts; Nietzsche's will to power; and so on. These tropes get transformed in the Industrial Age, through figures as diverse as Freud, Reich, Kristeva, and Deleuze, into a bioelectrical battery. The subject in formation becomes a giant biological Eveready® or Diehard®.

In primary repression the subject in becoming—the child as chora, little Eveready®—is first a social being, the object of processes, choices, and determinations outside itself that draw and quarter it into "a body in pieces." To become a conscious being it must assume a position within, through, and against the determining moments of the socius. It must condense the chora, channel its energies into a directed psyche, pull its self together, and begin to make its own history. Lacan described this development of the psyche as a sort of enclosure, a "closed precinct," an "internal organisation which up to a certain point tends to oppose the free and unlimited passage of forces and discharges of energy" (*Four Fundamental Concepts*, 60). It is only as enclosure that the field of energy, this chora that travels in waves over the body in pieces, can even begin to have direction and goal, to become understood as a drive. Primary repression should be understood positively, or at least dialectically; primary repression makes consciousness possible—just as it also makes universal consciousness impossible.

We can identify primary repression as a transhistorical prerequisite of consciousness, but we must be careful not to make the mistake of idealism. The category of primary repression must not be understood as standing outside history. A psychic process cannot exist outside material historical conditions. We cannot distinguish the elements that determine primary repression, the outside, as being transhistorical. Humans enter consciousness under circumstances directly encountered, given and transmitted from a sociohistorical setting. The outside from and through which psychic organization takes place is historically determined.

Primary repression flows over into secondary repression, making it difficult to distinguish them. Whereas primary repression is this act of closure, secondary repression is bound more firmly to culture, the outside that confronts the psyche or ego. Secondary repression is an experience that moves into consciousness but does not inhabit it fully. Primary repression, this process of subject formation, this closing of space, establishes an internal organization, but having once taken place, the enclosure does not end with infancy, and the ongoing establishment of the ego boundaries moves on into a secondary form. Not simply a defense of permanent walls but a constant reestablishment of ego boundaries, a portion of secondary repression thus remains outside conscious apprehension.

How are they distinct? Whereas primary repression moves a social being into consciousness, secondary repression moves it into subjectivity.[25] Secondary repression enables the ego enclosed by primary repression to become an active subject of history. It determines what kinds of activity are available to that subject. Secondary repression is bound to the experience of sociability. Only in a contained state can this psyche establish relations to others, to objects—in effect, become sociable. It attains a subject position, the I, *ich*, ego, a decentered subject position that connects the individual, little Eveready®, to others and allows little Diehard® to switch circuits. The psyche's greatest tool in this process is language, whereby it acquires its own subject.

Freud provided insight into the dynamic of secondary repression when he stated that "it is impossible to overlook the extent to which civilization [*Kultur*] is built up upon a renunciation of instinct, how much it presupposes precisely the non-satisfaction (by suppression, repression, or some other means?) of powerful instincts" (*Civilization*, 97). This description of the dynamic of culture lets secondary repression be understood as related to what Freud labeled the general force of renunciation present in culture, or what Foucault would simply have called power. It is important to recognize that the exercise of this repression takes multiple forms, characterized by Freud's parenthetical list: suppression, repression, or some other means. This list moves out from determinations on an unconscious or even presubjective level to determinations and experiences that are available to and recognized by the conscious mind. In their historical specificity the determinations of secondary repression are neither natural nor inherently necessary. They are imperatives. Freud's last timid option, "by some other means" moves into directions that are experienced consciously as imperatives of behavior, sometimes even violent imperatives. Nietzsche extensively analyzed the difficulty of developing a subject-oriented *I will* strong enough to counter the *You shall* of determining mores. I will examine this extensively in the next chapter, but at this point it is important to observe that the imperative *You shall* can take many forms: suggestion, recommendation, encouragement, incitement, stimulation, provocation, pressure, intimidation, coercion, oppression, obstruction, restraint, domination, force, brutalization, or authoritarianism.

In Freudo-Marxist social psychology in particular, but more generally as well, the discussion of repression has concentrated on its negative aspects. As I stated earlier, repression must, like determination, be understood dialectically (i.e., there is no subject without primary repression). Secondary repression must be recognized as containing positive and negative moments. Repression's dialectical nature marks the site of Foucault's insight and critique. Repression must be understood as both limitation and incitement, prohibition and stimulation. Focusing on its transhistorical form, secondary repression is the mutual price of sociability; more positively stated, sociability is one form of the profit that accrues to secondary repression. At the same time, a focus on the specific historical form makes it clear that not all forms of repression are the same—for example, the sociohistorical imperatives of the Third Reich were highly organized and hierarchical. Like Marx, Foucault was quick to point out that history gives specific forms to power/determination/repression, some of them more and some of them less equitable, more or less transformable. Nonetheless, the general force of renunciation in secondary repression is not inherently hierarchical, not inherently about domination. It should not be made synonymous with the forms of the Third Reich or reduced, for instance, to the arrangement of one subject disposing over another.

Subjects enter into sociability under circumstances directly encountered, given, and transmitted from a socio-historical setting. Having thus become historical beings, they then set about shaping and transforming these circumstances, responding to the imperatives of secondary repression. To incorporate this recognition the Freudo-Marxist social psychologists had to work against certain tendencies in psychoanalysis. Freud had sought to keep psychoanalysis separate from social questions. He had restricted his practice of psychoanalysis to an individual psychology with only limited applications to a broader level. This restriction provided the initial stumbling block for nascent social psychology of this sort. Freud of course had contributed a great deal to sexual reform and was himself committed to an "enlightened" social system: "Wo es war, muß ich werden" (where the id was, the ego must arise). Yet he had excluded as explananda primary structures of the socius, such as politics, economics, and social history. Freud's works on culture, for example, *Totem and Taboo* (1913) and *Beyond the Pleasure Principle* (1920), do examine cultural phenomena as they affect the individual psychic constitution. Yet culture acts as a metaphenomenon, transhistorical in nature. It is not approached in terms of social criticism. Freud did not seek to change society for his patients; rather, he sought to equip his patients with the tools to exist within the established society.

Marxism challenges the necessity of the imperatives of secondary repression. The determinations of the socius need not be accepted as a transhistorical given. Out of its Marxist commitment the social psychology examined here rejected Freud's timid description of secondary repression as culture for culture's sake.[26] A contemporary social psychology can follow this initiative. On the basis of the material clinical practice of psychoanalysis, revolutionary Marxism imbued social psychology with a commitment to the transformation of psychologically disturbing culture: a healthy psyche in a healthy socius.[27] Here a contemporary social psychology must diverge. The model of psychic health advocating the imposition of the heterocoital imperative withdrew knowledge from the subject. The model of social health advocated likewise withdrew governance from the subject. Both knowledge and governance were affirmed over self-knowledge and self-governance. The analyst was thereby aligned with a mode of authoritarianism. Contemporary social psychology must identify as its goal the increase of self-determination. Rather than accept the superego's control over the id, contemporary social psychology should bolster the *I will* of the individual against any totalizing *You shall*. Alternatively, to draw from Nietzsche, the goal of contemporary social psychology should be to help individuals become more of who they are.

Toward a New Mode of Social Psychology

From the initial problematic of the socius and the psyche I turned to Freudo-Marxist social psychology and its initial critique of homosexuality and fascism. I identified latency systems as the underlying theoretical error in this mode of social psychology. To reinvigorate the discourse of social psychology I suggested a paradigm of primary and secondary repression that negotiates the relationship of the socius and the psyche differently. Here the socius is acknowledged as a form of determination in the last instance. The psyche, however, consciousness and subjectivity, is affirmed as the site of the real human activity that produces, transforms, revolts, and makes history. With this paradigm of social psychology, can I return to the starting point and readdress the questions of sexuality, fascism, and latency?

In the earlier mode of social psychology heterosexuality appears as primary repression, but in truth it is secondary repression masquerading as primary. Heterosexuality is an erotic outcome of desire, not an erotic origin of desire. We must distinguish between desire and sexuality, a distinction that remains rather clouded in Freud's work.[28] The enclosure of primary repression makes it possible to identify certain directions of desire in the waves of energy. The imperatives of secondary repression give form to this desire. Heterosexuality does not create the ego, as was suggested by this social psychology. It is not a form of drive emanating from the ego. Heterosexuality confronts the ego as a behavioral imperative from outside the ego. Heterosexuality belongs to the socius, not the psyche.

If we understand heterosexuality as an aspect of secondary repression, one of the determining moments of sociability, then in one sense heterosexuality is a false repression, if false means that it appears as transhistorical. Of course, structure must exist, for otherwise sociability becomes impossible. Social philosophy breaks down into social psychosis. Here, however, a particular structure—heterosexuality—relies on an appearance of being outside history, comprising a transcendent aspect of sociability. This appearance is false. Heterosexuality as transhistorical is a disguise that masks the moment when heterosexuality slips into the closet and becomes a heterocoital imperative. This masking alone does not transform heterosexuality into a mode of domination. When any form of secondary repression appears as immutable, however, it robs subjects of the ability to transform themselves.

Subjects make their own history. Heterosexuality is one of the transmitted circumstances that they confront in making that history. And throughout the history of heterosexuality there have been revolutionaries. In the next chapter I discuss why there are revolutionaries, turning to Nietzsche to analyze the difficulty of developing a subject-oriented *I will.* The heterosexual *You shall* of determining mores makes it difficult to understand why anyone would be queer. The benefits that accrue to those who accommodate their will to the shall make it seem that those who do not are irrational, driven, asocial, perverse.

How can a new mode of social psychology approach fascism? The problem of fascism is not a failure of heterosexuality. Heterosexuality acts as a chief normativizing mechanism of fascism. It is part of the problem, not part of the solution. The Freudo-Marxist social psychologists discussed the family, schools, churches, military, and so on as blocks to heterosexual activity and thus the source of perverse sexuality. This argument, which resembles that of Engels examined in the previous chapter, blindly privileges heterosexuality. When these social psychologists approached such institutions of the socius, they failed to recognize that these institutions do not repress all sexuality. They might work to repress childhood heterosexuality, but they are all ultimately institutions of heterosexuality. They serve both to instill a heterocoital imperative and to suppress all other forms of sexuality, including nonreproductive heterosexuality.

If we ignore the significance of heterosexuality in their work, it becomes possible to recognize that the problematic they identified was not a problem of heterosexuality as such. Reich as well as Marcuse initiated an examination of the way monopoly capitalism relies on the restriction of orgasm as pleasure. The problem Reich described was one of orgasmic failure. For his part, Marcuse's description of a "one-dimensional man" sought to identify how capitalism has always sought to present a standardized, predictable, leveled humanity.

I have noted throughout this study that desire has experienced a varied history within capitalism. Some models of early capitalism sought to unleash desire. Beginning in the nineteenth century the predominant model sought to contain desire. This model cast desire as threat, irrationality, uncontrolled disruption, a destabilizing element that needed to be contained for the sake of sociability. It once had a positive accepted and socially promoted aspect. In the twentieth century, and with the Freudo-Marxist social psychologists, this leveling quality, the containment of desire, became an object of critique.

Albert Hirschman once expressed a certain puzzlement over the emergence of such a critique.

> Capitalism was precisely expected and supposed to repress certain human drives and proclivities and to fashion a less multifaceted, less unpredictable, and more "one-dimensional" human personality. This po-

sition, which seems so strange today, arose from extreme anguish over the clear and present dangers of a certain historical period, from concern over the destructive forces unleashed by the human passions with the only exception, so it seemed at the time, of "innocuous" avarice. *In sum, capitalism was supposed to accomplish exactly what was soon to be denounced as its worst feature.* (132)

Hirschman's puzzlement seems to have developed from an expectation that capitalism would remain stable. The analysis of Freudo-Marxist social psychology, however, prompted the recognition that this one-dimensionality, the containment of desire, had become capitalism's worst feature, and from our current perspective at the end of the consumer form of capitalism, it is hard to imagine that outlets for pleasure were once so fully blocked and restricted.

When Reich asked why the masses desired fascism, he answered, roughly, "because they were restricted from heterosexual coitus." Hence Reich viewed heterosexual liberation as the answer to fascism (along with all other social problems). Released from the theoretical support of the heterocoital imperative, I proffer a much simpler answer: the masses desired fascism because it offered pleasure. Fascism is an outlet for desire. Fascism provided this outlet in sexual and nonsexual forms.

Turning away from Reich's work and his narrow concentration on heterocoital orgasm as the only healthy form of drive discharge, we can recognize fascism as providing for the pleasurable discharge of energy. Fascism mitigated the "orgasmic failure" of capitalism by providing pleasure. For many of its participants, fascism was not a form of repression that instituted a roundabout path to a direct satisfaction; it did not present detours that the ego had to experience as unpleasure.[29] Capitalism in its fascist mode[30] offered a multitude of outlets for desire, including sexual outlets: rituals, ceremonies, rallies, public events, civic responsibility, public pride, awards, and so on. It counteracted the alienation of monopoly capitalism without undoing the structure of capitalism. Motherhood awards, child subsidies, Aryan brothels for SS officers, and so on established state support for sexuality. When Walter Benjamin observed that fascism rendered politics aesthetic, he recognized how, on the level of the mass rally, fascism provided "an aesthetic pleasure of the first order" (242). This experience of pleasure contrasted starkly with the orgasmic restrictions of nineteenth-century monopoly capitalism.

The problem of fascism is not secondary repression as such. The source of fascism is not homosexuality. The problem of fascism is neither power as such nor pleasure as such. The problem of fascism is a problem of the arrangement of power and the source of pleasure. In historical fascism a group "blocked a field of power relations, immobilized them, and prevented any reversibility of movement by economic, political, or military means" (Foucault, *Ethics*, 283). In short, a group managed to achieve domination. When we ask why the masses desired fascism, we speak of "Aryan" masses, heterosexual masses, masses willing to define their will through and within social imperatives but not against them. These masses dwindled ever more in their numbers until they became a select group. The problem of fascism is further that the pleasure of a select group was bought at the expense of a vast number of subjugated peoples: their unpleasure, the total disposition over their persons, their physical destruction.

The Freudo-Marxist social psychologists relied on a latency system. The understanding of drive-based psychoanalytic theories rested on something akin to a nature-culture dichotomy. The connection to nature, regardless of cultural development, was guaranteed by the existence of the essential universal drives found in humans, chief of which was the heterocoital sex drive. Bourgeois capitalist culture, however, drove the "healthy" sex drive into a latent state because of the sex negativity in this mode of production. And in the analysis of the social psychologists this false sexual repression gave rise to false sexual characters, such as homosexuals. In this conclusion Reich and all the social psychologists who followed this path falsely assessed the status of heterosexuality, aligning it with nature rather than with the determinations of secondary repression. Secondary repression appears only as domination, spawning a delusion of a subject outside or beyond power.

Latency continues to structure critical assessments of political subjects even within the various queer political movements. Several theoretical positions rest on the basis of an "if only . . . then . . ." phrase that marks this mode of politics. *If only* the subject were not exposed to secondary repression, *then* the individual would always emerge as . . . Depending on the movement to which the critic belongs, the outcome here would be heterosexual, homosexual, lesbian, polymorphous perverse, bisexual, proletarian species-being, or whatever version of health and utopic subjectivity the particular theorist has established as preferable. Contemporary constructions of desire are placed as a catachresis of real desire. As designated constructions, or imaginings, material determinations of the socius are then treated as somehow inauthentic. In the well-intentioned motivation to critique elements of secondary repression, it all too often seems that it is not enough simply to point out that acts such as gay bashing, discrimination, sexual abuse, homelessness, matricide, and genocide are undesirable results of social constructs and historical circumstances. A true base, a repressed wholeness, an unrealized potential must be identified as yearning to breath free. Ultimately, however, in the quest for liberty, our struggles cannot afford to attend to a difference based in the question, "Was I born this way, or did I become this way?"

Latency systems support the analyst's knowledge. They do not support self-knowledge or self-governance. It is possible that as individuals' activities align them with particular movements (e.g., intimate contact between men and the gay rights movement), the individuals will reanalyze their earlier behavior. They will construct a narrative that indicates that they were "always that way." Individuals will participate in projecting a latency period onto their own past. This is a matter of political alignment and narrative reanalysis, a confusion of cause and effect. It is not evidence for some latent essence. It is a problem of the manner in which the individual becomes a subject of history.

The repression attendant on the heterocoital imperative—that is, the suppression of queer sexualities—does not mean that without it we would all have "remained" lesbian, transgendered, or polymorphous perverse. The idea that individuals would freely choose everything in other, less repressed circumstances is deluded. Even if individual subjects could freely determine their object choices, it would be done within a field that they have not freely chosen. This field need not be immediately understood as a force of suppression. We desire what we desire. When the field we inhabit does not present the object of our desire, do we automatically cathect elsewhere, as is the popular image of men in prisons? When the field we inhabit does not allow us to cathect, do our desires get stalled as unrequited, unfulfillable longings? Do we repress or sublate them into other activities, such as cultural production and artistry? The imaginary answer to these questions is yes. The real answer to them is probably no.

Returning to the dynamic of antifascism and antihomosexuality, it is not enough to invert this formula and promote homosexuality. Homosexuality is not a guarantee against fascism. Nevertheless, heterosexuality holds a promise of fascism. The problem never was a problem of homosexuality. It was always a problem of domination. Where heterosexuality appears as transhistorical, as primary repression, it is removed from conscious perception as an object subject to human activity, production, transformation, revolution, and history. Heterosexuality becomes a block to the flow of power, a mechanism of domination. The problem of secondary repression is its ability to bring subjects into being through domination.

It is not homosexuals who are perverse but the situation in which they live. Such a statement does not automatically lead to the (naïve) position that the homosexual is free of perversion, a site of sociohistorical or socioeconomic purity and health. Yet we run the risk of adopting such a position when dealing with oppressed groups or individuals in alterior positions.[31] Thus the recognition of the perverse conditions of the homosexual lifeworld need not lead us to build a résumé of homosexual perversion or construct a pure (queer) revolutionary site; rather, it should lead us to review the conditions of the pathologizing society, to question the cause of or need for a pathologized, perverse homosexual. Oddly, in their analyses both Dannecker and von Praunheim failed to look away from the homosexual conditions to the social situation in which homosexuals find themselves. This problem is one of sociability and not of subjectivity.

Notes

1. Althusser's discussion of production and reproduction seems to have provided an answer by giving the superstructure an equal primacy in its effect on the mode of production. Given that the base is the mode of production, however, the primacy that Althusser granted was possible only by a sleight of hand by which he drew our attention to another term—ideology; see *Lenin and Philosophy, Reading "Capital,"* and *For Marx.*

2. Lewin's work was quantitative *and* qualitative. Lewin's work on behavioral fields or material determining structures, often involved projects of social experimentation and planning, for example, interventions in neighborhoods with racial, ethnic, or religions tension and attempts to raise quality of life as a means to solve social conflict. This work was significant for the social planning that the United States undertook from the 1930s to the 1970s. Lewin's most important lasting influence on social philosophy in the United States, however, seems to be his suggestion that real people in real situations can be represented mathematically; see Tesser; Marrow.

3. For more extensive discussion see my article "Between Marxism and Psychoanalysis." See also Hewitt; Litvak.

4. All translations of Reich are my own, drawn from the German originals. When Reich arrived in the United States, having been expelled from Germany, the Communist Party, and the psychoanalytic association, he reedited his works as they were translated into English, seeking to remove especially any traces of Marxism.

5. Character formation occurs from birth onward as a result of the interaction of individual drives with various forms of social organization. The force of the drives usually operates on an unconscious level: the child seeks discharge without reflecting on the source, intensity, or reason for the drive. The filiative moment predetermines the path of socialization. The concept of character presented here derives from Freud's developmental model of libido, a model that preceded the discussion of the Oedipus complex. The seminal work here is "Character and Anal Erotism," written by Freud in 1908. In this model the passage from the oral, through the anal, and to the genital stage sometimes stalls, leaving an individual caught in one phase and seeking primary pleasure through the mouth or the anus. As the individual grows and develops, this condition produces typical constellations of the libido that in turn produce behavior patterns designated as character. Most well known, perhaps, is the assertion of a rela-

tion between the anal stage and a compulsive or sadistic character. Reich's understanding differed little from work done by Freud, Rank, Ferenczi, and so on or what Fromm would describe; see, for example, Reich's discussion of character armor [*Charakterpanzer*], carried out primarily in *Der Triebhafte Charakter* and *Charakteranalyse*. It is in *Charakteranalyse* (1933), however, that Reich first made a connection crucial to the further development of his form of social analysis: "each social order [creates] for itself the type of characters which it requires for its continuation" (12). Although this book is remembered most as a study of resistance during the analytic process, *Character Analysis* shows Reich seeking to connect this conception of character to broad social phenomena—especially to class. He carried out the analysis of this connection in greater detail, however, in *The Mass Psychology* (*Massenpsychologie*).

6. It should be noted that psychoanalysis produced many "maps" with which the difficult terrain of sexual expression could be traversed. Freud himself followed a very different route here, avoiding a link between the individual homosexual psyche and any mass level. Surface and source, conscious and unconscious, were individual properties, not social ones. We see this displayed in his famous "Letter to an American Mother" (April 4, 1935). In this letter, perhaps his most "sympathetic" statement on homosexuality, Freud explained to a "concerned" mother that psychoanalysis would most likely be ineffective in "curing" her son of his homosexuality:

> By asking me if I can help, you mean, I suppose, if I can abolish homosexuality and make normal heterosexuality take its place. The answer is, in a general way, we cannot promise to achieve it.
>
> . . . What analysis can do for your son runs in a different line. If he is unhappy, neurotic, torn by conflicts, inhibited in his social life, analysis may bring him harmony, peace of mind, full efficiency, whether he remains a homosexual or gets changed. (*Briefe*, 416)

In this letter Freud opposed full efficiency, harmony, and peace of mind to the neurotic, conflictual state and inhibitions in social life. In the phrase "full efficiency" Freud imbued psychoanalysis with the ability to help the analysand become *sociable*. The neurotic homosexual posited by Freud exists as an incomplete member of society, the psyche of this individual being ill equipped for the demands of the socius. The goal of psychoanalysis is thus not implicitly to "cure" the disease homosexuality of an individual or to change society to accept the homosexual; rather it is to achieve sociability for the neurotic homosexual by removing his inhibiting neurosis, in effect linking an individual disconnected psyche to an existent socius.

7. For a discussion of the connection of the Red scare and the homosexual menace, see Edelman, *Homographesis*.

8. It is perhaps a sign of synchronicity that shortly after my first foray into the topic, Andrew Hewitt and Joseph Litvak also published analyses of the antihomosexuality of the Frankfurt School in general and Adorno in particular. At the same time Joel Whitebook managed to cover similar terrain and take no notice.

9. Female homosexuality played no role in their discussions. These social phenomena were analyzed as male. Presumably either women could not be fascists, authoritarians, anti-Semites, and so on, or their participation was only derivative. Hence the discussion of homosexuality was limited to males. Nevertheless, I hesitate to suggest that these social psychologists would have viewed lesbianism as positive.

10. Martin Dannecker, who was trained as a sociologist, is one of the more significant figures in the German gay rights movement. His study with Reimut Reiche published as *The Average Homosexual* provided the first statistical survey of homosexual practice in the Federal Republic of Germany. His collaboration with director Rosa

von Praunheim on the film *Not the Homosexual Is Perverse but the Society in Which He Lives* unleashed the gay rights movement there. His *Theories of Homosexuality* was one of the first comprehensive metaexaminations of the discourse of homosexuality. His numerous lectures, extensive written work, and ceaseless activism have furthered the position of gays and lesbians in Germany. He is truly one of the fathers of the modern gay rights movement, yet as that movement has expanded and taken on new directions, he has been increasingly involved in controversies around the form and direction of gay politics and gay theory, largely resistant to the emergence of queer theory.

11. Indeed, to be clear and explicit, I need to state that I have already engaged in a protracted debate with Martin Dannecker in the *Zeitschrift für Sexualforschung* (Journal for Sexual Science). The journal requested permission to republish my essay on antifascism and antihomosexuality in the Frankfurt School. Since the nineteenth century the journal has been at the heart of sexological and sexual scientific work. Its long history and various editorial incarnations placed it at the heart of a socially productive and socially fraught discourse. In its current configuration it has paid particular attention to the history of its own discourse, precisely the goal of my essay. The editors of the journal arranged for Martin Dannecker to respond to my essay in order to open up a debate in Germany around the problem. Reading his "response," I went from pleasure, to surprise, to befuddlement. Dannecker's "answer" quickly revealed itself as a caustic attack that forced me to wonder whether he had read my essay. His diatribe launched out on frequent examinations of my motives that, when strung together, ultimately made me laugh. Although "painfully naïve" I am supposedly "bitter," filled with a "rabid antipsychoanalytic ressentiment" arising from my "gay political correctness." Reading Dannecker's response was like reading a horoscope in a sports magazine: I know I am being hailed, but the system into which I am being interpolated has so little to do with my interests that I can only shrug my shoulders. "You got the wrong man." Let me be clear that I already took the time to respond to Dannecker at length in the *Zeitschrift* itself, but there is something in Dannecker's response, which condenses all the problems of the social psychological paradigm of homosexuality, that bears further reflection here.

12. All translations from Dannecker are my own. The original for this passage reads: "Fromm zielt, wie später . . . auch Horkheimer und Adorno, mit seinen Überlegungen zur Homosexualität nicht auf ein sexuelles, sondern auf ein geschlechtsbezogenes Verhalten, genau gesagt auf die zwischen Macht und Unterwürfigkeit oszillierende Beziehung der heterosexuellen Männer untereinander. Thematisiert wird von Fromm das Verhalten der Männer untereinander, dem er jedoch durch dessen Charakterisierung als homosexuell, eine sexuelle Konnotation verlieht" (23).

13. This direction is the one that appears in Mosse, *Nationalism and Sexuality.*

14. The original reads, "eine desexualisierte und zugleich charakteristische mann-männliche Beziehungsmodalität" (19).

15. Those natives who placed the old Aztec gods into the statues that adorn the new Christian churches seem to have held open the possibility of relishing the hidden depth.

16. Walter Benjamin, for instance, distinguished between the types of politics afforded by the National Socialists and the communists: an aestheticization of politics undertaken by the National Socialists versus a politicization of aesthetics undertaken by the communists. Of course, this distinction rings rather hollow if we look to the politics of Stalinism, but clearly with his invocation of communists Benjamin was thinking of the work of figures such as Bertolt Brecht. Nevertheless, in his distinction Benjamin sought to describe participation in fascist politics as false consciousness that made latent a real revolutionary politics. At this point I am trying only to dispute the mak-

ing latent of "real" political activity. See, for instance, Benjamin, 211–44. Operating according to the same assessment of political latency is Adorno, "Fascist Propaganda."

17. Dannecker uses the term *unbewußt* (unconscious), not *unterbewußt* (subconscious), in designating the conception of homosexuality in social psychology. This is at odds with the language of the theorists who vacillate between latency and repression, both of which are understood as subconscious processes. At least he avoided the construction of unconscious homosexuals.

18. Dannecker mistook the latency system in social psychology with psychoanalysis, or the "psychoanalytic situation." He seems unable to critically access appropriations of psychoanalytic language, understanding what the Frankfurt School developed to be synonymous with psychoanalysis—which is simply not the case.

19. The original reads, "Ausschlaggebend für die Einstufung eines Menschen unter den positiven Begriff von Homosexualität sind nicht seine sexuellen Handlungen, sondern seine sexuellen Phantasien und Wünsche" (31).

20. Also relevant might be all those "gentle" heterosexual males who, as a reward for being part of a movement that is "changing men," are identified as effeminate and suspected of homosexuality by "tough" heterosexuals. This would invert Adorno's "Tough Baby."

21. The original reads, "Als ob hinter dem von [Kinsey] vorgefundenen massenhaften homosexuellen Verhalten eine massenhaft vorkommende homosexuelle Disposition mit den ihr zugehörigen Wünschen stünde" (31).

22. The original reads, "Latente Homosexualität und bewußte Homosexualität [stehen] in einer komplementären Beziehung zueinander, und beide verweisen auf das Vorhandensein einer homosexuellen Disposition" (33).

23. The original reads: "Längst schon experimentieren die Menschen auch sexuell mit sich selbst, d.h. sie probieren an sich aus, ob gewisse sexuelle Verhaltensweisen und Praktiken, von denen sie gehört oder gelesen haben, nicht auch für sie reizvoll sein könnten. Auch wenn einige dadurch mit lebensgeschichtlich bedeutsamen frühen Erotisierungen in Berührung kommen mögen: Bei der Mehrheit der sexuell mit sich selbst Experimentierenden sind die auch den Wechsel des Geschlechts des Sexualobjektes einschließenden sexuellen Experimente nicht von einem inneren Wunsch motiviert, sondern vom gesellschaftlichen Befehl nach Abwechslung diktiert" (32).

24. Foucault states, for instance: "Indeed, it is not a question of denying the existence of repression. It's one of showing that repression is always a part of a much more complex political strategy regarding sexuality" (*Ethics*, 126). For a discussion of the "repressive hypothesis" see Foucault, *History of Sexuality*, vol. 1.

25. These two forms constitute a fundamental transformation of the Kantian paradigm of reason as the faculty that determines desire for the sake of sociability. In the psychoanalytic paradigm, sociability continues to be the main purpose of especially secondary repression. But the recognition of a primary repression moves sociality outside the control of reason. Indeed, whereas in Kant the desiring individual represses his desires through a rational will for the sake of sociability, here sociability becomes a force of repression distinct from reason.

26. Indeed, Reich, as well as the other Freudo-Marxist social psychologists, recognized in psychoanalysis a tendency toward a neoidealist philosophy, a tendency against which they struggled. Thus in his social psychology Reich explicitly preferred to write of social organization rather than use Freud's terms *culture* or *civilization*. Reich understood Freud's use of *Kultur* as too much an acquiescence to the forces of renunciation. These social psychologists recognized psychoanalysis first as a material clinical practice.

27. The quantitative social psychology, more of a sociological psychology, of the present era appears as farce in comparison, too timid to make demands; it responds to challenges with a by-all-means.

28. Freud's *Three Essays on Sexuality* shows this type of confusion very clearly. There Freud's emphasis on childhood sexuality draws into sexuality experiences that belong to the more general category of desire. Polymorphous perversity, for instance, describes a state of being that belongs to the more general category of desire. Later Freud sought to correct this position, as is indicated by a footnote like the one we find in *Three Essays* (130).

29. See Freud's discussion of the mechanisms of repression in *Beyond the Pleasure Principle*, esp. p. 27.

30. While fascism is not synonymous with capitalism, historically fascist states have relied on a capitalist economy. They may employ anticapitalist rhetoric, but this shows why we need to distinguish fascist ideology from fascist practice. The mode of exchange of capital in a fascist state is rarely synonymous with free-market economy, hence my use of the term "capitalism in its fascist mode."

31. A similar problematic appears in the somewhat ambivalent relationship of political leaders to the working class. The designation *Lumpenproletariat* marks an attempt to purify the revolutionary proletariat of the negative pathologies and criminal behaviors that might arise out of conditions of poverty. The *Lumpenproletariat* did not act as part of the class for itself; rather, those thus designated exhibited negative behavior, leaving *proletariat* as the designation for the "rightly guided" ones, the elect of the revolution. In anti-anti-Semitic positions the recognition that it is not "the Jew" who is perverse did not necessarily lead to a focus on Jewish purity; rather, it led to a focus on the negative structures of the political lifeworld that relied and continue to rely on anti-Semitism.

5 Nietzsche, Sociability, and Queer Knowing

> As a guarantee of [Nietzsche's] undiminished resistance, he is still as alone in this as in the days when he turned the mask of evil upon the normal world, to teach the norm to fear its own perversity.
>
> —Theodor Adorno

From Gay Science to Queer Knowing

Up to now the queer readings in this study have sought to find crucial points in what might appear as marginal discussions of sexuality and gender, which then are revealed as constitutive—a pleasure in finding the constitutive exclusions. Certainly this is a possibility with Nietzsche, although sexuality and gender play such a significant role in Nietzsche's texts that it would require an active blindness in order for a reader to overlook them. I would rather begin by noting the distortions of Nietzsche's positions on gender and sexuality that plague his interpreters.

I turn first to Nietzsche's preeminent commentator, Walter Kaufmann, who expressed certain anxieties regarding his translations, especially that of *The Gay Science*. Kaufmann's translations and commentary made possible the postwar reawakening of interest in Nietzsche. So many black-clad youths have spent hours in coffee houses poring over the Kaufmann translations, learning how to philosophize with a hammer, that while his legacy might be more utilitarian in terms of influence on Nietzschean studies, those of us who rely on a familiarity with Nietzsche in the English-speaking world owe Kaufmann a great deal. Before

Kaufmann, the first English-language translation of *Die Fröhliche Wissenschaft* appeared as *The Joyful Wisdom*.[1] Dissatisfied with that translation, Kaufmann put forward a translation of the work as *The Gay Science*, until the work of the Gay Liberation Front in the late 1960s made Kaufmann aware of a "new" denotation of *gay*. In the introduction to his full translation of *The Gay Science*, published first in 1974, Kaufmann noted that "meanwhile, the word 'gay' has acquired a new meaning, and people are beginning to assume that it has always suggested homosexuality" (4). Kaufmann explained further that while opting for a different translation to avoid any misunderstandings might be understandable, this really is not possible, because *"fröhlich* means *gay"* (4). Having locked himself into a direct correspondence between the linguistic fields of German and English, he found himself in a rather odd position, acknowledging that Nietzsche, like homosexuals, opted for "gay" because it implied a "light-hearted defiance of convention" (5).[2] Such defiance was in line with Nietzsche's immoralism and revaluation of values. Thus, it at first appears that Kaufmann recognized a similarity between Nietzsche's philosophy and the political activity of the gay rights movement.[3] Nevertheless, Kaufmann assured us that the title of the book does not imply that "Nietzsche was homosexual or that the book deals with homosexuality" (5). Counter to Kaufmann, Joachim Köhler has appeared to assert this charge of Nietzsche as a homosexual in his biography *Zarathustras Geheimnis*. So many "biographical" explanations of Nietzsche's work exist that it was only a matter of time. Counter to both Kaufmann and Köhler, however, I claim that while it does not matter one bit whether Nietzsche was homosexual, the book and Nietzsche's oeuvre in general are fundamentally queer. Nietzsche presented fundamental paradigms of queer knowing, and Nietzsche's *Gay Science* presents indeed a queer *Wissenschaft*, a *queer science*. One goal of this chapter is to distill this queer science from Nietzsche's joyful wisdom.

Nietzsche marks a significant transformation in the project of modernity. To be sure, Nietzsche's "antimodernity" joins Marx and Marxism in critically rejecting the liberal model of modernity and the cultural cost of social modernization. Likewise, it puts forward a hope in a general revolutionary transformation. As the preceding chapters showed, however, Marxism's "use value" is limited and must be distilled, because the discourse of Marxism still relies on a containment of desire that systematically generates its own disruptions. Nietzsche's epistemological shift breaks with this containment. I do not mean to suggest that Nietzsche has succeeded in cutting the knots of modernity that bind the desiring individual, somehow accomplishing human emancipation—to be "revealed" by wise and clever readings. Nietzschean overcoming, like Marx's revolution, defers a universal "break." Nevertheless, I do want to insist that Nietzsche offers the individual a knowledge-craft, a form of science, a way of knowing, that accommodates the contingencies of desire in the present, which is precisely what Nietzsche described as "gay science."

Nietzsche's gay science has proven productive in the generation of theory, influencing psychoanalysis, phenomenology, existentialism, deconstruction, and certainly queer theory. The success of the later theorizing, however, threatens to dissipate and overcome Nietzsche himself. Perhaps he would be pleased with the theoretical directions that have gone beyond him, given Zarathustra's admonitions to his disciples to overcome him. At the same time, I fear that this act of overcoming exposes Nietzsche's work to an active forgetting and that this active forgetting often undercuts the radical critical potential of Nietzschean social philosophy.[4] Let me be clear: in the following I do not seek to define an orthodox reading of Nietzsche—although there are misreadings and there are misreadings, and reading Nietzsche requires carefully weighing and valuing his terms, a familiarity with his larger corpus and not just a little bit of systematicity.

Nietzsche, Modernity, and Nihilism

Of what is this gay science made? How does the queer knowing that Nietzsche produces differ from previous social philosophy? What is new and modern and queer in Nietzsche? This study has already covered how the genesis of modernity has been variously attributed to Kant and Hegel. It has further contended that Marx likewise occupied a significant position in the project of modernity by opening philosophy to world-transforming practical activity. Many other scholars, however, have argued that Nietzsche rejected the project of modernity; was an antimodern royalist; or, in his delusions and ravings, simply stands outside any rational social philosophy.

As is well known, in the 1980s Habermas began an attack against contemporary developments in social philosophy and did so by marking Nietzsche's work as initiating a fundamental paradigm shift in the project of modernity, the emergence of a postmodern. He attacked in particular what he understood as an emphasis on indeterminacy and contingency in contemporary philosophy, which he recognized as derived from Nietzsche. Habermas is certainly right in identifying Nietzsche as instituting a break or shift in social philosophy, but we must be careful in assessing this shift. Although they might critique the cultural forms of modernity, Nietzsche and the Nietzscheans represent a direction in social philosophy that derives equally from the process of social modernization. The term *postmodern* cannot be deployed to undermine the coeval status of a philosophical discourse.[5]

In Habermas's vision of modern social philosophy, the future appears as the site of progress and ongoing development. Certainly for the most radical lines emerging from Hegel, the future contains the site of a revolutionary resolution to reified existence, and for even the conservatives it offers a site of material and spiritual compensation for present alienation, but such an openness to the future threatens to transform these philosophers into "despisers of the present." Nietzsche rejected any scientific claims of historiography and particularly the Hegelian understanding of history as a process of unfolding reason: "Insofar as it stands in the service of life, history stands in the service of an unhistorical power, and, thus subordinate, it can and should never become a pure science" (*Untimely*, 67). For Nietzsche, the measures whereby any progress can be assessed belong not to an external spirit or nation but rather to suprahistorical forces of life or the will to power. Thus, unlike the historians of the modern period, Nietzsche recognized not an unfolding of history guiding the socius but a historical method of social philosophy interpreting the socius and the psyche. In the concrete appearances of modernization, moreover, Nietzsche recognized not progress but only *progression.*

At the same time, Nietzsche bears certain similarities to the most radical philosophers of modernity. For instance, Nietzsche shared this historicized understanding of philosophy with Hegel, for whom modern philosophy is the history of philosophy, although Hegel viewed the modern period as the culmination of the philosophical past, whereas Nietzsche took the history of philosophy to reveal not only the debt to the past but also the possibility of radical breaks and disruptions with the past: progression, not progress. Furthermore, even though Nietzsche was not a political organizer, as Marx was, and he actually eschewed mass politics, he nevertheless purposefully popularized philosophy, transferring it from the academic setting to the literary market because he recognized its radical transformative potential. Marx's inversion of Hegel had given social philosophy a transformative instead of descriptive purpose, and Nietzsche continued in this direction. Furthermore, Marx viewed the period of capital as a transitional stage, and Nietzsche also recognized the present as transitional, although his terms construed it as a moment of pathology in the struggle of life toward health. Of course, the potential of transition in Nietzsche must be tempered by his recognition that the present, that gate where we stand in the great vicious circle of eternal return, is all we have, the only position we can occupy. Nevertheless, whereas Marx, in exploring the social dialectic of the individual and the collective, understood collective transformation as the goal of social philosophy and individual transformation as an outcome, Nietzsche understood individual transformation as the goal and collective transformation as an outcome. Although Nietzsche denied progress and recognized only progression, what he rejected is a historical progress that derives from a force outside or "behind the world." External determining factors, Hegelian mores, or Marx's base belong to such outside forces. Thus, while Nietzscheans might incorporate economics in their analysis, the economy does not have a structurally determining weight over and above the forces of life and will.

To be sure, Nietzsche advocated nihilism as a necessary step in his rigorous critique of every interpretive framework, but he approached nihilism as a point of necessary temporary negativity: "nihilism represents a pathological transitional stage" (*Will*, §13). Indeed, Nietzsche developed a specific understanding of nihilism; to offer a counterinstance to any stable nihilism among his contemporaries, he proposed a history of nihilism in which its negativity emerges not ex nihilo but out of a "will to truth."[6]

> Will to truth is a making firm, a making true and durable, an abolition of the false character of things, a reinterpretation of it into beings. "Truth" is therefore not something there, that might be found or discovered—but something that must be created and that gives a name to a process, or rather to a will to overcome that has in itself no end—introducing truth, as a *processus in infinitum*, an active determining—not a becoming-conscious of something that is in itself firm and determined. It is a word for the "will to power." (*Will*, §552)

In this sense Nietzsche's untimeliness cannot be counted as simply post- or premodern. While it does contain a great deal of futurity, it differs from the modern "despisers of the present" by expressing a radical contemporaneity. It is not trying to return to an archaic past, nor, in its relationship to the past, does it speak against the torture chamber of humanity's history.

In his discussion of nihilism Nietzsche did recognize an unfolding over time that appears vaguely like progress, a *processus;* the history of philosophy reveals not the unfolding of the spirit of freedom but the unfolding of life, specifically of will to power. It is precisely this history of nihilism that has kneaded, prepared, formed "man," that made it possible to go beyond being the animal, beyond species-being to something else. This history is indeed "*pregnant with a future,*" such that there is a glimpse of something beyond: "as if man were not a goal but only a way, an episode, a bridge, a great promise" (*Genealogy*, pt. 2, §16). The unfolding in the history of nihilism, this *processus*, is an active overcoming that gives rise to the overman. Nihilism is a period of revaluation of all values but also a transitional state whose negativity must be overcome by optimism, by laughter, by will to truth, by *gay science*.

Nietzsche's influence on Foucault is well known. When the historian Foucault describes human history as one of self-fashioning, he employs a historical mode of analysis based on progression, not progress. Nietzsche provided inspiration to Foucault's discussions of power/knowledge in discourse. Nevertheless, Foucault's productive recognition of discourse is a step in nihilism and thus not a final step; it is not yet positive queer science. For Nietzsche, it would appear as one step in the unrelenting process of the revaluation of values: "For why has the advent of nihilism become *necessary*? . . . Because we must experience nihilism before we can find out what value these 'values' really had.—We require, sometimes, *new values*" (*Will*, 4). By following Nietzsche in questioning the basis of scientific questioning, Foucauldian "discourse" helped recognize the value of "values," yet it must itself be overcome by new *queer* knowing. In Foucault the nexus power/knowledge remains primarily descriptive, even as it establishes an alternative to the historical narratives inspired by Hegel and Marx, offering a history without telos, filled with rationales but not reason.[7] By contrast, the queer science that will exceed nihilism is not merely descriptive or critical but must and does strive to provide positive knowledge.

This tension between Nietzsche and Foucault may be illustrated in the title of the passage Nietzsche calls "The Uses and Disadvantages of History for Life," which, rather than pin down "epistemes," subordinated historiography to a larger principle, that of "life" as a force that stands outside history. Thus Nietzsche strove to find some position outside discourse on which knowledge could be based. When Nietzsche critiqued epistemology and ontology, he offered in their place something that appears as both a principle of knowledge and material practice. "In so far as the word 'knowledge' has any meaning, the world is knowable; but it is *interpretable* otherwise, it has no meaning behind it, but countless meanings.—'Perspectivism.' It is our needs that interpret the world; our drives and their For and Against. Every drive is a kind of lust to rule; each one has its perspective that it would like to compel all the other drives to accept as a norm" (*Will*, §481). Nietzsche's radical critique of epistemology and ontology does not throw us into chaotic unknowing, nor does it rely on an unknowable noumena "behind the world." If it is without reason, as Habermas suggests, it is not without rationale. It leaves us with a material world on which life acts, defining its for and against along the frictions and contours of the body. Queer knowledge begins with perspectivism as the practice of interpretation in which bodies confronting materiality engage. In this way queerness offers the site of a positive and active production of knowledge.

The Nietzschean Socius: What Is Lived Is Real, and What Is Real Serves Life

Perspectivism is fundamentally related to a process of overcoming in life. Nietzsche derived a fundamental optimism from events or qualities that are typically described as negative, that are assessed as having had a bad outcome for history; in such phenomena Nietzsche still recognized the presence of a positive force at work. Life overcomes nihilism. Seemingly paradoxically, "even the most harmful man may really be the most useful when it comes to the preservation of the species" (*Gay Science*, §1). In this vein Nietzsche advised us to ignore mores and "pursue [our] best or . . . worst desires, and above all perish" (ibid.), which means that *what is lived is real, and what is real serves life.*

Of course, reason had been a central concern to social philosophy well before Nietzsche, yet given perspectivism, Habermas was correct to claim that Nietzsche marked a shift in the relation of social philosophy to reason as such. With the advent of the modern era, the project of social philosophy involved the establishment of universal standards of rationality—or in Hegelian terms, Reason—which would establish the socius as a homogeneous society. Kant had already construed reason as defining psyche, subjecting psyche to homogenizing morality. At the same time, however, the project of modernity is based on an autonomy of action in the socius, a space in which the free development of the individual should take place. To actualize this project, the socius would have to be imbued with a heterogenizing principle that would stand in tension with the principles of universal reason. Hegel's solution, an absolute spirit that stands above and outside any individual, "resolved" the split philosophically through the assertion of totalization over universalization: *what is real is rational, and what is rational is real.* Hegel's statement serves totalizing systems, whereas the position I ascribed to Nietzsche describes dynamic processes of transforming reason.

Habermas sought to overcome this diremption central to modernity by remaining with Hegel but shifting the separation from socius and psyche to reason and activity. His systematic explanatory scheme of universal pragmatics, communicative action (*Kommunikatives Handeln*), offers a solution through a linguistic turn; it shifts the absolute of reason from metaphysical spirit to material communicative action. *What is communicated is rational, and what is rational is communicated.* Such a position, however, is still an insufficient response to Nietzsche. Nietzsche's greatest communicator, Zarathustra, is a prophet who teaches his followers not to listen to him but to find their own ways, a relentless condemnation of the life of the herd. What Habermas describes as communication, Nietzsche describes as herd mentality. Whereas Habermas hopes to find a democratic equalizing of power in communicative action, Nietzsche recognizes the result of a socius organized around debt. Communication, discourse, negotiation, memory, and consciousness itself all derive from an imbalance of power inherent to the socius. *"Consciousness has developed only under the pressure of the need for communication; that from the start it was needed and useful only between human beings (particularly between those who commanded and those who obeyed)"* (*Gay Science*, §354).[8] Thus communication itself is based on imbalance of power, and Nietzsche did not aspire to a socius without power. For Nietzsche, the socius and the psyche derive from the play of power (although we can distinguish between power as hegemony and power as domination).

What is lived is real, and what is real serves life. The socius of that statement derives not from a contained Kantian rational sociability, a universal Hegelian ethical spirit, a Marxian social humanity, or a universal Habermasian communicative community but rather from a contingent and conflictual sum of relations. Sociability in itself has no value other than as an affective state. Society is not a space brought into being by a necessary regulation; rather, it is a term simply defining an enclosure, a whole much like the astronomic term *universe*, which simply defines all that exists within certain limits. This entirety has no exterior from which it can be guided or judged, no ground for moral transcendence, no absolute spirit. "One is necessary, one is a piece of fate, one belongs to the whole, one is in the whole—there exists nothing which could judge, measure, compare, condemn our being, for that would be to judge, measure, compare, condemn the whole . . . But nothing exists apart from the whole! . . . this alone is the great liberation—thus alone is the innocence of becoming restored" (*Twilight*, "Four Great Errors," 8). Nietzsche and the Nietzscheans introduced a new tradition of critique of the socius, one characterized by its obliviousness to telos. In the Nietzschean socius, Hegelian rationality and spirit give way to radical individualism; for Nietzsche, a healthy socius is based on a becoming of radical affiliation, which means that the subordination of the psyche to reason for the sake of sociability ceases to be the repository of all emancipatory potential. Whereas with Kant emancipation and freedom are brought forth through subjugation to a lawful, public, external coercion, the Nietzschean individual attains emancipation by overcoming such subjugation. Thus the rejection of Kantian emancipation is not the same as a rejection of emancipation. On this point Habermas is simply wrong. Obviously, Nietzsche did aspire to a form of emancipation in the overman—an emancipation from humanity. Nor does Nietzsche's rejection of reason defined by the subjugation of sociability mean that he abandoned reason as such for its "other," some "archaic" process of "self-discovery." Nietzsche repeatedly asserted his own commitment to reason, albeit a reason deriving from sources other than absolute spirit. "[There is a] misunderstanding of passion and reason, as if the latter were an independent entity and not rather a system of relations between various passions and desires; and as if every passion did not possess its quantum of reason" (*Will*, §387). The individual psyche is neither subordinated to the reason of the socius nor aligned with its own autonomous passion but rather intertwines both in the energy of "life" and the "will to power." Thus Nietzsche strove for a sort of inversion that subordinates reason to life and its contingencies and thereby frees reason from totalization. The rational can be only that which prepares consciousness to apprehend the "reality" of life.

The Subject of Gender

The queer readings in this study primarily examine works of particular philosophers to find crucial and constitutive points in their discussions of sexuality and gender. And clearly the problem of gender in Nietzsche's social philosophy must be addressed directly, not least because it has provided many misreadings and much fodder for blanket rejections. For example, Kaufmann remarked: "What Nietzsche says about Germans and Jews tends to be unconventional and leads us to see things in a new light. It is often thought-provoking even if after due reflection we do not agree with him. He broke the tyranny of stereotyped views that were false and made it possible for us to take a fresh look. His reflections on women, on the other hand, generally have little merit and originality" (in Nietzsche, *Gay Science*, §24).[9] Kaufmann actively defended Nietzsche against criticisms of his "supposed anti-Semitism" yet accepted his supposed misogyny, taking his provocative comments on women at face value. Kaufmann's disavowal on this point has the quality of a rather gentlemanly effort to protect the "ladies" from Nietzsche's viciousness. It is a "kindness" that threatens to turn Kaufmann's scholarship into an apologetics of the type that Nietzsche himself abhorred.

Nietzsche's discussion of gender offers a better glimpse of the central points discussed in the preceding sections: what constitutes queer knowing, what it means to deny sociability as the highest goal, what it means to overcome nihilism with positivity, what it might mean to bring subjective consciousness in line with the "reality" of life. These in turn suggest a few other questions: what does it mean to consciously occupy a Nietzschean *socius*, and if sociability is no longer the highest goal, what does it mean to be a political subject? In this section I attempt to explore these questions and their answers by picking up my strategy of queer readings.

To begin with, we have to overcome a tendency on the part of the "Nietzscheans" to consider his remarks on women as marginal to his social philosophy even though they possess great merit and originality. The remarks on women are not marginal, since Nietzsche said a great deal about the issue, frequently linking the discussion to terms such as *makeup, finery, mask,* and *role.* In his discussion of simulation Derrida acknowledged that Nietzsche was addressing a fundamental and classical connection between the philosophical notion of truth and the concept of the feminine, a relationship to which I want to attend. Nevertheless, Nietzsche's discussion of the "makeup" of gender also reveals a clear understanding of what currently predominates in queer theory as performativity. Nietzsche began book 2 of *The Gay Science* with an explicit discussion of the power of the performative. I quote at length a passage that deftly portrays performativity's connection to the Kantian legacy of appearance, morality, and subjectivity, all within deceptively simple reflections. As one reads this passage, it must be kept in mind that the subsequent aphorisms in *The Gay Science* are devoted specifically to discussions of women. Gender, then, comes to provide the first example of the performative principle of life.

> *Only as creators!*—This has given me the greatest trouble and still does: to realize that what things *are called* is incomparably more important that what they are. The reputation, name, and appearance, the usual measure and weight of a thing, what it counts for—originally almost always wrong and arbitrary, thrown over things like a dress and altogether foreign to their nature and even to their skin—all this grows from generation unto generation, merely because people believe in it, until it gradually grows to be part of the thing and turns into its very body. What at first was appearance becomes in the end almost invariably, the essence

and is effective as such. How foolish it would be to suppose that one only needs to point out this origin and this misty shroud of delusion in order to *destroy* the world that counts for real, so-called *"reality."* We can destroy only as creators.—But let us not forget this either: it is enough to create new names and estimations and probabilities in order to create in the long run new "things." (§58)

Contemporary discussions of performativity have productively analyzed the problematic relationship of being and identity, the inability of identity to signify being, but they have stalled on this point. More recent attempts to discuss the relationship of power and performativity have primarily turned to Kant and Hegel, but such explorations of this knot of modernity, although productive, have proven insufficient (see Butler, Laclau, and Žižek). Nevertheless, Nietzsche's discussion of roles, make-up, appearance, reputation, name, and so on establishes the significance of becoming rather than being for social philosophy and "restores" a possibility of acts rather than identity as defining subjectivity.[10] As Nietzsche broke with Kant and Hegel, his gender performance already addressed the political impasse experienced by queer theory to this date.

Nietzsche's analysis of the performative inverts the Hegelian order of essence followed by appearance, suggesting that "what at first was appearance" has become "essence and is effective as such," which complicates any reading of Nietzsche on gender. If gender—that is, the name *woman* or *man*—was once appearance tossed over the body, in the Nietzschean inversion it becomes an *essence placed under erasure*. This ~~essence~~ gives gender its heft, its ability to organize the socius.[11] It also fills Nietzsche's own style of addressing the topic of women with an apparent misogyny that puts off many readers. Others get trapped in certain terms of his discussion, distilling only those passages about women and ignoring how they interlock with other terms such as *masculinity, artistry, truth, roles, masks, democracy, will to power*—indeed, all aspects of Nietzsche's works.[12] He strategically deploys various terms vis-à-vis gender and sexuality, for instance, *Frau* and *Weib*.[13] Such terms are not necessarily deployed in a systematic fashion, although distinctions between *Frau* and *Weib* do indicate an attempt to distinguish between femininity as a performative and those bodies determined by that performative.[14] His deployment of terms, however, is based precisely in the process of revaluation described in the previous quotation. His terms create new names, estimations, and probabilities ultimately to create new "things." Nietzsche peels the "dress" of gender designations away from bodies, leaving them in a philosophically transgendered state. Nietzsche often uses the term *third sex* much as Hirschfeld did. Notice, moreover, the manner in which gender and sex disjoin in this remark from *The Gay Science:* "*Great man.*—From the fact that somebody is 'a big man' we cannot infer that he is a man; perhaps he is merely a boy, or a chameleon of all the ages of life, or a bewitched little female" (208). Clearly the final inclusion of the "bewitched little female" throws body sex and gender traits into confusion, where to hold one stable destabilizes the other.[15] Thus the revaluation of gender that Nietzsche undertook affects not only femininity but also masculinity. Furthermore, we must pay attention to the terms as we read, always recognizing the possibility that they are used ironically, cleverly, reveling in their own performativity.

A closer reading of his use of *Frau* and *Weib* turns up passages such as those in *Beyond Good and Evil*, where Nietzsche writes: "Women [*die Weiber*] themselves still retain in the background of all personal vanity their impersonal scorn—for 'Woman' [*das Weib*]" (§86). *Das Weib* here comes to indicate the performative of woman that determines all women. The relationship of *personal* vanity and *impersonal* disgust women have for woman indicates a tension of determination and action: the personal subject constituting necessity versus an impersonal knowledge-oriented field of action. Such a tension has reappeared in contemporary discussions of performativity, where much work has been undertaken to offset a sense of voluntarism that filled the term's initial reception in the last decades of the twentieth century. Discussions of subjectivization responded to voluntarism by indicating that the subject is constituted performatively, so that the determination of the performative is inescapable.[16] Here, however, Nietzsche's aphorism suggests that even if performativity is inaccessible for a particular subject, locked in the background as determination or unconscious, a foreground of queer knowledge can be actively aware of the performative's work at all levels. Queer knowledge begins to change names, estimations, and probabilities to create new "things." Indeed, the initial wave of voluntaristic appropriation of performativity—for example, "genderfuck" as a means to overthrow patriarchy or kiss-ins against homophobia—while simplistic in their political strategy, exhibited a desire to act and not react, a hunger for the exercise of queer knowledge.

Seven Points

Under these conditions of destabilization, bringing a certain amount of systematicity to Nietzsche's text will facilitate our ability to read Nietzsche on women, which is to say on gender, which is to say on queer knowledge. We need to differentiate seven points of analysis of woman in his texts.

First, when Nietzsche addressed the enslavement of women in patriarchy, he made strong, pointed criticisms of the double standard of sexuality: women's chastity enforced by ignorance versus men's sexual activity allowed by knowledge. Pushing his analysis of this social condition onto a social philosophical level, however, he recognized this double standard as the central metaphor for truth in philosophy. He opened *Beyond Good and Evil* by asking, "Suppose, that truth is a woman—how?" It is a question posed not at women but skeptically at the position of woman in philosophy. Nietzsche went on the attack against the metaphysics of patriarchy, in which woman is a feminine truth in that sense proposed by Hegelian essentialism, where woman appears philosophically as the other of masculinity and, as such, a knowledge that ultimately must remain outside the apprehension of the masculine philosopher. This truth, based on enslavement, gives way to *skepticism*, but not in the philosopher, who remains unobstructed in his will to "truth."[17] Women, however, are doubly skeptical because, as Nietzsche described, masculinity fails to sustain truth. Masculine sexuality can keep itself as truth only by keeping women in ignorance of sexuality, yet that ignorance must inevitably give way as masculine sexuality reveals itself in the completion of the sex act, at which point skepticism appears. Nietzsche wrote of the skepticism at the heart of the "revelation" in the sex act: "Thus a psychic knot has been tied that may have no equal. Even the compassionate curiosity of the wisest student of humanity is inadequate for guessing how this or that woman manages to accommodate herself to this solution of the riddle. . . . far-reaching suspicions must stir in her poor, unhinged soul—and how the ultimate philosophy and skepsis of woman casts anchor at this point!" (*Gay Science*, §71).

A second point thus emerges as Nietzsche discusses women's experience of that truth of philosophy, and here the doubled basis for women's skepticism becomes clear. If *woman* bears the "truth" of social philosophy for men, *women* enter into social philosophy as inherently skeptical and not just vis-à-vis masculinity, making women clever, dangerous nihilists. Femininity as a truth without knowledge has appearance, not essence; it is something distinct from and external to women's lived experience. The relationship of women to the philosophical "truth" of femininity is again one of skepticism, whereby this external femininity becomes style. Nietzsche wrote of this second kind of skepticism: "*Skeptics.*—I am afraid that old women are more skeptical in their most secret heart of hearts than any man: they consider the superficiality of existence its essence, and all virtue and profundity is to them merely a veil over this 'truth,' a very welcome veil over a pudendum" (*Gay Science*, §64).

These two points of analysis define a fundamental dynamic of modern social philosophy.

Skepticism is nihilistic, not a stable dynamic or an end in itself, and to remain skeptical is a sign of decay and degeneration—a positive process for Nietzsche vis-à-vis morality but ultimately a negative process vis-à-vis life. If life is to benefit, skepticism must be overcome so that positive knowledge can be produced. Nietzsche recognized skepticism as leading to various reactions in the socius that I suggest continue to limit possible social action today. Therefore, the third of Nietzsche's points is his frequently drawn connection between the activity of the artist and women. He praised both for their ability to engage in a form of affirmative creativity. Simultaneously, he connected this creativity to the art of the actor in which the role that is assumed and performed becomes reality. The actor conflates appearance and essence. The aesthetic repulsion of reality forces the artist into a dream state to reconcile appearance and essence, soul and form, with an active ignorance of what is natural.[18] The dreamlike state of appearance ultimately is a decadent undertaking that leads to decline.[19] Fourth, Nietzsche connected the activity of women to that of priests. He recognized an analogous form of resistant will to power in their expression of ressentiment against their masters. There is little praise for this form of "resistance," which develops by limiting and containing the desire of the master. The actions of ressentiment, in Nietzschean social philosophy, succeed only in drawing everyone into decline.

Fifth, there is the response of feminism, which Nietzsche assessed with a viciousness that is often hard to comprehend. His antifeminism belongs to a strategy similar to his anti-anti-Semitism, but it is not a parallel antimisogyny. His antifeminism stemmed from the dilemma of appearance, which feminism irrevocably confused with essence and refused to advance any further. I suggest that this different status, anti-anti-Semitism versus antifeminism, in part derives from the difference in the status of knowledge produced by Judeo-Christians and that produced by the first wave of feminism. In the political movement of feminism, according to Nietzsche, women seek to occupy the same position as men, deploying the same "science" and "objectivity" that men deployed in marking women as different. Paradoxically women begin to instruct men on the *Weib* in itself, but in doing so, they fail to create new names, estimations, and probabilities. In *Beyond Good and Evil* in particular, Nietzsche criticized the knowledge produced by feminism (see §232). Following those injunctions of masculine power that reinforced patriarchy for centuries, "woman should be silent in the church" and "woman should be silent in politics," aphorism 232 ends with hopes for the injunction "woman should be silent about women"—an explicit rejection of projects such as *écriture feminine*. At the same time, the critique of feminine ~~essence~~ does not allow a masculine ~~essence~~ to remain intact, nor does it allow for the retention of a masculine knowledge. It does remind us that will to truth must derive from will to power to produce knowledge. No system of domination was overturned as a "reasonable" response to a petition or the simple production of new knowledge. In producing knowledge according to the same propositions, feminism thus ultimately fails to overcome the operations of a corrupt and decadent science.

The famous or infamous "old woman" represents a sixth type of analysis as well as a specific form of response to the dynamic of gendered domination. Here the old woman reveals to Zarathustra the famous truth, "When you go to women do not forget to take the whip" (*Zarathustra*, 67). This truth derives from a recognition of the social principles of masculinity and femininity, and Zarathustra's need to be reminded of this only underscores their nature as a role awkwardly occupied. The old women's injunction confronts Zarathustra with his own masculine ~~essence~~; he is the whip bearer. It is the old woman who teaches Zarathustra of the values of these "values"; in this statement the old woman confronts Zarathustra with an essentially nihilist recognition and a central problem of all attempts at "radical politics." The overcoming of appearance as essence cannot take place simply through a rejection of ~~essence~~. There is not an outside to the system unless it is created.

The seventh analysis then requires the overcoming of nihilism and the creation of new values around gender. This analysis emerges in the metaphors in Nietzsche's works, particularly the positive tropes and images of gender relations, because although Nietzsche and the Nietzscheans did not accomplish a transformation of gender paradigms, "it is enough to create new names and estimations and probabilities in order to create in the long run new 'things.'" Thus in book 3 of *Zarathustra*, originally conceived as the final chapter to the book, Life appears as a woman and dance partner, and as Zarathustra dances with her, he raises a whip to count time. Life, however, protests that as lovers the two have gone to an island beyond good and evil, and Zarathustra no longer needs this whip. Life also berates Zarathustra because she knows that he is unfaithful to her and will soon leave her. Zarathustra whispers to her of his knowledge of the eternal return that overcomes death and restores Zarathustra to life. The next section then turns to a praise of eternity as woman. These women, no longer defined by femininity as derived from the master-slave relationship, open up new possibilities of existence, even as they have become metaphors (as has Zarathustra's masculinity). They have come to represent a part of Zarathustra himself. These women are in effect aspects of an ever-so-gay Zarathustra freed from nihilism and pessimism. The fourth book presents a new woman, that of desire, who is likewise bound to eternity and likewise an aspect of Zarathustra. Zarathustra's masculinity is not a masculinity that consumes femininity, as does the truth of the master philosopher. Rather, this trope makes of Zarathustra's very existence an advancement of the supersession of gender difference, beyond masculine and feminine, beyond good and evil, beyond ressentiment, and the performance of gender here goes beyond appearance and ~~essence~~ to a positive relationship to life.

Such metaphors seem oddly distant from lived life. They are untimely in that their thrust to create new names for the long run binds them to a futurity. Their action is distant from the present. In the following section I focus more closely on Nietzsche's general discussion of life. This discussion, bound into the history of nihilism, focuses more specifically on the possibilities inherent in the present and more clearly on their possible resolution in a not so distant future.

Life, the Subject of Will

Nietzsche's Zarathustra takes up a gay dance with life, a cheerful rhythm that restores them both. As Nietzsche's writings develop, they move away from Schopenhauer's pessimistic conception of life toward a fundamental optimism. Nietzsche counterposed a will to life to what he characterized in Schopenhauer as will to nothingness. Life, or what Schopenhauer termed "will," is a force driving the subject into pain, which is to be avoided through aestheticism. Nietzsche accepted pain as defining the relationship of will to life, yet he rejected the relationship of displeasure to pain. Life or willing does not proceed according to pleasure or the avoidance of displeasure. What Nietzsche posited in opposition to the pessimistic position of will is something very different from the will of Kant's willed reason or a Hegelian will defined as essence, or for that matter a Habermasian *Willensbildung*, willed consensus. Nietzsche further rejected Schopenhauer's understanding of the will as essence or noumena. He asserted instead the materiality of the will, will as act of willing, an inseparable action or activity. It is not a will subject to outside force or determination; to the contrary, it is an outwardly directed action. It might be weak or strong, passive or active, but will cannot be thought abstractly outside its specific appearance in activity.[20]

The Nietzschean concept of subject emerges from this understanding of will: "There is no 'being' behind doing, effecting, becoming; 'the doer' is merely a fiction added to the deed—the deed is everything" (*Genealogy*, pt. 1, §13). This will defined in activity fundamentally denies the existence of the subject as a category, or a thing in itself. For Nietzsche the Kantian subject is a changeling, an inversion of order. The Nietzschean subject is perhaps exemplified in Freud's description of the ego perched precariously atop the massive steed of the id. Like the id in that description, will drives action, and while the "subject" may strive to be the directing force, life is ultimately served not by the subject but by the attainment of a goal or an aim. Will is the gale-force winds driving the vessel of a helmsman, who as subject negotiates with the wind to take him toward a distant shore.

Like that vessel, Nietzschean subjectivity identifies its locus in the body, a contained *field of will*, which produces deeds and activity. When Nietzscheans such as Deleuze conceptualized the nomadic and rhizomatic, the body without organs, the interface with technology, the protocyborg, as an antidote to the Kantian subject, they misunderstand both the nature of the subject here and the role of the body as *field of will* in Nietzsche. The response to power is not to make the body a conduit or, worse, an assimilated mitochondrial energy source. It is rather to strengthen and extend the bounds of the body.[21] Such a misrecognition perhaps derives from the fact that Nietzsche never engaged in abstract discussions of will, but in such instances the term functions ultimately as an empty signifier requiring specific form and content, specific activity. Will requires a field within which it is articulated, for otherwise it would have a noumenal status. This was recognized by both Freud and more current discussions of the body-ego. Such a body comes to be in two ways: as a result of damned-up energy that discharges and as an intentional activity with purpose. The latter is an action that strengthens subjectivity. The active direction of will characterizes a higher species.

The shift in the overcoming of nihilism toward optimism is the shift from a state of subjugation to one of subjectivization, a shift from subjectivity defined by relations of domination and reaction to one of subjectivity defined by heterogeneity and action. There is a confusion of these two terms in queer theory and in leftist political theory in general. It perhaps derives from the overwhelming concentration on the lord and bondsman dialectic in Hegel and the failure to read about twenty-five pages further to discover that Hegel found a paradigm of resolution in the heterosexual love relationship. This resolution relies on essence. Nietzsche, however, rejected such ~~essence~~ for a material process of overcoming. His genealogy passes beyond the subjugation of the bondsman to the lord and beyond the heteronormative bourgeois subject that Hegel proposed as solution. Out of the debtor relationship, or a relationship of domination, arises the possibility of a subjectivity beyond domination and beyond subjugation.

In *The Genealogy of Morals* Nietzsche described man as the species with a memory, the feature that distinguishes man's subjectivity. The history of nihilism reveals that this memory emerged through the tortures of debt; this history is a long and bloody process in which debt shaped and formed man as fully subjugated and circumscribed by a coercive and totalizing sociability. Like nihilism in general, however, this state now needs to be overcome. The key to this overcoming lies in the nature of memory itself. Memory is "an active *desire* not to rid oneself, a desire for the continuance of something desired once, a real *memory of the will*: so that between the original 'I will,' 'I shall do this' and the actual discharge of the will, its *act*, a world of strange new things, circumstances, even acts of will may be interposed without breaking this long chain of will" (*Genealogy*, pt. 2, §1). Here memory serves as a tool to bring about intentional activity. The I and the will stand interconnected in the statement "I will." Memory conjoins the two, allowing for direction, planning, struggling—in short, creation. Nietzsche described a state of immoral autonomy that emerges through and from this sociability that would have given Kant nightmares.

> Then we discover that the ripest fruit is the *sovereign individual*, like only to himself, liberated again from morality of custom, autonomous and supramoral (for "autonomous" and moral are mutually exclusive), in short the man who has his own independent, protracted will and the *right to make promises*—and in him a proud consciousness, quivering in every muscle, of *what* has at length been achieved and become flesh in him, a consciousness of his own power and freedom, a sensation of mankind come to completion. This emancipated individual and the actual *right* to make promises, this master of a *free* will, this sovereign man. (*Genealogy*, pt. 2, §2)

This form of sovereignty makes subjectivization possible. The "free" will of the "sovereign" individual does not (any longer) freely choose that which is required, finding freedom in all-encompassing sociability. The freedom of this sovereign individual derives not from a self-control based in morality, which is precisely the form of duty that circumscribes the subject as Kant defined it.[22] Neither is this sovereign individual a Hegelian subject, permanently subjugated, positioned within an institutional setting, and circumscribed by the morality of mores, *die Sittlichkeit der Sitten*.[23] Finally, the sovereignty of the individual derives not from the freedom to or from of institutional subjugation but rather from a freedom of willing. Playfully Nietzsche suggested that "one must be able to lose oneself occasionally if one wants to learn something from things different from oneself" (*Gay Science*, §305). The subjectivity that can account for a "loss of self" relies on an instability of institutions, an active traversing of lifeworlds. This subject develops its *I will* in the "for and against" of action, not from a static location of subjectivity unto itself.

Sex and Radical Affiliation

There is certainly more to say about sexuality in Nietzsche than the crass distillation of "immorality" that has been simplistically deployed to allow promiscuity and fornication; cows too breed freely in the pasture. Nietzsche spoke about sex in connection with various topics: Christianity, despisers of the body, sensuality, artistry, Dionysian principles, drives, will to power, marriage, love, and so on. I will not concentrate on those passages where he wrote about sex and sexuality explicitly; rather, I will rely on the topic of sex and sexuality to think further through the Nietzschean negotiations of socius and psyche and to clarify what life means in his work.

As Kant grounded the categorical imperative in a contained heterosexual desire, Nietzsche began *Beyond Good and Evil* with a sexual propositioning of truth; recall that the first line of the preface begins "suppose, that truth is a woman" and goes on to suggest that all philosophers to that point had been (like Kant) quite inadequate as suitors. Indeed, Plato's metaphysics, with its essential division of the noumenal and phenomenal world and its nonapprehendability of pure spirit or good in itself, established in this analogy an impossibility of heterosexual union, transforming philosophy into a propositioning by permanent bachelors, pronouncements of faith by celibate Jesuits. The philosopher could do no more than write about pleasures and joys he could never experience. Keeping with this metaphor, Nietzsche identified philosophy to that point as a failure of heterosexuality perpetrated by "corruptors of youth," such as Socrates. Nevertheless, rather than seek homophobically to distance himself from the history of philosophy, to shore up the institution by holding out the possibility of union of philosopher and truth—rather than present himself as a successful paramour, the philosophical libertine who finishes the tradition—Nietzsche took a typical and radical step, setting himself up as a "free, very free spirit" beyond good and evil. It is not that he left behind the sexuality of truth altogether, but he did fully abandon its heterosexuality. Unlike the trope of woman in *Zarathustra*, the discursive questioning of truth as a woman, an external existence in itself, gives way to other possibilities. Nietzsche did not abandon the possibility of truth, but he abandoned the relationship to truth as one of heterosexual desire, the philosopher's lust for an exterior object. Instead, the desire for truth becomes bound to the individual, the material, the perspectival. When, in the first aphorism, of the book he identified a "will to truth" as foundational to philosophy, truth ceased to be a woman, to have an essential exterior existence, and became a drive for itself, internal, part of the individual. The image of truth becomes a drive, one of many drives, all "*herrschsüchtig* [power hungry]" (§6), all an expression of the fundamental will to power.

I previously suggested that the Nietzschean socius rejects a structure based in a sociable containment of desire. The Nietzschean socius is thus not a closed system but the cacophony of social interaction, a socius that allows the individual access to a freedom of becoming. This *radical individualism* requires and is offset by the possibility of *radical affiliation*, a break with concepts of duty, an ability to overcome debt and history (see also *Will*, §736). Sex provides a particularly precise explication of these points. In the general phantasm that promiscuity and bisexuality present to the "moral" world, there lurks a recognition that sexual union is a fundamentally affiliative act. Even Kant's definition of marriage, the external granting of legitimacy to the mutual use of each other's sex organs, both dreaded and regulated the affiliative quality of sexual union. Sex is one of the most dreadful forces vis-à-vis morality. Nietzsche observed that historically "man affirm[ed] himself most strongly" in "sexuality, avarice, lust to rule, cruelty" (*Will*, §786), and hence these became the objects of prohibition in a morality based on sociability. Sexuality is not simply a site of control. As a form of self-affirmation sex has a particularly significant potential to disrupt normativity and oppose coercive social imperatives; in other words, sex has a queering potential. In a Nietzschean framework immoral sex, queer sex, affirms radical individualism in a moral society. It draws the individual out of decadence and degeneration to a practice healthy for "life." Using different terms Marcuse suggested that in alienated existence sex provides a sense of unalienated existence.

Throughout Nietzsche's work the term *sex*, like the more general terms *nature* or *life*, appears as a code for instinct and inclinations.[24] For Nietzsche, sexuality belongs to the psyche. It is a drive or an impulse; it is need, want, desire. This assessment was certainly not new, but what was new was the idea that sex is not the opposite of will or subject to willed reason but an incitement to willed action.[25] Nietzsche invoked this willed action against an external morality, an anti-Kantian moment that elevates precisely those aspects that Kant excluded from reason as the basis for a rationale of action (see, e.g., *Gay Science*, §294).

We must, however, not confuse Nietzsche's antimorality with a recommendation to "do whatever feels good." An ethics structures Nietzsche's response to morality. In his rejection of morality he began from a point similar to Kant's, discounting behavior motivated by feelings of pleasure—this is not a behaviorism in which humans are motivated by pleasure and flee displeasure. Nor was Nietzsche a hedonist advocating a pursuit of pleasure to corrupt morality. When in an anti-Kantian moment he advocated a eudaemonistic approach to ethics, promoting the pursuit not of pleasure but of happiness, this eudaemonia referred to an ethics of the good life as developed by the Stoics. He likewise praised the transformation of philosophy undertaken by the Epicureans—"philosophy as an art of *living*" (*Will*, 449)—yet regarding their relationship to Aristotle and the Stoics, he shifted and praised the Stoic "hard morality," which he esteemed as a form of self-defense against decadence and dissipation. His praise of the Stoics must be understood within his analysis of the process of historical nihilism. In Stoicism and especially Platonism he recognized the beginnings of Christian asceticism. Indeed, in his critique of the philosopher in "Schopenhauer as Educator," Stoicism provides the philosopher with distance from the world, supporting the will to knowledge, but it also establishes a limit to knowledge because Stoicism gives way to asceticism. Nietzsche directed his critique of Schopenhauer against precisely his rejection of the body, of sensuality, of displeasure and pleasure. Nietzsche responded to Schopenhauer's estimation of life as painful, and hence as something that must be avoided or circumvented, with his own affirmation of life. Moreover, as Nietzsche explored the question of will, he moved further from terms such as *nature* and *life*. Having already denied the significance of pleasure and displeasure in his break with Schopenhauer, he then denied happiness and pain as motivating will (see, e.g., *Gay Science*, §326). He radicalized the "good life" or this "art of living" and identified the higher man not as the one who pursues happiness but as the one who wants to expand in strength even at the cost of suffering and "going under" (*Will*, §222).

An ethics thus operates in Nietzsche's development of the critique of morality. Whereas Kant's morality creates sociability, Nietzsche's ethics might appear to promote "asocial" actions. Nietzsche's denial of the individual ego as a state of distinct being, however, ultimately undoes the possibility of an asocial position. Only as *being* can the individual appear as an asocial atom. A morality in which the individual must either conflict selfishly with society or be lost in the herd can develop only when the individual is taken as being. For Nietzsche, the individual is an unsteady site of becoming, transforming yet unique only as a result of the trajectory assumed in the crossing of lifeworlds. The "dissatisfaction" that propels such a crossing is the "germ of ethics" (*Will*, §333). Hence, Nietzsche's ethics require a selfishness in this becoming derived from radically affiliative actions. Strong feelings support this radical affiliation: "wild spirits, voluptuousness, triumph, pride, audacity, knowledge, self-assurance, happiness as such" (*Will*, §296). Nevertheless, Nietzsche's recognition of a connection among sexuality, greed, lust for power, and cruelty should not be taken as a promotion of cruelty. Nietzsche esteemed self-affirmation, and the rest is historical detritus resulting from the actions of morality against such selfishness.

Sexuality nevertheless has no essence, no being. As with will in general in Nietzsche's work, sexuality is action. Sexuality, a subset of the broader categories of need, instinct, drives, impulses and so on that Nietzsche deployed, provides (unconscious) motivations for action, out of which will coalesces. The more organized the need, the more apparent the will. Lacking fulfillment, need can fail to become will and give way to desire. The longer one desires, the more distant and overwhelming the object of desire threatens to become. In the case of a desire for unfulfillable ideals, desire directs itself toward a dream and away from action, proving ultimately detrimental, decadent. "'Willing' is not 'desiring,' striving, demanding: it is distinguished from these by the affect of commanding. There is no such thing as 'willing,' but only a willing *something*: one must not remove the aim from the total condition. . . . That state of tension by virtue of which a force seeks to discharge itself—is not an example of 'willing'" (*Will*, §668). Thus sexuality as willing appears only in action. This distinction is significant. *The aim cannot provide essence*; to speak of sexual *identity* is to give a depth to sexuality incommensurate with its surface goal. In designations such as homosexuality, sexuality appears to have particular essence, but there is no homosexual and heterosexual depth to sexual willing. The object nature of the willing can differentiate only appearance and manifestation, not an essence.[26]

If morality limits and directs the possible objects of sexuality, if it restricts the possibilities of affiliation, it does transform the appearance of sexuality. Nevertheless, Nietzsche's radical individualism can discern the lack of essence behind the apparent determination: "There is no place, no purpose, no meaning, on which we can shift the responsibility for our being, for our being thus, and thus" (*Will*, §765). Queerness constitutes an "interior" force, a genius that propels *becoming* beyond determining factors. There are those individuals who push aside the influence of material conditions, who disdain all the privilege, security, and safety that accrue to those whose actions concur with the heterocoital imperative. When homosexuals make the claim that they were born "that way," they announce some strange force that motivates them, that overtakes their lives. The announcement appears much as an epileptic seizure or possession must have appeared in the past. Such an external genius brings individuals into conflict with their milieus, surprising other members of their lifeworlds and often the person announcing his or her homosexuality. The announcement leads them to wonder how such a "thing" could have happened. It appears as something radically altering beyond material determination, which frustrates the expectation of the milieu with a radically altering force. It leads to a certain confusion and bafflement, and rather than accept this path-altering announcement as an expression of power, those who confront it will even initiate a search for the origins of this "thing" (as if it could be eliminated) or for the cause of this "thing" (as if the aim could produce the willing). We can either pursue the "cause" or "origins" of homosexuality or take queerness in general as indicating the possibility that the ego can throw off material determining conditions.

At the same time, asking after the goal and effect of the assertion "I was born this way" reveals a different presence of determination. There are two possible rationales of will behind the statement, one reactive, the other active. Both assert a will beyond subjectivity, a force outside the control of the ego, but the question is how the ego aligns itself with that force and in that alignment invites material determination to play a role. The reactive rationale results from powerlessness, the fear of losing material well-being, employment, accommodation, limb, or even life. An individual facing such fears can wield "I was born this way" as a morality of ressentiment. Reactively, "I was born this way" presents homosexuality as a handicap that must be accommodated, a nonthreatening but lifelong disease that must be accepted. This "disability" requires an accommodation of rights granted by the "healthy." Such a reactive assertion, even as it displays its suffering and begs for forgiveness, strives for an equality of "rights" that will prevent the already powerful from growing in power (see *Will*, §86). If successful, it results in a material limitation on the powerful, yet such morality leads to decadence and decline.

The active rationale aligns the ego with a will beyond subjectivity. Actively, "I was born this way" presents homosexuality as a confrontation, a heterogenizing force beyond the ego and milieu. Active assertion of this will rejects morality and denies conventions; it forces the universal claims of morality to appear before the ego as they are, normativizing, totalizing. The active announcement of queerness reveals the cost of the heterocoital imperative, "how much taming, self-overcoming, severity toward ourselves it requires" (*Will*, §281). Unless material conditions allow otherwise, however, the ego that accepts its "birthright" by aligning itself actively with this assertion may inflict material costs on the individuals making this claim. Their rising up as "evil" becomes likewise decadent, leading to their declines and deaths. Such "evilness" corrupts morality *and* transforms material conditions. When material conditions allow the active response to sustain such "evilness," however, freedom and justice become increasingly insignificant terms for such an ego, which then no longer speaks of its "rights." The active response becomes simply creative and life sustaining.

———

For queer theory, the use of sex vis-à-vis the socius may constitute a dreadful attack on morality, but it would be absurd to reduce queer theory to an exercise in shocking bourgeois morality. Sex is not a solution but a problem to be overcome. Nevertheless, sexuality and homosexuality in particular will continue to provide the beginning point for queer theoretical work. As long as marriage and children remain the signification of "proper" heterocoital activity in social philosophy, they will reinforce "proper" sex and gender polarities and produce a badge of "conformity" for the public sphere, masking the "perversions" and "deviations" that are as proper to the bourgeois bedroom as to any other site of sexual activity. Queer sexuality is an appearance, not a structure. Starting with genital-anal or -oral contact, we could create a lengthy list of activities (and nonactivity) that appear in the most sanctified bourgeois bedroom and go well beyond heterosexual genital contact, for example, those involving garments, leather, silk, diapers, plastics, lucite, batteries, tubes, role-playing, tantrums, passivity, exhibitionism—all the way to intentional abstinence from "perversions" or the jouissance of stringently denying oneself access to what one desires. Although all these acts appear in the bourgeois bedroom, as "improper" to heterosexual desire they become public taboo for the middle-class heterosexual couple, not to be discussed or even acknowledged. Sexuality and homosexuality in particular then appear in such a system as its negation, and in achieving a position as the negation of heterosexuality, they become mysterious and fascinating. It seems that the norm can do nothing but think about perversions.

At the same time, sexuality and homosexuality in particular cannot be elevated as an inherently radical or progressive position. Homosexuals, who appear in this economy of desire as some of the primary perverts, are simply skeptics—or rather, homosexuals are not by nature skeptical but are forced into skepticism by the economy of desire in which they must live. We must refrain from an overestimation of skepticism. Certainly homosexuals can see through heterosexuality just as women can see behind masculinity, and both women and homosexuals know how disappointing it is to look behind the curtain of their own mysteries only to find the most quotidian and unexceptional concerns; for some this peek behind the curtain results in a flight from the horror of their own "normalcy" (see Martin). But such a position does not necessarily contain the possibility of quantitative, let alone qualitative, transformation. At best it offers progressus.

Nietzsche indicated that skepticism is unstable, nihilistic, and ultimately unhealthy; it must be overcome. In its sociopolitical effects, queer sexuality in general, and homosexuality in particular, breaks down into the same responses I noted regarding the struggle for gender emancipation. The first response appears in the artistry of drag, camp, or even body manipulation and reconstruction. These are positive yet aesthetic and often become goals in themselves, so that the performer hopes to be overcome by the role rather than to overcome it. The second response appears in the legally oriented ressentiment that lurks in civil rights efforts and hate crimes legislation, the ressentiment that morally outs others to scandalize those in power, thereby only coercing and totalizing. The third response manifests itself in those gays and lesbians who search earnestly for the "causes" of their existence, searching their genes and psyches for some origin. They educate parents, friends, and legislators about the naturalness of their desires. In a plethora of venues they produce endless accounts of determination on where and what gays eat; how lesbians mate; how homosexuals live, travel, and have sex—in short, accounts of the beauty of the ghetto. They even assist in exploring their own bodies for extra gonads, enlarged ear canals, abnormal glands, going all the way to identifying kinks in their DNA.

Fourth, there are those, like Zarathustra's old woman, who reject their essence and seek to struggle through their appearance. Such radical nihilism appears as the most dangerous yet politically decadent position. It has a strong effect yet remains reactive, a response, caught up in a dialectic of sexuality. A concentration on the negation of queer sexuality yields a problematic alignment. Clearly a concentration on acts or behavior defines queers by (perverse) sexual behaviors "prohibited" to heterosexuals. When this position is adopted as a reaction, these acts become esteemed as the site of identity and politics. For instance, if straight men appear as men who engage in heterocoital contact with women, the queer position is taken up by men who define themselves through engaging in oral- or anal-genital contact with other men and who then build out of this a political position. If monogamy is advanced publicly as the positive ideal of heterosexuality, then promiscuity is claimed as the positive ideal of queerness. Queers assert and "celebrate" their position outside "normalcy," while straight women and men are trapped in it. We can see this political tactic adopted repeatedly, from the aesthetic decadents near the end of the nineteenth century, through to the Gay Liberation Front of the 1970s,[27] to queer manifestos such as "I Hate Straights" and "Tremble Hetero Swine."

Monogamy and promiscuity, oral- and anal-genital contact, have at best only contingent political significance deriving from the position of negation. The negative or abject as a site of essential political energy or self-description serves only satirical or cynical purposes.[28] It is a dead end. Which is not to say that homosexuals' attempts to adopt a "positive" position, for example, in support of monogamy, derive any less from a position of negation. Sexuality, particularly queer sexuality, constitutes a site of a great deal of contestation, of the exercise of power, but to overcome the skepticism and nihilism, the position of negation, we must look to *social philosophy and not to sexuality.* We must go beyond critical queer theory to generate a positive queer social philosophy.

Notes

1. This is the translation to which Barbara Harlow turned in her translation of Derrida's *Spurs,* presumably moving from the French translation, *Gai Savoir.*

2. This reliance on transparency of language is a bit odd. Kaufmann seems to suggest that Nietzsche would have chosen *fröhlich,* which in German has no relationship to homosexuality, because of its meanings in English.

3. Kaufmann noted a further parallel between Nietzsche and male homosexuals in that "Nietzsche says some very unkind things about women, and he extols friendship and the Greeks" (in *Gay Science,* §5). In this equation Kaufmann seems to indicate that his familiarity with male homosexuals was drawn from a limited group of misogynist classicists.

4. For instance, the fact that we can trace Freud's initial formulation of the id (*es*) back to Nietzsche may obscure the radical difference Freud's formulation of the unconscious has from anything in Nietzsche. Freud's famous "wo es war, muß ich werden" supports an expansion of ego at the expense of id. Nietzsche's admonition to replace "thou shalt" with an "I will" likewise supports an expansion of ego, but at the expense of what Freud would describe as the superego. In the one, instinctual life suffers at the expense of sociability; in the other, sociability plays little role. In general this argument is contained in Nietzsche's responses to the effects of morality. *Zarathustra* contains, in the context of eternal return, a discussion of the relationship of "I will" to an "it was" that is, "*es war*" (137–42). *The Will to Power* sets forward this opposition in terms of a historical analysis (§940; see also §275). Ostensibly Nietzschean writers have often brought forward propositions significantly divergent from Nietz-

sche's, going as far as proposing a Nietzschean theology or restoration of morality. Thus a return to Nietzsche is in order if only to discover what is specific to his work.

5. In *The Philosophical Discourse of Modernity* Habermas drew a distinction between social and cultural modernization that further distinguishes between institutions and values. Since both the social and the cultural are forms of modernization, it appears that economic development plays an equal part in both, yet Habermas makes social modernization primary to cultural. I shift this distinction to cultural modernity and social modernization to maintain a last instance more clearly.

6. This presents an inversion of Hegelian terms of history. Neither freedom nor positive elements propel history. Long before Adorno, Nietzsche described the activity of the negative in history.

7. As much as Foucault described "that" history happens, this does little to explain why the "epistemic" shifts propelling history occur. Foucault occupied the position that Nietzsche described as the "critical historian," who lives and suffers in the present and disrupts the past seeking a transformation in the future.

8. He stated, furthermore: "My idea is, as you see, that consciousness does not really belong to man's individual existence but rather to his social herd nature; that, as follows from this, it has developed subtlety only insofar as this is required by social or herd utility" (*Gay Science*, 354).

9. I want to caution against singular readings of gender and sexuality in Nietzsche. His lengthy and significant discussions of gender, which appear in texts such as *The Gay Science* and *Beyond Good and Evil*, take place alongside discussions of other identities, other states of supposed being: German, Jew, Christian, socialist, animal, artist. All these discussions include a rejection of what we would call "identity politics." Kaufmann commented rigorously on the conflux of the first two, German and Jew, reading Nietzsche as neither the rabid nationalist nor the anti-Semite that the Nazi era made of him. Rather, Kaufmann found the opposite in his writings; Nietzsche's break with Wagner resulted in an antinationalist position that opposed especially German nationalism. Certainly from *The Gay Science* onward Nietzsche frequently spoke out against the anti-Semitism that attended German nationalism so closely, yet in these works he adopted a position as anti-anti-Semite that did not collapse into a "philo-Semitism," or a valorization of a Jewish essence. He adopted a difficult position that did not defend Judaism or the Jews from his general and scathing critiques of religion, although even there he directed his critique more directly at Christianity. Nietzsche's rejection of nationalism and religious affiliation reveals a radical individualism opposed to essentialism that forms the basis of his philosophy, from which derives a clear rejection of any form of identity politics. His remarks on women must be understood as belonging to this framework. At the same time, Nietzsche adopted an antifeminist position rather than the equivalent of an anti-anti-Semite position, an antimisogynist position. It remains to be seen whether his own misogyny is on par with his critiques of the Judeo-Christian tradition.

10. As Thomas DiPiero has famously pointed out, the ultimate outcome of the discussions around performativity in the 1990s was to bring us "back" to that period Foucault identified at the beginning of *The History of Sexuality* as the period before sexual identity. That is, although they did not "undo" the significance of sexual identity, these debates undermined the understanding of sexuality as a state of being and allowed us to recognize the significance of acting vis-à-vis sexuality (see DiPiero, *White Men Aren't*).

11. The poststructuralist orthographic play that abounded in the 1980s has grown somewhat tiresome, so that I am a bit hesitant to resort to what may appear as such play, yet I find myself turning to ~~essence~~ out of necessity. ~~Essence~~ will designate my

recognition that this notion has had great social philosophical impact and hence I must address it as a concept, but the deconstructive orthographic convention of "placing it under erasure" allows me to discuss essence without actually falling into an essentialist position. I hope you, gentle reader, will recognize the necessity that drives my use of this convention.

12. Generally scholars who critique Nietzsche on the basis of sex or gender isolate particular comments on women and do not seek to situate them within an overall analysis of the text or within an analysis of the historical context within which they emerged. Anglo-American feminists have exhibited a tendency to engage in close readings of Nietzsche's texts, seeking out solely the statements related to women; see Clark; Bergoffen. Alternatively, they dismiss them as simply a matter of historical context; see, e.g., Kennedy.

13. *Frau* is the word commonly used for "woman," although it derives from the noble title meaning "lady." *Weib* is an archaic word, formerly the common term for "woman." It subsequently took on a negative connotation, alluding to prostitution, something like *wench* or *vixen*.

14. Much recent scholarship has described Nietzsche as a much more "untimely" thinker, finding in him positions from which to mount critiques of the contemporary feminist movement. Yet much of this scholarship has also suggested that Nietzsche was "not fully consistent in his attitude toward the opposite sex" (Higgens, 145). Some have even suggested a lack of sustained thinking about women; see Allen. While I hesitate to describe in Nietzsche the systematic outlines of a Kant or Hegel, his work on gender and sex does follow certain consistent trajectories overall.

15. See also *Gay Science*, where he discusses the "function" of gender and the possibility of "women who transform themselves into some function of a man" (§119).

16. For a significant text that provided a discussion of subjectivization in response to performativity, see Butler, *Psychic Life of Power*.

17. In this vein Nietzsche writes of "*Ultimate skepsis.*—What are man's truths ultimately? Merely his *irrefutable* errors" (*Gay Science*, §265).

18. As illustration, in *The Gay Science*, immediately following the discussion of creators, Nietzsche turned his attention to "we artists," ironically including himself among them, and he began by observing what happens when "we" love a woman. (There is, however, no reason to understand the artist lesbophobically as a position reserved solely for men.) "When we love a woman, we easily conceive a hatred for nature on account of all the repulsive natural functions to which every woman is subject" (59). This "repulsion" propels the artist simultaneously toward both appearance and essence. "Then we refuse to pay any heed to physiology and decree secretly: 'I want to hear nothing about the fact that a human being is something more than *soul and form*'" (§59; see also §§293, 361, 369, 376).

19. See, for instance, *The Gay Science*, esp. §361 but also, in connection with the relationship between motherliness and artistic creativity, §§369 and 376.

20. Nietzsche's following remark illustrates the understanding of will as a form of activity even in passivity:

> What is "passive"?—To be hindered from moving forward: thus an act of resistance and reaction.
> What is "active"?—reaching out for power. (*Will*, 657)

This passage also illustrates how the will serves to stabilize a field of power, or what Deleuze might describe as territorialization.

21. Nietzsche wrote on this point: "Greater complexity, sharp differentiation, the contiguity of developed organs and functions with the disappearance of the interme-

diate members—if that is perfection, then there is a will to power in the organic process by virtue of which dominant, shaping, commanding forces continually extend the bounds of their power and continually simplify within these bounds: the imperative grows" (*Will*, 644).

22. Not only does *The Genealogy of Morals* characterize the sovereign individual as developing through a free will based in an immoral consciousness; in notes collected in *The Will to Power*, Nietzsche modified his assessment of free will to a more skeptical position. He actually radicalized the anti-Kantian aspects of his description. Again understanding the term *free will* nihilistically, Nietzsche recognized that it created the "right for man to think of himself as cause of his exalted state and actions" (*Will*, §288). At the same time, however, he demoted consciousness, recognizing more than conscious willing involved in "free will." Will as willed desire, as we saw with Kant, positions man as the primary cause of his own actions. Consciousness loses its position obtained in the Kantian bipartite system and becomes an aftereffect, not a cause, a performer and not a director.

23. This institutional subjugation is clearly addressed by Althusser in his discussion of the state apparatus and interpellation. It is, however, a mistake to recognize Althusser's description of subjectivity as resulting in a stable or singular subject. Interpellation is a temporary state, or rather, the institution's call is always doomed to failure, to incompleteness, and must be constantly "restated." The subject hailed by ideology is not permanently called into being. Even according to his own discussion, the dynamic of interpellation that Althusser identified must be only temporary to allow the possibility that humanity may be differently hailed.

24. Early on it is apparent that "nature" is at work. The discussion of nature is not a pantheism, however, in that it occurs in conjunction with discussions of life, even a will to life, where nature actually relates directly with the instincts as positive preserving forces for life. Nature is not an external spirit. For early discussions see Nietzsche, *Untimely Meditations*, book 2 in general and book 3, section 3, in particular.

25. "The multitude and disaggregation of impulses and the lack of any systematic order among them result in a 'weak will'; their coordination under a single predominant impulse results in a 'strong will'" (Nietzsche, *Will*, §46). Nietzsche's thought on the will changed over time. We need only compare the preceding remark to a subsequent one in *The Will to Power* (84) to recognize contradictions in his thinking on will. There is, however, a trajectory that begins with the influence of Schopenhauer that he overcomes for a more positive appraisal of life. This gives way increasingly to reflections on the nature of will and then on will to power in particular. This trajectory makes it difficult to accept Heidegger's ability to discern a definitive reading of will in Nietzsche. The following passage provides a glimpse of this trajectory:

> Is "will to power" a *kind* of "will" or identical with the concept "will"? Is it the same thing as desiring? Or *commanding*? Is it that "will" of which Schopenhauer said it was the "in-itself of things"?
>
> My proposition is: that the will of psychology hitherto is an unjustified generalization, that this will *does not exist at all*, that instead of grasping the idea of the development of one definite will into many forms, one has eliminated the character of the will by subtracting from its content, its "whither?"—this is in the highest degree the case with *Schopenhauer*: what he calls "will" is a mere empty word. It is even less a question of a "will to live"; for life is merely a special case of the will to power;—it is quite arbitrary to assert that everything strives to enter into *this* form of the will to power. (*Will*, §692)

26. Nor did Freud follow such a differentiation in *Three Essays on Sexuality,* developing the understanding of libido from Nietzschean willing. He insisted there that the object nature of the libido is not sufficient to differentiate homosexuality and heterosexuality.

27. In their leaflets the Gay Liberation Front proclaimed: "We are fighting an entire culture. . . . We must be 'rotten queers' to the straight world and for them we must use camp, drag, etc., in the most 'offensive' manner possible. And we must be 'freaks' to the gay ghetto world. Our very existence must provoke a questioning of society" (qtd. in Watney, 72)

28. Examples of attempts to negate the negation appear in positions assumed by authors as diverse from one another as Jean Genet, John Rechy, and more recently, Dennis Cooper. The historian Jeffrey Weeks has been attentive to these developments of gay identity and gay politics, and in this respect his book *Invented Moralities* is of interest.

Conclusion:
Prolegomena to a Queer Social Philosophy

Social Philosophy after Nietzsche

The survey of critical social philosophy undertaken here should not be confused with a rejection of the various formulations; rather, it should be understood as an attempt to assess the descriptive and analytic potentials of each—indeed, to continue the practice that drove each of the figures explored in the preceding chapters. None of them was content with the work of his predecessors, each figure identifying previous limits and weaknesses and establishing new formulations. For my part, in attempting to give the queer its due, I have repeatedly sought to identify those moments where queer reason disrupts the rationales of the social philosophy under examination. In placing Nietzsche at the end of the book, however, I sought to mark a fundamental challenge to each of the formulations explored. Nietzsche presented a critique of modern philosophy, not a rejection. He owed a debt to the developments of his predecessors, but he also sought to overcome them, thereby moving his critique from a negative, reactive position to a positive, active one. Queer social philosophy begins with this critique but must likewise go beyond it. I want to take a moment to review the possibilities.

Kantian philosophy identifies structures of the psyche that continue to define modern psychology. Kant's social philosophy, an example of the

best of bourgeois revolutionary thought, continues to infuse liberal political theory. Yet his moral philosophy proceeded from a desire to change
real conditions. Not content with his own period's social organization,
Kant established principles that would influence future social structures.
He sought to do this by defining a form of self-governance proper to a universal human psyche. His system, however, relies not on what he recognized as human interests but on a metaphysical human nature. He did recognize the psyche as a field of heterogeneous desires and interests, yet in
his characterization of the real existing social conditions as fetters to the
free development of all humanity, he established the homogenization of
the psyche as basis of self-governance. Of course, not all subjects recognize the heterocoital imperative, and the categorical imperative is not an
a priori structure. It is instead a principle that any individual can apply as
a guiding maxim to lead a moral life. Yet for Kant, only those who recognize these imperatives can be considered moral. For a Kantian rational
socius to work, all individuals must live morally, for only then can they
live in line with reason. Immoral individuals are irrational, living in a
heteronomous state and thereby losing control over their own persons. Out
of such a person is born the desiring individual, the core of the queer of
modern social philosophy. Nietzsche drew on Kant's description of the
bipartite consciousness and the move to a socius defined by self-governance, but his social philosophy reveals a problem here: what Kant defined
as immoral, irrational, and antisocial proves *constitutive* of the socius.
Nietzsche began with human interests and not a universal human essence
that lies somewhere behind a future humanity. Nietzsche thus offered a
principle of "immorality" and "irrationality" that radicalizes the dynamic
autonomy of Kantian social philosophy.

Much of what can be said about Hegel's social philosophy has already
been said about Kant's, yet Hegel certainly knotted up the threads his
predecessor spun. Further, Hegel offered a secularization of history that
allows humans to become not just subjects but agents of their own history. Determining structures are undeniably significant here—the world
is one of conflict and coercion—but Hegel also recognizes human consciousness as a subject of its own determination and human conflict as
a structure of ultimate freedom and harmony. The history Hegel describes
is a grand narrative with a happy end. Nevertheless, its reliance on the
heterocoital imperative to structure this harmonious state transforms
Hegelian social philosophy into a totalizing rather than a universalizing
philosophy. The moral-ethical stability that Hegel defined as ending history and bringing about harmony becomes a queer apparatus engender-
ing perpetual resistance and dynamic historical transformation. In his

essay "On the Use and Abuse of History for Life" Nietzsche rejected the Hegelian telos of history, and in the *Genealogy of Morals* he radicalized the history of morality present in Hegel to the point where morality loses any transcendence. Nietzschean genealogical analysis accounts for historical development but refuses a systematic rational plan. Humans may be animals with memories, but they have no certainty of a future. Likewise, in his critique of the herd, Nietzsche radicalized the significance of autonomy, refusing state institutions of governance as higher instances, and in his recognition of eternal recurrence, the future loses all significance. There is no world or time behind or in front of this one. Hence the highest goal of the individual is in the living moment.

Unlike Nietzsche, Marx adopted an orientation toward a definite future, thus opening up a fundamental critique of the project of modernity. Social philosophy here goes beyond a critical, descriptive mode to become a guiding force in social transformation. Marx made resistance to coercion central to social philosophy. Like his predecessors, he expressed a discontentment with the existing order, but in response he identified the possibility of social organization beyond the state. Marx's resolution of the problem of coercion does not rely on a principle of moral rationality, filiation, or state totalization. Rather, Marx began with the recognition that the activity and labor of humans make them social. Fundamentally, Marx's critique of industry and ideology recognizes the role of desire in constituting individual subjects. While participation in the socius presents the psyche with a homogenizing dynamic that can become coercive, the system of desiring relations that result from human intercourse nevertheless holds the key to resolving any queer conflict. The structures of relations of production, however, particularly the economic forces unleashed by capitalism, led to a socius structured by inequitable and coercive relations. Marx recognized a solution within capitalism itself, in that the economic pauperization of individuals also forces them into a universal lifeworld as proletariat. Yet Marxism could not exceed the limits that heteronormativity places on desire. Marx failed to account for the heterogeneity of subjects. Presuming a universal, homogeneous human subject, he hoped that once forced into participation in a single lifeworld, this proletarian collective subject could resolve economic and historical conflict. The subsequent developments of Marxism sought to accomplish this homogenization by establishing the proletariat as a performative. Instead of ending coercion, Marxism generated its own unique queering apparatus.

In the final analysis, however, Marx and Nietzsche are not necessarily antithetical. Although it would be too much to describe Nietzsche as a materialist, the two shared both an anti-idealist approach and an understanding of philosophy as an activity of radical social transformation. Nevertheless, the critique of herd mentality and rejection of performativity set Nietzschean social philosophy in a different direction. As I have discussed, Nietzschean material change relies on a transformative heterogeneity, striving for a universality without totality. For the first time in the history of modern social philosophy, Nietzsche's emphasis on willing and becoming, his position that there is no being behind doing, allowed for an analysis that did not take the desiring individual as a negative other to the rational and thus moral citizen-subject. Nietzsche, however, in his rejection of the herd and moral debt, failed to recognize the significance of human industry and the dynamic of sociability for subjectivity. Zarathustra enters into society only because he is overflowing with his own wisdom; otherwise the prophet of the overman is content to remain isolated on a mountain top. Such disdain for the social proves too weak to counter the effects of coercion, and it threatens to reduce the entire system of Nietzschean philosophy to an individualism that cannot carry out the transformation toward which it strives.

I have so far distinguished two sources of queerness. One is a heterogenizing principle of the psyche, the differentiating principle of self-consciousness that makes it fundamentally queer. The other form derives from what I have referred to as a queering apparatus, those systems or institutions that seek to counter heterogeneity, coercing a homogeneity in psyche and socius. The former source of queerness is constitutive and inescapable. The latter is aggressive, a destructive line of force that may evoke resistance. In keeping with the positive, socially transformative role Marx recognized for social philosophy, a queer social philosophy should describe the intellectual equipment with which one can counter coercion and foster heterogeneity. It must be active, not simply reactive.

These considerations lead into three general areas of concern for queer social philosophy: its relation to individual queer practice in the world, or "philosophical activism"; its relation to larger collective activity, or "queer emancipation"; and its ability to generate distinct questions and perspectives, or "queer science."

Philosophical Activism

There is a type of individual engagement with the world that we might describe as *reactive activism* since, although it does respond to given conditions and seek to change them, it accepts the basic configuration of given conditions. The individual engages in such activism out of an experience of coercion explained because of an essence: they hate me because I am gay, black, smarter, prettier, or free. The reactive struggle against the coercion emerges from the essence. The struggle is informed by a certain empiricism that accepts the organizing institutions of public life (e.g., marriage, political parties, the military, the police, churches, country clubs, and schools) and seeks inclusion into them without demanding their fundamental redefinition. The quest for equal rights is then a quest for equate-ability: to be treated just like. Succeeding in such a quest is certainly an act of emancipation within the present order, but ultimately such emancipation is a minoritizing change with limited effect on the majority. It is possible that, as Hegel suggested, sufficient quantitative change of this sort can force institutions to change qualitatively as well, but qualitative change is not the express goal of this type of activism. With a focus on acceptance into the organizing institution of the socius, practical political activity need be informed only by a tendentious and limited theory.

Queer theory has been primarily critical, negative, and deconstructive—in other words, reactive. Contingency, heterogeneity, deviation, divergence, and difference—the queer elements of socius and psyche—have all had advocates in the long history of social philosophy, yet it has been the effort to contain them through coercion, totalization, homogeneity, and filiation that has dominated social philosophy's responses to its own discoveries. Few have sought to understand queer elements as means to qualitative change. Locked in ghettos of 10 to 1 percent, what is identified as queer appears quantitatively minor, able to accomplish a politics of only reform and integration. In rejecting these premises of modern social philosophy, queer theory established a very significant domain of criticism and thus offered individuals new ways of confronting circumstances directly encountered, given, and transmitted from the past.

Unfortunately queer theory has often been accused of being distant from political practice, too difficult for the nonspecialist academicians and of no use to activists. I find such accusations disappointing, albeit sometimes understandable. Political activists know how complicated the world is. Why would the theoretical analyses of that world be simple? Difficult experiences are difficult to describe. Complicated systems require complicated language. Nevertheless, there is a relationship between queer theory and queer activism, and queer theory has understood its audience to exceed the walls of academia. Queer theory has struggled in its own way to uphold Marx's effort to commit social philosophy to social change.

Interestingly, even as it has been denounced as distant from activist interests and needs, queer theory has often had to confront the deployment of highly complicated analyses in simplistic ways, as when Judith Butler's analysis of performativity unleashed a wave of performance. I am not sure we need to express too much anxiety about "misappropriations" of queer theory. It would be better to take this as a sign that queer theory helps to allow individuals determined by histories of negation and abjection to make their own history, revolutionize themselves, create things that have never existed, break with the spirit of the past, and find their ways in a language of the future. Queer theory has struggled to go beyond a primarily critical negative position and enter concrete positive praxis. The generation of a queer social philosophy results from such a shift.

Writing in *The Chronicle of Higher Education* Lennard Davis reported the tale of his son, who went off to college, took a course on queer theory with an adjunct, read some Judith Butler on performativity and Leslie Feinberg on stone butches, and as a result announced that he was transgendered. This story may seem a bit nightmarish for unassuming parents and might incite us to expend a great deal of energy to recuperate the radical critical potential of queer theory from appropriation by a juvenile practice of genderfuck. To be sure, the story of Davis's child provokes a suspicion that the son is not an authentic trannie but rather a freshman in a state of rebellion, engaged in a juvenile act of experimentation. The tale provokes this suspicion because it seems filled with Davis's anxiety about his ability to accept his son as he really is. It seems a mistake to concentrate on the question of the daughter's essence: is s/he genuinely trans or not? That type of questioning only instantiates essentialism of gender, sex, and sexuality. What I find interesting is the idea that the child went off to college and came back with a backpack full of queer studies and a head filled with the philosophical insights of queer theory. Perhaps the first-year student engaged in a naïve reading of the works, although by all accounts his father, a professor of English and expert on disability studies, was unable to outwit his new daughter's philosophical weapons. The encounter with queer theory brought forth an intellectual and emotional tenacity with which the student was able to defend his self-consciousness. This story shows that queer theory can offer a direct practical outcome. It can lead to a type of *philosophical activism*, an engagement with the world informed by theory that allows the boy to explore new possibilities and the girl to find new forms of expression, to critically test the world—and maybe in the process provoke the parents as well.

Perhaps after sufficient testing the child will change in new, unexpected directions. The outcome of the story does not matter, however, because this philosophical activism is not a terminable project, finished after the attainment of a single goal. The critical consciousness developed from philosophical activism may exceed gender, sex, and sexuality. In this way the principles of philosophical activism become available for the exploration of all the lifeworlds the subject inhabits.

Queer Emancipation

The preceding section focused primarily on the individual's relationship to queer social philosophy, but individualist solutions are not enough to counter the collective effect of homogenizing institutions and totalizing coercion. Grander schemes of human interaction and social arrangement—that is, the political—therefore become an urgent domain for queer social philosophy. Indeed, it would be a sad reduction if queer social philosophy were confused with an advocacy of "Western individualism." My analysis has made it clear that queer politics derives from a dynamic of affiliative sociability and self-governance based in specific interests. The question for a conclusion is how such a politics might appear and where we might find traces of it in the present order.

Coming out continues to be fundamental to gay and lesbian politics, although coming out has also passed into the general culture to become an activity open to everyone from victims of abuse to chocoholics. Eve Sedgwick's critique of coming out has become a classic of queer theory. Coming out might thus offer a useful starting point. Sedgwick observed that no individual steps out of the closet into a stable being. She described coming out as interminable process that can never provide the freedom it promises, because in a heteronormative socius that being must be constantly reasserted. Homosexuals become bound to the closet for their social being. This critique was a necessary stroke of genius, because the act of coming out had become a central rationale of gay rights activity. Nevertheless, in coming out an active striving for liberation does comprise the substance of the matter.

It might be helpful to distinguish two types of coming out. Sedgwick focused on the coming out that takes place *across* lifeworlds, when the individual comes out as a type to other types. Historically the politics of gay coming out derived from the outing as addressed to heterosexuals, but a second coming out can be localized to a particular lifeworld, a sort of "coming in." Coming out as gay is also an entry into the desired that was once off limits, into the underground, the subculture, the scene, the lifestyle; it is an act of affiliation with a new lifeworld, an expansion of choice. This coming out precedes the other and might be described as a coming to self-consciousness.

Of course, the possibilities and import of coming out are already defined by arrangements of lifeworlds. To come out as a heterosexual is unnecessary given the heteronormative presumptions that currently order the socius. To come out as a chocoholic might be a bit daring in a size- and health-conscious society but really risks little. Nevertheless, it makes a rather mundane desire decadent and perverse and allows a community of chocoholics to form, much as coming out as a raunch pig does. Of course, when coming out the raunch pig, the trannie girl, and the bear cub face conditions different from those facing the chocoholic. Coming out can expose the individual to a great deal of danger if it is a coming out across lifeworlds in a coercive relationship. The trannie girl coming out to her parents could wind up on the street. The raunch pig could wind up in jail. The bear cub may find himself being dragged behind a pickup truck.

Coming out across lifeworlds is a limited method of confronting coercion, especially if it confronts the other with only a truth of being. There is coming out on a small scale, telling parents, friends, or co-workers, "I am lesbian, and I was born this way." The hope is that the others will appear interested, learn more about the lesbian and her community, and thereby lose their fears and come to a position of *tolerance* for this difference. Tolerance has been a political goal for minority groups since the Enlightenment; indeed, it is inherently a minoritizing position. The form of acceptance offered by tolerance relies on a sort of forgetting of the differences of the other, a certain anonymity to which both parties contribute: on the one hand, the tolerated accommodate themselves, passing, fading into the homogeneity of the socius; on the other hand, those doing the tolerating express a sort of active disregarding, active ignorance: "Don't tell, and we don't need to know." "Okay, maybe now you can get on with your life." Tolerance might reduce a threat of violence, but it is not a counter to coercion.

There is, of course, a stronger means of countering coercion that we discern in coming out. There is a grand process of affiliation that strives for *emancipation*. One attests to a difference of being by coming out as a particular species, but to make it known, it has to be made visible, it has to be flaunted—repeatedly made visible, as Sedgwick noted. Kiss-ins, parades, pins, T-shirts, bumper stickers, rainbow baby strollers, petitions, rallies, pickets, and marches all become necessary performatives to say, "We're here. We're queer. Get used to it." Emancipation is the action not of an individual but of a group and thus derives from the *expansion* of a lifeworld. Emancipation requires a certain visibility, group cohesion, and, as the numbers grow, even a form of coercion that moves "identification with" toward "identity as." In numbers lie strength and community. Historically and typically, perhaps, the homosexual rights movement relied on tolerance, whereas the gay rights movement relied on emancipation.

A stronger method of confronting coercion operates through *the power of the state.* This method focuses on removing the violent and coercive force of the state itself. Weber, we recall, defined the state as the human community that within a certain territory "successfully upholds the claim to the *monopoly* of the *legitimate* use of physical force in the enforcement of its order" (*Economy and Society*, 1:54). To confront coercion and end the threat of physical violence, queer communities have often sought to reduce the state's exercise of heteronormative force. In 1898 Magnus Hirschfeld presented the first petition to Germany's parliament on behalf of homosexual emancipation, the first address of this kind to a modern state. As subsequent experience demonstrated, however, to get police to stop raiding the parks and legislators to repeal sodomy laws does indeed require an active, coordinated "10 percent" of the population. There is of course the further possibility of acquiring state power. Emancipation challenges the monopoly of the state apparatus not to undo that monopoly but at most to reform it and most often to prove the "respectability" of the subjects of the lifeworld. In return for licit behavior, the subjects receive the surety that the state will exercise physical force "on their behalf" in the future; that is, it stabilizes the group, making them into a special interest group integrated into the coercive apparatus with a political agenda. Unfortunately, queer social philosophy of this route ultimately leads away from self-governance and sociability. It offers political emancipation and progress in the present order, but queer social philosophy should also attend to what Marx described as human emancipation. Human emancipation can rely on the services of legality and the state, but it is ultimately a question of discovering self-governance. The move from governance to self-governance is ultimately a move from the state into the realm of culture as the arena of emancipation.

Let me return to the dynamic of coming out to suggest a further corrective to Sedgwick's critique. That corrective helps illustrate the cultural form of *queer liberation.* Given that coming out has a cultural history as a gay act, the explosion of nongay comings-out and the spread of *outing* as a term across linguistic and cultural barriers indicate individuals' willingness to affiliate themselves with an illicit, immoral, nonnormative, queer act. Self-outing in the media and on talkshows might seem social philosophically trivial, but such acts betray a queer heterogenizing desire on even the most mundane level, and thus queer social philosophy is immanent in these quotidian attempts to uncontain self-governance and coordinate new forms of sociability. But if coming out were advised by queer social philosophy, it would fulfill further emancipatory potentials: even if coming out offers entry into new lifeworlds, the individual who comes out does not arrive at a fixed, stable social being. It would be so only if coming out were no more than a presentation of a type to other types rather than a method for discovering new possibilities of acting and becoming.

Queer Science

Some years ago the neurobiologist Simon LeVay published a book with the provocatively Nietzschean title *Queer Science: The Use and Abuse of Research into Homosexuality*, but nothing is more anti-Nietzschean than this work. LeVay was at the forefront of the search for a biological cause of homosexuality. He conducted research mostly on hormones and the size of the hypothalamus until the 1990s, when criticism of his methodology led him to abandon his research position and become a freelance writer. LeVay cited Magnus Hirschfeld's third-sex model as an influence on his own work. Hirschfeld did indeed propose the third-sex model to account for sexual development, but he differed from LeVay by proving to have been an amazing documentarist of a diversity of gender identifications, sex configurations, and sexual practices (see Steakely, "*Per scientiam*"). His research on sexual intermediaries, his vast library and photoarchive, would have been a lasting legacy to the world, but the great mound of material went up in flames at the famous Nazi book burning of May 1933, lost forever to a terrible active ignorance.

There is a connection between Hirschfeld and LeVay, and yet there is also a world of difference. LeVay's work, more of a queer creationism than a queer science, promotes the essentialist logic of being. LeVay searched for origins and causes to homosexuality: I was born this way. Hirschfeld's work, empirical and painstaking, queered standard scientific protocols by relying on survey forms, calipers, cameras, and so on to challenge the dominant heteronormative model of sexual dimorphism. He did not look for causes or origins but sought *existing* human diversity: We are born this way *and* that. I hold up these two figures to give insight into the directions queer social philosophy might take in instituting a *queer science, a queer way of knowing*. A vibrant queer social philosophy necessarily gives rise to such queer knowledge.

Hirschfeld's work represents some elements of a queer science, notably by helping us see what we do not normally see very well. Ultimately his research bypasses questions of essentialism or antiessentialism and stridently challenges stereotypes and other coercive normative mechanisms that restrict our field of vision, our ways of knowing. It institutes ways of seeing difference and in doing so establishes new ways of seeing. A queer social philosophy coordinates with a queer science, mutually generating knowledge and activism.

The "born this way" model, in which LeVay participated, resonates in popular culture and gay politics, posing the antithesis to a challenge from the Christian right that attacks the "homosexual lifestyle." We might describe it as a battle between probirth and pro-lifestyle-choice camps, designations that evoke the deadlock in the abortion debate. The probirth position wins liberal multicultural tolerance, but the circumstances of determination do not guarantee a particular outcome. "I was born this way" does not guarantee the equal treatment or the form of rights in the socius for which it hopes; indeed, it can just as easily open the possibility of violent coercion—and we do not need to look to Nazi Germany to recognize this. Indeed, the discovery of a gay gene might lead to a rash of abortions. In 1997 James Watson, a codiscoverer of DNA, supported a woman's right to abort a gay fetus. In the same year Jonathan Tolins wrote the popular play (now a movie available on video, *The Twilight of the Golds*) about just this scenario. Also around that time the queer icon Quentin Crisp opined that he would encourage such abortions. Knowledge of the cause of homosexuality would surely become knowledge of a cure for homosexuality, unless it existed in an environment in which diversity and difference already structured the rationale of the socius. The problem is normativity, not etiology.

Interestingly, the lifestyle position of the Christian right acknowledges a heterogeneous psyche, but they deploy a Kantian rational-moral argument to limit that heterogeneity forcefully. There is no reason to accept this argument, and I have spent a great deal of time here critiquing it. The problem is normativity, specifically heteronormativity. Queer science would provide further knowledge of the means by which this argument comes to have coercive force in the socius. It need not remain a critical negative knowledge, however; rather, it can generate positive queer social philosophy and queer activism. Nevertheless, if I suggest that queer science is antinormative, that suggestion should not be confused with an admonition to "do as you please" or a blanket celebration of multicultural difference. Such knowledge would only assert the integrity of a heterogeneity of essences. It would run the risk of simply asserting difference while leaving the status quo intact.

The history of modern social philosophy is filled with attempts to address the recognition of difference. I have revealed a tension between difference and sameness, between heterogeneity and homogeneity, between a Kantian universality and a Hegelian determinate specificity. When Hirschfeld set out on the voyage of discovery described in *The World Journey of a Sexologist* (1933), he was certainly not the first to search the world for difference. The voyages of discovery and colonization of the New World made difference a central problem of modernity. Anthropologists likewise have long sought to document human diversity. They have set out to explore the world, looking for signs of universal humanity and for forms of cultural difference. Depending on they way they approached this information, social philosophers have produced very different knowledge. Kant began by asserting universality and thereby treated difference as incidental. Herder and Hegel rejected this position but accounted for difference as support for an evolutionary theory of human development that ended outside their windows. Hegel in particular recognized difference as a problem of conflict but exposed it to a totalizing resolution. Marx recognized capitalism as a totalizing force, crushing all difference into universality. Nietzsche attended to the inherent difference of the other, emphasizing a diversity that existed for itself yet was drawn into universality by a will to power.

In learning from all that heritage, queer science begins to approach difference with a new kind of sensibility. Difference is an object of knowledge for queer science not simply so that it can be understood, justified, tolerated, or accepted. Rather, queer science apprehends difference in the same way that Nietzsche apprehended history: if history must be approached in terms of its usefulness to life, so must the knowledge of difference be approached. Thus difference is significant to the extent that it tells us something that the available socius cannot tell us or something that the psyche does not house in its hidden, secret depths. Queer science distills from difference transformative hints of the self, hints pertaining to that which is not in the status quo but which has the capacity to go beyond it and, in doing so, enrich the world. In this way, queer science becomes both a tool for emancipation and the anchor of philosophical activism.

BIBLIOGRAPHY

Adorno, Theodor. *Drei Studien zu Hegel.* Frankfurt am Main: Suhrkamp, 1963.
———. "Freudian Theory and the Pattern of Fascist Propaganda." *The Essential Frankfurt School Reader.* New York: Continuum, 1982.
———. *Hegel: Three Studies.* Cambridge, Mass.: MIT Press, 1994.
———. *Minima Moralia: Reflections from Damaged Life.* London: Verso, 1974.
———. *Negative Dialectics.* New York: Continuum, 1973.
———. *Problems of Moral Philosophy.* Stanford, Calif.: Stanford University Press, 2000.
———. "Sexual Taboos and Law Today." *Critical Models: Interventions and Catchwords.* New York: Columbia University Press, 1998.
———, et al. *The Authoritarian Personality.* New York: Harper, 1950.
Albelda, Randy, Elaine McRate, Edwin Melendez, and June Lapidus. *Mink Coats Don't Trickle Down: The Economic Attack on Women and People of Color.* Boston: South End, 1988.
Allen, Prudence. "Nietzsche's Tension about Women." *Lonergan Review: A Multidisciplinary Journal* 2 (1993): 42–67.
Allison, David B., ed. *The New Nietzsche.* Cambridge, Mass.: MIT Press, 1986.
Althusser, Louis. *For Marx.* London: Verso, 1982.
———. *Lenin and Philosophy.* London: New Left Books, 1971.
———. *Reading "Capital."* London: Verso, 1979.
Altman, Dennis. "Global Queering." *Australian Humanities Review* 2 (1996), available at <http://www.lib.latrobe.edu.au/AHR/archive/Issue-July-1996/altman.html>.
———. *Global Sex.* Chicago: University of Chicago Press, 2001.
———. *Homosexual: Oppression and Liberation.* New York: Avon Books, 1973.
Amott, Teresa, and Julie Matthaei. *Race, Gender, and Work: A Multicultural Economic History of Women in the United States.* Boston: South End, 1991.
Anderson, Michael. *Approaches to the History of the Western Family, 1500–1914.* London: Macmillan, 1980.
Aronowitz, Stanley. *The Crisis in Historical Materialism: Class, Politics, and Culture in Marxist Theory.* Minneapolis: University of Minnesota Press, 1990.
Baeumer, Max. "Winckelmann's Formulierung der klassischen Schönheit." *Monatshefte* 65 (1973): 61–75.
Bamyeh, Mohammed. *The Ends of Globalization.* Minnesota: University of Minnesota Press, 2000.
Bataille, Georges. *On Nietzsche.* St. Paul, Minn.: Paragon House, 1992.
———. *Visions of Excess: Selected Writings 1927–1939.* Minneapolis: University of Minnesota Press, 1985.

Baxandall, Rosalyn. "Marxism and Sexuality: The Body as Battleground." *Marxism in the Postmodern Age: Confronting the New World Order.* Ed. Antonio Callari, Stephen Cullenberg, and Carole Biewener. New York: Guilford, 1995.

Beck, Gunnar. "From Kant to Hegel: Johann Gottlieb Fichte's Theory of Self-Consciousness." *History of European Ideas* 22, no. 4 (1996): 275–94.

Beiner, Ronald, and William James Booth, eds. *Kant and Political Philosophy: The Contemporary Legacy.* New Haven, Conn.: Yale University Press, 1993.

Beiser, Frederick C., ed. *The Cambridge Companion to Hegel.* Cambridge: Cambridge University Press, 1993.

Benhabib, Seyla. "On Hegel, Women, and Irony." *Feminist Interpretations and Political Theory.* Ed. Carole Pateman and Mary Lyndon Shanley. University Park: Pennsylvania State University Press, 1991.

Benjamin, Harry. *The Transsexual Phenomenon.* New York: Ace, 1966.

Benjamin, Walter. *Illuminations: Essays and Reflections.* New York: Schocken Books, 1969.

Bergoffen, Debra B. "Nietzsche Was No Feminist." *International Studies in Philosophy* 26, no. 3 (1994): 23–32.

Berlant, Lauren. *The Queen of America Goes to Washington City: Essays on Sex and Citizenship.* Durham, N.C.: Duke University Press, 1997.

Berlant, Lauren, and Michael Warner. "Sex in Public." *Critical Inquiry* 24 (1998): 547–66.

Bersani, Leo. *Homos.* Cambridge, Mass.: Harvard University Press, 1995.

Blasius, Mark, and Shane Phelan, eds. *We Are Everywhere: A Historical Sourcebook of Gay and Lesbian Politics.* New York: Routledge, 1997.

Bloch, Iwan. *The Sexual Life of Our Time in Its Relations to Modern Civilization.* London: W. Heinemann, 1928.

Boon, L. J. "Those Damned Sodomites: Public Images of Sodomy in the Eighteenth Century Netherlands." *The Pursuit of Sodomy: Male Homosexuality in Renaissance and Enlightenment Europe.* Ed. Kent Gerard and Gert Hekma. New York: Harrington Park, 1989.

Bray, Alan. *Homosexuality in Renaissance England.* London: Gay Men's Press, 1982.

Breines, Paul. "Revisiting Marcuse with Foucault: An Essay on Liberation Meets the History of Sexuality." *Marcuse: From the New Left to the Next Left.* Ed. John Bokina and Timothy J. Lukes. Lawrence: University Press of Kansas, 1994.

Brown, Wendy. *States of Injury: Power and Freedom in Late Modernity.* Princeton, N.J.: Princeton University Press, 1995.

Butler, Judith. *Antigone's Claim: Kinship between Life and Death.* New York: Columbia University Press, 2000.

———. *Bodies That Matter: On the Discursive Limits of "Sex."* New York: Routledge, 1993.

———. *Excitable Speech: A Politics of the Performative.* New York: Routledge, 1997.

———. *Gender Trouble: Feminism and the Subversion of Identity.* New York: Routledge, 1990.

———. "Imitation and Gender Insubordination." *The Lesbian and Gay Studies Reader.* Ed. Henry Abelove, Michèle Aina Barale, and David M. Halperin. New York: Routledge, 1993.

———. *The Psychic Life of Power: Theories in Subjection.* Stanford, Calif.: Stanford University Press, 1997.

———. *Subjects of Desire: Hegelian Reflections in Twentieth-Century France.* New York: Columbia University Press, 1987.

Butler, Judith, Ernesto Laclau, and Slavoj Žižek. *Contingency, Hegemony, Universality: Contemporary Dialogues on the Left.* London: Verso, 2000.

Butler, Judith, and Joan Wallach, eds. *Feminists Theorize the Political.* New York: Routledge, 1992.

Butt, David. "Randomness, Order and the Latent Patterning of Text." *Functions of Style.* Ed. David Birch, Michael O'Toole, and M. Halliday. London: Pinter, 1988.

Cadava, Eduardo, Peter Connor, and Jean-Luc Nancy, eds. *Who Comes after the Subject?* New York: Routledge, 1991.

Califia, Pat. *Sex Changes: The Politics of Transgenderism.* San Francisco: Cleis, 1997.

Champagne, Rosaria. "Queering the Unconscious." *South Atlantic Quarterly* 97 (1998): 281–97.

Cheah, Pheng. "Introduction Part II: The Cosmopolitical—Today." *Cosmopolitics: Thinking and Feeling beyond the Nation.* Ed. Pheng Cheah and Bruce Robbins. Minneapolis: University of Minnesota Press, 1998.

Clark, Danae. "Commodity Lesbianism." *The Lesbian and Gay Studies Reader.* Ed. Henry Abelove, Michèle Aina Barale, and David M. Halperin. New York: Routledge, 1993.

Clark, Maudmarie. "Nietzsche's Misogyny." *International Studies in Philosophy* 26, no. 3 (1994): 3–12.

Clarke, Eric O. *Virtuous Vice: Homoeroticism in the Public Sphere.* Durham, N.C.: Duke University Press, 2000.

Coker, F. W. *Organismic Theories of the State: Nineteenth-Century Interpretations of the State as Organism or as Person.* New York: Columbia University Press, 1910.

Copjec, Joan, ed. *Supposing the Subject.* London: Verso, 1995.

Cornwall, Richard. "Incorporating Social Identities into Economic Theory: How Economics Can Come Out of Its Closet of Individualism." *A Queer World: The Center for Lesbian and Gay Studies Reader.* Ed. Martin Duberman. New York: New York University Press, 1997.

———. "Queer Political Economy: The Social Articulation of Desire." *Homo Economics: Capitalism, Community, and Lesbian and Gay Life.* Ed. Amy Gluckman and Betsy Reed. New York: Routledge, 1997.

Crompton, Louis. "Gay Genocide: From Leviticus to Hitler." *The Gay Academic.* Ed. Louie Crew. Palm Springs, Calif.: ETC, 1978.

Crowe, Michael J. *The Extraterrestrial Life Debate, 1750–1900: The Idea of a Plurality of Worlds from Kant to Lowell.* Cambridge: Cambridge University Press, 1986.

Dannecker, Martin. "Die Kritische Theorie und ihr Konzept der Homosexualität: Antwort auf Randall Halle." *Zeitschrift für Sexualforschung* 10 (1997): 19–36.

Darwin, Charles. *The Descent of Man, and Selection in Relation to Sex.* New York: Appleton, 1874.

David-Menard, Monique, ed. *Feminist Interpretations of Immanuel Kant.* University Park: Pennsylvania State University Press, 1997.

Davis, Lennard J. "Gaining a Daughter: A Father's Transgendered Tale." *Chronicle of Higher Education*, 24 Mar. 2000, B4.

Deleuze, Gilles. *Masochism*. New York: Zone Books, 1991.

Deleuze, Gilles, and Félix Guattari. *Anti-Oedipus: Capitalism and Schizophrenia*. Minneapolis: University of Minnesota Press, 1983.

———. *Nietzsche and Philosophy*. New York: Columbia University Press, 1983.

———. *A Thousand Plateaus: Capitalism and Schizophrenia*. Minneapolis: University of Minnesota Press, 1987.

Dellamora, Richard. *Masculine Desire: The Sexual Politics of Victorian Aestheticism*. Chapel Hill: University of North Carolina Press, 1990.

D'Emilio, John. "Capitalism and Gay Identity." *The Lesbian and Gay Studies Reader*. Ed. Henry Abelove, Michèle Aina Barale, and David Halperin. New York: Routledge, 1993.

———. *The World Turned: Essays on Gay History, Politics, and Culture*. Durham, N.C.: Duke University Press, 2002.

Derks, Paul. *Die Schande der heiligen Päderastie: Homosexualität und Öffentlichkeit in der deutschen Literatur, 1750–1850*. Berlin: Rosa Winkel, 1990.

Diagnostic and Statistical Manual of Mental Disorders. 4th ed. Washington, D.C.: American Psychiatric Association, 1994.

Dick, Steven J. *Plurality of Worlds: The Origins of the Extraterrestrial Life Debate from Democritus to Kant*. Cambridge: Cambridge University Press, 1982.

DiPiero, Thomas. *Dangerous Truths and Criminal Passions: The Evolution of the French Novel, 1569–1791*. Stanford, Calif.: Stanford University Press, 1992.

———. *White Men Aren't*. Durham, N.C.: Duke University Press, 2002.

Di Stefano, Christine. "Masculine Marx." *Feminist Interpretations and Political Theory*. Ed. Carole Pateman and Mary Lyndon Shanley. University Park: Pennsylvania State University Press, 1991.

Dohm, Wilhelm von. *Über die bürgerliche Verbesserung der Juden*. Berlin: Friedrich Nicolai, 1781.

"Domesticated Bliss: New Laws Are Making It Official for Gay or Live-In Straight Couples." *Newsweek*, 23 Mar. 1992, 62–63.

Duberman, Martin, ed. *A Queer World: The Center for Lesbian and Gay Studies Reader*. New York: New York University Press, 1997.

Duberman, Martin, Martha Vicinus, and George Chauncey Jr., eds. *Hidden from History: Reclaiming the Gay and Lesbian Past*. New York: New American Library, 1989.

Dülmen, Richard von. *Die Gesellschaft der Aufklärer: zur bürgerlichen Emanzipation und aufklärerischen Kultur in Deutschland*. Frankfurt am Main: Fischer Taschenbuch, 1986.

Duyves, Mattias, Gert Hekma, and Paula Koelemij. *Onder Mannen Onder Vrouwen: Studies van Homosociale Emancipatie*. Amsterdam: SUA, 1984.

Dynes, Wayne R. "Wrestling with the Social Boa Constructor." *Forms of Desire: Sexual Orientation and the Social Constructionist Controversy*. Ed. Edward Stein. New York: Routledge, 1992.

Edelman, Lee. *Homographesis*. New York: Routledge, 1994.

Egger, Oswald. *Knigge mehr als heute Kant ("hat jemand gesagt"), Knigge als Kant*. Vienna: Prokurist, Verein für Organisation und Austausch von Kunst und Kultur, 1994.

Elshtain, Jean Bethke. *Meditations on Modern Political Thought: Masculine/Feminine Themes from Luther to Arendt.* University Park: Pennsylvania State University Press, 1992.

Epstein, Barbara. "Postwar Panics and the Crisis of Masculinity." *Marxism in the Postmodern Age: Confronting the New World Order.* Ed. Antonio Callari, Stephen Cullenberg, and Carole Biewener. New York: Guilford, 1995.

Escoffier, Jeffery. *American Homo: Community and Perversity.* Berkeley: University of California Press, 1998.

———. "The Political Economy of the Closet: Notes toward an Economic History of Gay and Lesbian Life before Stonewall." *Homo Economics: Capitalism, Community, and Lesbian and Gay Life.* Ed. Amy Gluckman and Betsy Reed. New York: Routledge, 1997.

———. "Sexual Revolution and the Politics of Gay Identity." *Socialist Review* 15 (1985): 119–53.

Faderman, Lillian, and Brigitte Eriksson, eds. *Lesbian-Feminism in Turn-of-the-Century Germany.* Weatherby Lake, Mo.: Naiad, 1980.

Fausto-Sterling, Anne. "How to Build a Man." *Constructing Masculinity.* Ed. Maurice Berger, Brian Wallis, and Simon Watson. New York: Routledge, 1995.

———. *Myths of Gender: Biological Theories about Women and Men.* New York: Basic Books, 1992.

Feinbloom, Deborah Heller. *Transvestites and Transsexuals: Mixed Views.* New York: Delacorte, 1976.

Fernbach, David. "Towards a Marxist Theory of Gay Liberation." *Pink Triangles: Radical Perspectives on Gay Liberation.* Ed. Pam Mitchell. Boston: Alyson, 1980.

Field, Nicola. *Over the Rainbow: Money, Class, and Homophobia.* London: Pluto, 1995.

Forbes, Kipling D. *Hegel on Want and Desire.* Wakefield, N.H.: Hollowbrook, 1992.

Formisano, Ronald P., and Constance K. Burns, eds. *Boston, 1700–1980: The Evolution of Urban Politics.* Westport, Conn.: Greenwood, 1984.

Foucault, Michel. *Ethics: Subjectivity and Truth.* New York: New Press, 1994.

———. *The Foucault Effect: Studies in Governmentality.* Chicago: University of Chicago Press, 1991.

———. *The History of Sexuality.* 3 vols. New York: Vintage Books, 1980–86.

———. *Remarks on Marx: Conversations with Duccio Trombadori.* New York: Semiotext(e), 1991.

———. "What Is Enlightenment?" *The Foucault Reader.* Ed. Paul Rabinow. New York: Pantheon, 1984.

Fout, John C., ed. *Forbidden History: The State, Society, and the Regulation of Sexuality in Modern Europe.* Chicago: University of Chicago Press, 1992.

Freud, Sigmund. *Beyond the Pleasure Principle. The Standard Edition of the Complete Psychological Works of Sigmund Freud.* Vol. 18. London: Hogarth Press, 1966.

———. *Briefe 1873–1939.* Frankfurt: S. Fischer, 1960.

———. "'A Child Is Being Beaten': A Contribution to the Study of the Origin of Sexual Perversions." *The Standard Edition of the Complete Psychological Works of Sigmund Freud.* Vol. 17. London: Hogarth Press, 1966.

———. *Civilization and Its Discontents. The Standard Edition of the Complete Psychological Works of Sigmund Freud.* Vol. 21. London: Hogarth Press, 1966.

———. "The Economic Problem of Masochism." *The Standard Edition of the Complete Psychological Works of Sigmund Freud.* Vol. 19. London: Hogarth Press, 1966.

———. *On Narcissism: An Introduction. The Standard Edition of the Complete Psychological Works of Sigmund Freud.* Vol. 14. London: Hogarth Press, 1966.

———. *Three Essays on the Theory of Sexuality. The Standard Edition of the Complete Psychological Works of Sigmund Freud.* Vol. 7. London: Hogarth Press, 1966.

Frevert, Ute. *Frauen-Geschichte zwischen bürgerlicher Verbesserung und neuer Weiblichkeit.* Frankfurt am Main: Suhrkamp, 1986.

Fromm, Erich. "Über Methode und Aufgabe einer Analytischen Sozialpsychologie." *Zeitschrift für Sozialforschung* 1 (1932): 28–55.

———. "Die psychoanalytische Charakterologie und ihre Bedeutung für die Sozialpsychologie." *Zeitschrift für Sozialforschung* 3 (1932): 253–78.

———. "Sozialpsychologischer Teil." *Studien über Autorität und Familie: Forschungsberichte aus dem Institut für Sozialforschung.* Paris: F. Alcan, 1936.

Gailey, Christine Ward. *Kinship to Kingship: Gender Hierarchy and State Formation in the Tongan Islands.* Austin: University of Texas Press, 1987.

Gallop, Jane. *Intersections: A Reading of Sade with Bataille, Blanchot, and Klossowski.* Lincoln: University of Nebraska Press, 1981.

Gauthier, Jeffrey A. *Hegel and Feminist Social Criticism: Justice, Recognition, and the Feminine.* Albany: State University of New York Press, 1997.

Gerard, Kent, and Gert Hekma, eds. *The Pursuit of Sodomy: Male Homosexuality in Renaissance and Enlightenment Europe.* New York: Harrington Park, 1989.

Geyer-Kordesch, Johanna, and Annette Kuhn, eds. *Frauenkörper, Medizin, Sexualität: Auf dem Wege zu einer neuen Sexualmoral.* Düsseldorf: Schwann, 1986.

Gimenez, Martha E. "The Production of Divisions: Gender Struggles under Capitalism." *Marxism in the Postmodern Age: Confronting the New World Order.* Ed. Antonio Callari, Stephen Cullenberg, and Carole Biewener. New York: Guilford, 1995.

Gluckman, Amy, and Betsy Reed, eds. *Homo Economics: Capitalism, Community, and Lesbian and Gay Life.* New York: Routledge, 1997.

Gordan, Rupert H. "Kant, Smith, and Hegel: The Market and the Categorical Imperative." *Paradoxes of Civil Society: New Perspectives on Modern German and British History.* New York: Berghahn Books, 1999.

Green, Richard, and John Money. *Transsexualism and Sex Reassignment.* Baltimore, Md.: Johns Hopkins Press, 1969.

Greenberg, David. *The Construction of Homosexuality.* Chicago: University of Chicago Press, 1988.

Grell, Ole Peter, and Roy Porter, eds. *Toleration in Enlightenment Europe.* Cambridge: Cambridge University Press, 2000.

Gustafson, Susan. *Men Desiring Men: The Poetry of Same-Sex Identity and Desire in German Classicism.* East Lansing, Mich.: Wayne State University Press, 2002.

Habermas, Jürgen. *The Philosophical Discourse of Modernity.* Cambridge: Polity, 1987.

————. *The Structural Transformation of the Public Sphere: An Inquiry into a Category of Bourgeois Society.* Cambridge, Mass.: MIT Press, 1991.

————. *The Theory of Communicative Action.* 2 vols. Boston: Beacon, 1987.

Halle, Randall. "Between Marxism and Psychoanalysis: Anti-Fascism and Anti-Homosexuality in the Frankfurt School." *Gay Men and the Sexual History of the Political Left.* Ed. Gert Hekma, Harry Oosterhuis, and James Steakley. New York: Haworth, 1995.

————. "Lesbian and Gay Culture in Germany." *The Encyclopedia of Contemporary German Culture.* New York: Routledge, 1999.

————. "Political Organizing and the Limits of Civil Rights: Gay Marriage and Queer Families." *Relatively Speaking.* Ed. Mary Bernstein and Renate Reiman. New York: Columbia University Press, 2000.

Halperin, David. *One Hundred Years of Homosexuality: And Other Essays on Greek Love.* New York: Routledge, 1990.

Haraway, Donna. *Simians, Cyborgs, and Women: The Reinvention of Nature.* New York: Routledge, 1991.

Hegel, Georg Wilhelm Friedrich. *Elements of the Philosophy of Right.* Cambridge: Cambridge University Press, 1991.

————. *The Phenomenology of Spirit.* Oxford: Clarendon, 1977.

Heidegger, Martin. *Nietzsche.* San Francisco: Harper and Row, 1987.

Hennessy, Rosemary. "Incorporating Queer Theory on the Left." *Marxism in the Postmodern Age: Confronting the New World Order.* Ed. Antonio Callari, Stephen Cullenberg, and Carole Biewener. New York: Guilford, 1995.

————. *Profit and Pleasure: Sexual Identities in Late Capitalism.* New York: Routledge, 2000.

Herder, Johann Gottfried von. *Reflections on the Philosophy of the History of Mankind.* Ed. Frank Edward Manuel. Chicago: University of Chicago Press, 1968.

Hermann, Barbara. "Could It Be Worth Thinking about Kant on Sex and Marriage?" *A Mind of One's Own: Feminist Essays on Reason and Objectivity.* Boulder, Colo.: Westview, 1993.

Herve, Florence, ed. *Geschichte der deutschen Frauenbewegung.* Cologne: Pahl-Rugenstein, 1983.

Hewitt, Andrew. *Political Inversions: Homosexuality, Fascism, and the Modernist Imaginary.* Stanford, Calif.: Stanford University Press, 1996.

Higgens, Kathleen Marie. "Gender in the *Gay Science.*" *Feminist Interpretations of Friedrich Nietzsche.* Ed. Kelly Oliver and Marilyn Pearsall. University Park: Pennsylvania State University Press, 1998.

Hippel, Theodor. *Über die bürgerliche Verbesserung der Weiber.* Berlin: G. Reimer, 1828.

Hirschfeld, Magnus. *Transvestites: The Erotic Drive to Cross-Dress.* Buffalo, N.Y.: Prometheus Books, 1991.

Hirschman, Albert. *The Passions and the Interests: Political Arguments for Capitalism before Its Triumph.* Princeton, N.J.: Princeton University Press, 1977.

Hocquenghem, Guy. *Homosexual Desire.* 2d ed. Durham, N.C.: Duke University Press, 1993.

Holub, Robert C. *Friedrich Nietzsche.* New York: Twayne, 1995.

Honneth, Axel. "Pathologies of the Social: The Past and Present of Social Philosophy." *The Handbook of Critical Theory.* Ed. David M. Rasmussen. Oxford: Blackwell, 1999.

Hoof, Dieter. *Pestalozzi und die Sexualität seines Zeitalters: Quellen, Texte, und Untersuchungen zur historischen Sexualwissenschaft.* St. Augustin: H. Richarz, 1987.

Horkheimer, Max, and Theodor Adorno. *Dialectic of Enlightenment.* New York: Continuum, 1996.

Hubschmid, Hans. *Gott, Mensch und Welt in der schweizerischen Aufklärung; eine Untersuchung über Optimismus und Fortschrittsgedanken bei Johann Jakob Scheuchzer, Johann Heinrich Tschudi, Johann Jakob Bodmer und Isaak Iselin.* Affoltern am Aachen: J. Weiss, 1950.

Hull, Isabel V. *Sexuality, State, and Civil Society in Germany, 1700–1815.* Ithaca, N.J.: Cornell University Press, 1996.

Hunt, Nancy. *Mirror Image.* New York: Holt, Rinehart and Winston, 1978.

Hutchison, John, ed. *Biological Determinants of Sexual Behavior.* Chichester, N.Y.: Wiley, 1978.

Institut für Sozialforschung. *Studien über Autorität und Familie: Forschungsberichte aus dem Institut für Sozialforschung.* Paris: F. Alcan, 1936.

Jauch, Ursula Pia. *Immanuel Kant zur Geschlechterdifferenz: aufklärerische Vorurteilskritik und bürgerliche Geschlechtsvormundschaft.* Vienna: Passagen, 1988.

Kando, Thomas. *Sex Change: The Achievement of Gender Identity among Feminized Transsexuals.* Springfield, Ill.: Thomas, 1973.

Kant, Immanuel. *Anthropology from a Pragmatic Point of View.* The Hague: Nijhoff, 1974.

———. *Critique of Practical Reason.* Trans. Lewis White Beck. New York: Macmillan, 1956.

———. *Critique of Pure Reason.* Trans. Paul Guyer. Cambridge: Cambridge University Press, 1998.

———. *Foundation of the Metaphysics of Morals and What Is Enlightenment?* New York: Macmillan, 1990.

———. *Groundwork of the Metaphysics of Morals.* Trans. Mary Gregor. Cambridge: Cambridge University Press, 1998.

———. "Idea for a Universal History with a Cosmopolitan Purpose." *Kant: Political Writings.* Cambridge: Cambridge University Press, 1991: 41–53.

———. *Kant's Cosmogony, as in His Essay on the Retardation of the Rotation of the Earth and His Natural History and Theory of the Heavens.* New York: Greenwood, 1968.

———. *The Metaphysics of Morals.* Trans. Mary Gregor. Cambridge: Cambridge University Press, 1991.

———. "Toward Perpetual Peace: A Philosophical Sketch." *Kant: Political Writings.* Cambridge: Cambridge University Press, 1991: 93–130.

Katz, Jonathan Ned. *The Invention of Heterosexuality.* New York: Dutton, 1995.

Kaufmann, Walter. *Hegel: Reinterpretation, Texts, and Commentary.* Garden City, N.Y.: Doubleday, 1965.

Kennedy, Ellen, "Nietzsche: Women as *Untermensch*." *Women in Western Political Philosophy: Kant to Nietzsche.* Ed. Ellen Kennedy and Susan Mendus. New York: St. Martin's, 1987.

Klossowski, Pierre. *Nietzsche and the Vicious Circle.* Chicago: University of Chicago Press, 1997.

Kocka, Jürgen. "The European Pattern and the German Case." *Bourgeois Soci-*

ety in Nineteenth-Century Europe. Ed. Jürgen Kocka and Allen Mitchell. Oxford: Berg, 1993.

Kogel, Jörg-Dieter, ed. *Knigge für Jedermann: vom Umgang mit Menschen.* Frankfurt am Main: Insel, 1999.

Köhler, Joachim. *Zarathustras Geheimnis: Friedrich Nietzsche und seine verschlüsselte Botschaft: eine Biographie.* Reinbek: Rowohlt, 1989.

Koselleck, Reinhart. *Preußen zwischen Reform und Revolution: allgemeines Landrecht, Verwaltung und soziale Bewegung von 1791 bis 1848.* Stuttgart: Klett, 1967.

Krafft-Ebing, Richard Freiherr von. *Psychopathia sexualis, eine klinisch-forensische Studie.* Stuttgart: Enke, 1886.

Kristeva, Julia. *Revolution in Poetic Language.* New York: Columbia University Press, 1984.

Kuzniar, Alice A., ed. *Outing Goethe and His Age.* Stanford, Calif.: Stanford University Press, 1996.

Lacan, Jacques. *The Four Fundamental Concepts of Psycho-Analysis.* New York: Norton, 1978.

———. "Kant with Sade." *October* 51 (1989): 55–58.

Laqueur, Thomas. *Making Sex: Body and Gender from the Greeks to Freud.* Cambridge, Mass.: Harvard University Press, 1990.

Laslett, Peter. *Household and Family in Past Time.* Cambridge: Cambridge University Press, 1972.

Lautmann, Rüdiger. *Der Zwang zur Tugend: die gesellschaftliche Kontrolle der Sexualitäten.* Frankfurt am Main: Suhrkamp, 1984.

LeGuin, Ursula K. *Left Hand of Darkness.* New York: Ace Books, 1969.

LeVay, Simon. *Queer Science: The Use and Abuse of Research into Homosexuality.* Cambridge, Mass.: MIT Press, 1996.

Litvak, Joseph. *Strange Gourmets: Sophistication, Theory, and the Novel.* Durham, N.C.: Duke University Press, 1997.

Lothstein, Leslie Martin. *Female-to-Male Transsexualism: Historical, Clinical, and Theoretical Issues.* Boston: Routledge and Kegan Paul, 1983.

Lukenbill, Grant. *Untold Millions: Gay and Lesbian Markets in America.* New York: HarperCollins, 1995.

Lütge, Friedrich. *Deutsche Sozial- und Wirtschaftsgeschichte.* Berlin: Springer, 1966.

Lyotard, Jean François. *The Differend: Phrases in Dispute.* Minneapolis: University of Minnesota Press, 1988.

Marcus, Steven. *The Other Victorians.* New York: Basic Books, 1964.

Marcuse, Herbert. *One-Dimensional Man: Studies in the Ideology of Advanced Industrial Societies.* Boston: Beacon, 1964.

———. *Reason and Revolution: Hegel and the Rise of Social Theory.* London: Oxford University Press, 1941.

Marrow, Alfred F. *The Practical Theorist: The Life and Work of Kurt Lewin.* New York: Basic Books, 1969.

Marshall, Bill. "Gays and Marxism." *Coming On Strong: Gay Politics and Culture.* Ed. Simon Shepherd and Mick Wallis. London: Unwin Hyman, 1989.

Martin, Biddy. *Feminity Played Straight: The Significance of Being Lesbian.* New York: Routledge, 1996.

Marx, Karl, and Frederick Engels. *Karl Marx, Frederick Engels: Collected Works.* 49 vols. to date. New York: International, 1975–.

Mayer, Hans. *Outsiders: A Study in Life and Letters.* Cambridge, Mass.: MIT Press, 1982.

McCubbin, Bob. *The Gay Question: A Marxist Appraisal.* New York: World View, 1976.

McGrath, Patrick, and Simon Richter. "Representing Homosexuality: Winckelmann and the Aesthetics of Friendship." *Monatshefte* 86 (1994): 45–58.

McIntosh, Mary. "The Homosexual Role." *The Making of the Modern Homosexual.* Ed. Kenneth Plummer. London: Hutchinson, 1981.

Meijer, Irene Costera, and Baukje Prins. "How Bodies Come to Matter: An Interview with Judith Butler." *Signs: Journal of Women in Culture and Society* 23 (1998): 275–87.

Mendus, Susan. "Kant: An Honest but Narrow-Minded Bourgeois?" *Women in Western Political Philosophy: Kant to Nietzsche.* Ed. Ellen Kennedy and Susan Mendus. New York: St. Martin's, 1987.

Merton, Robert K. *Social Theory and Social Structure.* Glencoe, Ill.: Free Press, 1957.

Middleton, Richard. *Colonial America: A History, 1607–1760.* Cambridge, Mass.: Blackwell, 1992.

Mitterauer, Michael. *The European Family: Patriarchy to Partnership from the Middle Ages to the Present.* Chicago: University of Chicago Press, 1982.

Mittwoch, Ursula. *Genetics of Sex Differentiation.* New York: Academic, 1973.

Money, John. *Gay, Straight, and In-Between: The Sexology of Erotic Orientation.* New York: Oxford University Press, 1988.

Money, John, and Patricia Tucker. *Sexual Signatures: On Being a Man or a Woman.* Boston: Little, Brown, 1975.

Morton, Donald, ed. *The Material Queer: A LesBiGay Cultural Studies Reader.* Boulder, Colo.: Westview, 1996.

———. "Review: The Class Politics of Queer Theory." *College English* (1996) 58: 471–82.

Mosse, George Lachmann. *The Crisis of German Ideology: Intellectual Origins of the Third Reich.* New York: H. Fertig, 1981.

———. *Nationalism and Sexuality: Respectability and Abnormal Sexuality in Modern Europe.* New York: H. Fertig, 1985.

———. *The Nationalization of the Masses: Political Symbolism and Mass Movements in Germany from the Napoleonic War through the Third Reich.* New York: H. Fertig, 1975.

Mulvey, Laura. *Visual and Other Pleasures.* Bloomington: Indiana University Press, 1989.

Mutari, Ellen, Heather Boushey, and William Fraher. *Gender and Political Economy: Incorporating Diversity into Theory and Policy.* Armonk, N.Y.: M. E. Sharpe, 1997.

Nietzsche, Friedrich. *Beyond Good and Evil: Prelude to a Philosophy of the Future.* Trans. Walter Kaufmann. New York: Vintage Books, 1966.

———. *The Gay Science.* New York: Vintage, 1978.

———. *On the Genealogy of Morals; Ecce Homo.* New York: Vintage, 1967.

———. *Thus Spoke Zarathustra: A Book for None and All.* New York: Penguin, 1978.

————. *Twilight of the Idols, or, How to Philosophize with a Hammer.* Oxford: Oxford University Press, 1998.

————. *Untimely Meditations.* Cambridge: Cambridge University Press, 1983.

————. *The Will to Power.* New York: Vintage, 1968.

Nipperdey, Thomas. *Deutsche Geschichte 1866–1918.* Munich: C. H. Beck, 1998.

————. "Verein als soziale Struktur in Deutschland im späten 18. und frühen 19. Jahrhundert." *Gesellschaft, Kultur, Theorie: Gesammelte Aufsätze zur neueren Geschichte.* Göttingen: Vandenhoeck und Ruprecht, 1976.

Norris, Christopher. *The Truth about Postmodernism.* Cambridge, Mass.: Blackwell, 1993.

————. *Uncritical Theory: Postmodernism, Intellectuals, and the Gulf War.* Amherst: University of Massachusetts Press, 1992.

Okin, Susan Moeller. *Justice, Gender, and the Family.* New York: Basic Books, 1989.

Parker, Kevin. "Winckelmann: Historical Difference and the Problem of the Boy." *Eighteenth-Century Studies* 25 (1992): 523–44.

Patton, Cindy. "Tremble, Hetero Swine!" *Fear of a Queer Planet: Queer Politics and Social Theory.* Ed. Michael Warner. Minneapolis: University of Minnesota Press, 1993.

Penelope, Julia, ed. *Out of the Class Closet: Lesbians Speak.* Freedom, Calif.: Crossing, 1994.

Perrot, Michelle. *A History of Private Life.* Cambridge, Mass.: Belknap, 1991.

Piercy, Marge. *Woman on the Edge of Time.* London: Women's Press, 2000.

Raffo, Susan, ed. *Queerly Classed.* Boston: South End, 1997.

Rancour-Laferriere, Daniel. *The Mind of Stalin: A Psychoanalytic Study.* Ann Arbor, Mich.: Ardis, 1988.

Rawls, John. *Kant's Transcendental Deductions: The Three "Critiques" and the "Opus Postumum."* Stanford, Calif.: Stanford University Press, 1989.

————. *A Theory of Justice.* Cambridge, Mass.: Harvard University Press, 1971.

Raymond, Janice G. *The Transsexual Empire: The Making of the She-Male.* Boston: Beacon, 1979.

Reich, Wilhelm. *Charakteranalyse.* Berlin: privately printed, 1933.

————. *Dialektischer Materialismus und Psychoanalyse.* Copenhagen: Verlag für Sexualpolitik, 1934.

————. *Der Einbruch der Sexulmoral: zur Geschichte der Sexuellen Ökonomie.* Copenhagen: Verlag für Sexualpolitik, 1935.

————. *Die Funktion des Orgasmus.* Leipzig: Internationaler Psychoanalytischer Verlag, 1927.

————. *Massenpsychologie des Faschismus.* 2d ed. Copenhagen: Verlag für Sexualpolitik, 1934.

————. Review of *Das Geschlechtsleben der Wilden in Nordwestmelanesien,* by Bronislaw Malinowski. *Zeitschrift für Sozialforschung* 1 (1932): 232.

————. *Der Triebhafte Charakter.* Leipzig: Internationaler Psychoanalytischer Verlag, 1925.

————. "Über Spezifität der Onanieformen." *Frühe Schriften.* Cologne: Kiepenheur und Witsch, 1977.

Rey, Michel. "Police and Sodomy in Eighteenth-Century Paris: From Sin to Disorder." *The Pursuit of Sodomy: Male Homosexuality in Renaissance and En-*

lightenment Europe. Ed. Kent Gerard and Gert Hekma. New York: Harrington Park, 1989.

Richardson, Lynda, Katrine Ames, Christopher Sulavik, Nadine Joseph, Lucille Beachy, and Todd Park. "Proud, Official Partners: Gay and Other New Yorkers Using Law." *New York Times* 1 Aug. 1993.

Richter, Simon. "Winckelmann's Progeny: Homosocial Networking in the Eighteenth Century." *Outing Goethe and His Age.* Ed. Alice Kuzniar. Stanford, Calif.: Stanford University Press, 1996.

Rockmore, Tom. *Before and after Hegel: A Historical Introduction to Hegel's Thought.* Berkeley: University of California Press, 1993.

Rosenbaum, Heidi. *Formen der Familie: Untersuchungen zum Zusammenhang von Familienverhältnissen, Sozialstruktur und sozialen Wandel in der deutschen Gesellschaft des 19. Jahrhunderts.* Frankfurt am Main: Suhrkamp, 1982.

Roters, Karl-Heinz. *Reflexionen über Ideologie und Ideologiekritik.* Würzburg: Königshausen und Neumann, 1998.

Rousseau, Jean-Jacques. *"The Social Contract" and "Discourses."* London: J. M. Dent, 1986.

Rubin, Gayle. "Thinking Sex: Notes for a Radical Theory of Sexuality." *The Lesbian and Gay Studies Reader.* Ed. Henry Abelove, Michèle Aina Barale, and David M. Halperin. New York: Routledge, 1993.

———. "The Traffic in Women." *Toward an Anthropology of Women.* Ed. Rayna Rapp Reiter. New York: Monthly Review Press, 1975.

Santner, Eric. *My Own Private Germany: Daniel Paul Schreber's Secret History of Modernity.* Princeton, N.J.: Princeton University Press, 1996.

Schama, Simon. *The Embarrassment of Riches: An Interpretation of Dutch Culture in the Golden Age.* Berkeley: University of California Press, 1988.

Scheuner, Ulrich. *Der Beitrag der deutschen Romantik zur politischen Theorie.* Opladen: Westdeutscher, 1980.

Schutz, Alfred. *Life Forms and Meaning Structure.* Boston: Routledge and Kegan Paul, 1982.

———. *The Phenomenology of the Social World.* Evanston, Ill.: Northwestern University Press, 1967.

Sedgwick, Eve Kosofsky. *Between Men: English Literature and Male Homosocial Desire.* New York: Columbia University Press, 1985.

———. *Epistemology of the Closet.* Berkeley: University of California Press, 1990.

———. *Performativity and Performance.* New York: Routledge, 1995.

———. *Tendencies.* New York: Routledge, 1994.

Seidman, Steven. "Identity Politics in a 'Postmodern' Gay Culture: Some Historical and Conceptual Notes." *Fear of a Queer Planet: Queer Politics and Social Theory.* Ed. Michael Warner. Minneapolis: University of Minnesota Press, 1993.

Shell, Susan. "Kant's Political Cosmology: Freedom and Desire in the 'Remarks' Concerning 'Observations on the Feeling of the Beautiful and the Sublime.'" *Essays on Kant's Political Philosophy.* Ed. Howard Williams. Chicago: University of Chicago Press, 1992.

Siegel, Jerrold. *Marx's Fate: The Shape of a Life.* Princeton, N.J.: Princeton University Press, 1978.

Sieyès, Emmanuel Joseph. "What Is the Third Estate?" *The Nationalism Reader.*

Ed. Omar Dahbour and Micheline Ishay. Atlantic Highlands, N.J.: Humanities, 1995.

Silverman, Hugh. *Philosophy and Desire.* New York: Routledge, 2000.

Simmel, Georg. *Georg Simmel 1858–1918: A Collection of Essays.* Ed. Kurt H. Wolff. New York: Harper and Row, 1965.

———. *Georg Simmel: On Women, Sexuality and Love.* New Haven, Conn.: Yale University Press, 1987.

———. *Hauptprobleme der Philosophie.* Berlin: De Gruyter, 1964.

———. *Kant: Sechzehn Vorlesungen gehalten an der berliner Universität.* Munich: Duncker und Humblot, 1918.

———. *On Individuality and Social Forms.* Chicago: University of Chicago Press, 1971.

———. *Philosophische Kultur.* Frankfurt am Main: Suhrkamp, 1996.

———. *Schriften zur Soziologie.* Frankfurt am Main: Suhrkamp, 1983.

———. *Schopenhauer and Nietzsche.* Amherst: University of Massachusetts Press, 1986.

———. *Simmel on Culture: Selected Writings.* London: Sage, 1997.

Sklar, Kathryn Kish, Anja Schuler, and Susan Strasser, eds. *Social Justice Feminists in the United States and Germany: A Dialogue in Documents, 1885–1933.* Ithaca, N.Y.: Cornell University Press, 1998.

Smith-Rosenberg, Carroll. "Discourses of Sexuality and Subjectivity: The New Woman, 1879–1936." *Hidden from History.* Ed. Martin Duberman, Martha Vicinus, and George Chauncey Jr. New York: Penguin, 1989.

Steakley, James D. *The Homosexual Emancipation Movement in Germany.* New York: Arno, 1975.

———. *"Per scientiam ad justitiam:* Magnus Hirschfeld and the Sexual Politics of Innate Homosexuality." *Science and Homosexualities.* Ed. Vernon A. Rosario. New York: Routledge, 1997.

Stein, Edward, ed. *Forms of Desire: Sexual Orientation and the Social Constructionist Controversy.* New York: Routledge, 1990.

Stepelvich, Lawrence, ed. *The Young Hegelians: An Anthology.* Atlantic Highlands, N.J.: Humanities, 1997.

Stoller, Robert J. *Sex and Gender.* 2 vols. London: Karnac Books, 1976.

Stychin, Carl F. *A Nation by Rights: National Cultures, Sexual Identity Politics, and the Discourse of Rights.* Philadelphia: Temple University Press, 1998.

Tate, John W. "Kant, Habermas, and the 'Philosophical Legitimation of Modernity.'" *Journal of European Studies* 27, no. 3 (1997): 281–322.

Tesser, Abraham. *Advanced Social Psychology.* New York: McGraw-Hill, 1995.

Thompson, John B., and David Held, eds. *Habermas: Critical Debates.* Cambridge, Mass.: MIT Press, 1982.

Tilly, Charles. *Coercion, Capital, and the European States, A.D. 990–1990.* Cambridge, Mass.: Blackwell, 1990.

Tobin, Robert. *Warm Brothers: Queer Theory and the Age of Goethe.* Philadelphia: University of Pennsylvania Press, 2000.

Todorov, Tzvetan. *The Conquest of America: The Question of the Other.* New York: Harper and Row, 1984.

Trentman, Frank, ed. *Paradoxes of Civil Society: New Perspectives on Modern German and British History.* New York: Berghahn Books, 1999.

Vierhaus, Rudolf. *Deutschland im 18. Jahrhundert: Politische Verfassung, soziales Gefüge, geistige Bewegungen.* Göttingen: Vandenhoeck und Ruprecht, 1987.

———. *Deutschland im Zeitalter des Absolutismus, 1648–1763.* Göttingen: Vandenhoeck und Ruprecht, 1978.

Vovelle, Michel. *Der Mensch der Aufklärung.* Frankfurt am Main: Fischer Taschenbuch, 1998.

Waite, Geoff. *Nietzsche's Corps/e: Aesthetics, Politics, Prophecy, or, The Spectacular Technoculture of Everyday Life.* Durham, N.C.: Duke University Press, 1996.

Warner, Michael. *Publics and Counterpublics.* New York: Zone Books, 2002.

———. "Something Queer about the Nation-State." *After Political Correctness: The Humanities and Society in the 1990s.* Ed. Christopher Newfield and Ronald Strickland. Boulder, Colo.: Westview, 1995.

Watney, Simon. "The Ideology of GLF." *Homosexuality, Power, and Politics.* Ed. Gay Left Collective. London: Allison and Busby, 1980.

Weber, Max. *Economy and Society: An Outline of Interpretive Sociology.* 2 vols. Berkeley: University of California Press, 1978.

———. *The Protestant Ethic and the Spirit of Capitalism.* New York: Routledge, 1992.

Weeks, Jeffrey. *Coming Out: Homosexual Politics in Britain from the Nineteenth Century to the Present.* London: Quartet, 1990.

———. *Sex, Politics and Society: The Regulation of Sexuality since 1800.* London: Longman, 1977.

Weil, Eric. *Hegel and the State.* Baltimore, Md.: Johns Hopkins University Press, 1998.

Weininger, Otto. *Sex and Character.* New York: Putnam's, 1906.

Westphal, Carl Friedrich Otto. *Gesammelte Abhandlungen.* Berlin: A. Hirschwald, 1892.

Whitebook, Joel. "Fantasy and Critique: Some Thoughts on Freud and the Frankfurt School." *The Handbook of Critical Theory.* Ed. David M. Rasmussen. London: Blackwell, 1999.

Williams, Howard. *Essays on Kant's Political Philosophy.* Chicago: University of Chicago Press, 1992.

Wingrove, Elizabeth. "Interpellating Sex." *Signs: Journal of Women in Culture and Society* 24 (1999): 869–91.

Yack, Bernard. "The Problem with Kantian Liberalism." *Kant and Political Philosophy: The Contemporary Legacy.* Ed. Ronald Beiner and William James Booth. New Haven, Conn.: Yale University Press, 1993.

Žižek, Slavoj. *The Abyss of Freedom.* Ann Arbor: University of Michigan Press, 1997.

———. *For They Know Not What They Do: Enjoyment as a Political Factor.* New York: Verso, 1991.

———. *The Plague of Fantasies.* New York: Verso, 1997.

———. *The Sublime Object of Ideology.* New York: Verso, 1989.

———. *Tarrying with the Negative: Kant, Hegel, and the Critique of Ideology.* Durham, N.C.: Duke University Press, 1993.

INDEX

Adorno, Theodor, 12, 15, 63, 92, 117, 122–25, 127, 138–41, 146, 150, 174; and homosexual dread, 140–44; and latency systems, 151–52, 154; and the state, 75–78

affiliation, 78, 82, 84–85, 111–13, 139, 143, 152; and affiliative politics, 112; and coming out, 212–14; of desire, 85–86; radical, 181–82, 192–99. *See also* filiation

autonomy, 7, 32, 37–38, 40, 45–48, 55, 69, 70–76, 79, 121, 128, 206–7; characteristics of, 45, 47, 59; and citizens, 47; and heteronomy, 50–51; and heteronormativity, 80–86; and individuals, 47, 56–57, 180, 182, 191; and lifeworlds, 67, 79–80. *See also* freedom

Bacon, Francis, 149

base, 17, 133. *See also* economics

bisexuality, 44, 116, 118, 156, 167, 193. *See also under* sexuality

body-sex morpheme, 16. *See also under* gender; sexuality

butch-femme dyad, 18. *See also under* gender

Califa, Pat, 145

categorical imperative, the, 25, 27–33, 42, 55, 57, 73–74, 87, 90, 192, 206; and coercion, 29; identification with, 32; and the libertine, 27; procedure (CI-p), 55; and the will to power, 33

Christian right, 144, 215

circle of manipulation, 123. *See also under* economics; need

citizen, the, 26, 37, 47–49, 57, 66–67, 72–76, 97–98, 125, 208; and desire, 74; emancipation of, 101–2; and ethics, 75; ideal, 74; and the nation-state, 77–78, 86, 91; passive, 47. *See also under* socius; state

civil society, 7, 57, 70–73, 78–80; and coercion, 83; and emancipation, 101–4, 106, 111, 115; and family, 84; and heterocoital imperative, 103; as need, 79, 92, 106. *See also* socius; state

Clover, Carol, 145

coercion, 72, 76, 82, 145, 212–13; and coercive totalizing, 5, 102; and deep structures, 142; as domination, 72; and pleasure, 86–87; resistance to, 207; and will, 88–89. *See also under* power

coming out, 145, 195–97, 211–13; as active, 211–12; as affiliation, 212; and latency, 145; as reactive, 211; and tolerance, 212; as type (transgendered, bear cub, raunch pig, etc.), 211

common sense, 14, 20, 157

conflict, ideological, 119

consumer capitalism, 122; and satiety, 124. *See also under* economics

Crisp, Quentin, 8

culture industry, 122–23, 126–29; and latency, 149, 153–54; and standardization, 125. *See also under* economics

Dannecker, Martin, 145–48, 154–57

deep structure, 151–52, 157; and order, 152. *See also* psyche

Deleuze, Gilles, 190

D'Emilio, John, 113–15

democracy, 6, 7, 10, 47, 57, 80, 124, 181, 184. *See also under* state

Derrida, Jacques, 4

desire, 1, 3, 8–9, 13, 15, 41, 45, 53–55, 58, 67–68, 98, 138, 160, 168, 180, 182, 189, 191, 211–12; affiliation of, 85–86; autonomous, 121; and bio-need, 120; and categorical imperative, 27–33; configurations of, 7–8; and conflict, 119; and consumer

Joan of Arc, 8
Justi, Johann Heinrich Gottlob von, 42, 52

Kafka, Franz, 27–28
Kaufmann, Walter, 174–75; on gender, 182–83
knot, defined, 14–15; of modernity, 33
Kristeva, Julia, 145, 160
Kritik, 22n9
Kuzniar, Alice, 8, 9

Lacan, Jacques, 157, 160
Lacquer, Thomas, 19
latency, 12; and biology, 150; and dreams, 148, 149; and futurity, 151; and homosexuality, 136–43, 144–45; and latent configuration, 149; and latent process, 149; and latent self, 149; and linguistics, 150; and nationalism, 150; and politics, 167–68; and repression, 151–52; and transparency, 151
latency phase, 149
latency system(s), 148–54; and authoritarian knowledge, 153–54, 156; culture industry as, 149, 153–54; four characteristics of, 151–54; and need, 153–54; and order, 152–53
law, 57–58, 73–74; and loss of transcendence, 29; moral, 31; premodern, 28; reform in, 29; rule of the sovereign as, 28, 31, 32
Le Vay, Simon, 214–15
Lewin, Kurt, 134–35
liberation, 97–99, 106, 112–17, 121, 127–29, 153, 211–16; and the gay rights movement, 114–16; heterosexual, 166–67; homosexual, 147–48
lifeworlds, 64, 67–68, 69, 72–73, 76–78, 86–88, 98, 102, 105, 113, 125–26, 141, 192, 195, 212–13
linguistics of sexuality, 16; expansion of communication in, 17, 18, 19
love, 90, 92
Lyotard, Jean-François, 4

Mahlsdorf, Charlotte von, 8
Marcuse, Herbert, 125–26, 127, 159, 165
marriage, 41; and love, 84–85; and procreation, 84; same-sex, 42
masochism, 7; ethics of, 75. *See also* sadism

matriarchy, 108
Merton, Robert K., 149
military rights, 6
modernity, 25, 33–36, 68, 176–78; knot of, 14–15, 33; and modern subject of desire, 26; and progress, 177–78
morality, 34, 38–39, 70, 72, 74–75, 104, 180, 187, 194–96, 205–9; and freedom, 86–93; and heterosexuality, 13, 20, 51, 109–10, 136; and homosexuality, 37, 58; and immoralism, 175; and moral law, 27–33; and moral minimalism, 103; of subsistence, 120; and willed reason, 43, 46, 52–56, 58. *See also under* ethics; freedom; heteronormativity; totality
morbid projection, 138
Mulvey, Laura, 145

nation-state, 89–91, 98; and coercion, 76–8; and eugenics, 77; and governmentality, 72; as queering apparatus, 67. *See also* socius; state
need, 10, 29, 52–54, 84, 87, 92, 107, 110, 120–29, 153–54, 160, 179, 181, 193, 195, 210; bio-need, 118–19, 120, 127; and civil society, 79, 92; collective, 56; human, 106–7; and necessity, 121; retroactive, 123; sexual, 58–59
negation, 3, 10, 76, 86, 89, 102, 105, 116–20; as abjection, 10, 210; queer, 3, 10, 116, 119, 197–99; total, 76, 117
nihilism, 111, 178–80; overcoming, 188, 190; and queer science, 179; radical, 198–99

performativity, 183–84; and becoming, 184; and performance, 210; and voluntarism, 185
perspectivism, 179–80; and reason, 180
perversion, 19; and health, 15
philosophical activism, 209–10
Plato, 8
pleasure, 10, 31, 41, 43–44, 46, 50, 53–55, 75, 104, 108–9, 189, 194; and freedom, 86–93; and labor, 121–22, 165; univeralizing, 91. *See also under* desire; drives; sexuality
political agency, 11
political emancipation, 63–64; and civil society, 101; and minorities, 100–101
power, 4–5, 14–15, 29–30, 33, 44, 46–47, 50, 104, 167–68, 196; bio-, 50, 67,

RANDALL HALLE is an associate professor of
German studies and film studies at the University of
Rochester. His research and publications cover wide-
ranging topics, including social philosophy, queer theory, visual representation, and globalization. He has
written numerous essays and is the coeditor of *Light
Motives: German Popular Film in Perspective* and the
double special issue of *Camera Obscura* entitled
"Marginality and Alterity in European Cinema." He is
currently completing a book on German cinema in
the transnational era.

The University of Illinois Press
is a founding member of the
Association of American University Presses.

Composed in 9.5/12.5 Trump Mediaeval
by Jim Proefrock
at the University of Illinois Press
Manufactured by Thomson-Shore, Inc.

University of Illinois Press
1325 South Oak Street
Champaign, IL 61820-6903
www.press.uillinois.edu